PreDumb

Before I Came To L.A.

Mark Hayes

Copyright © Mark Hayes, 2014

http://www.markhayes.tv

First Edition: March 2014

The author has asserted his moral rights.

First published in 2014 by
RanDumb House

Imprint of T.M.I

ISBN: 978-0-6159925-94

A CIP record for this title is available from the British Library.

Cover design Iskon Design

Formatting Polgarus Studio

This book is sold subject to the condition that it shall not, by way of trade or otherwise, be lent, resold, hired out or otherwise circulated, without the author's prior consent, in any form other than that in which it is published and without a similar condition including this condition being imposed on the subsequent publisher. No part of this publication may be reproduced or transmitted in any form or by any means, electronic or mechanical, including photocopying, recording or storage in any information or retrieval system, without the prior permission of the author in writing.

Dedicated to my new mighty new niece Anna.

(Don't make me regret this.)

FOREWORD

What's this man doing in my garden so?

ROBBIE WILLIAMS, 2014

Chapter 1
Is God Watching?

"Simply the best!" Music is booming over the sound system. A stage is already set up in Daunt Square, the wide, open, cobbled area between Virgin Records and McDonalds, right in the heart of Cork. Bands have played gigs before and the whole city shut down for them so I imagine this is the case for mine as well. Biggest event this city has ever seen.

A huge crowd has already gathered to see a band but they never showed up. Thousands of impatient people. Grumbles. Rumbles. Mumbles. All about to leave. This is when I fly in from stage right – A tall, mysterious, young, spikey brown haired boy still in his school uniform, here to entertain and appease. Music booming. *"Better than all the rest!"*

A draft of wind rattles my bedroom window, jolting me out of my daydream. If I looked out my window, all I'd see is gloom. If you looked in my window, you'd just see my room. And me. Lying on my bed. Slowly gyrating up and down.

I'm at home in Rochestown. Cork. Ireland. Back in the 90s. I'm about fourteen-years-old. And I'm daydreaming the gloomy Irish weather away. Face down. Eyes shut. Mind open. Trying to stay warm as I lie on my navy blue ThunderCats duvet cover. Arms tucked tight in by my sides. Still wearing my Douglas Community School uniform. Navy wooly jumper. Crisp white shirt. Itchy grey pants. Shoes off. Socks on. Head in the pillow. Burrowing. Furrowing. Daydreaming. Escaping for dear life.

Start having this one dream. I want to be the best singer in the world. Better than Bono. Bigger than the Beatles. Badder than Michael Jackson. And not just the best singer. I want to have written the greatest songs ever written too. Writer. Singer. Performer. I want to be a star!

I like to keep my daydreams logical so they seem more realistic. The deal I've made with myself in this daydream is that I can go through music lists and handpick all my favourite songs i.e. the ones people have told me are classics. These songs then just disappear from people's memories and reappear when I release them, like some sort of songwriting swooping. U2. Beatles. Rolling Stones. Maybe Michael Jackson. Prince?

I'll have to keep them all kind of similar to each other in style otherwise I'd just be an unfocused artist who's all over the place and people don't know what to make of them. So I'll try to swoop all the best songs and keep them within my range. Throw some Blur and Oasis in there. Few other one-offs that I really like. Ocean Colour Scene perhaps. Although they might never have been big if I take away their best songs. No Ocean Colour Scene. I don't want these other bands to disappear or anything. I just want to take their best songs and present them to the world as my own. Writer. Producer. Singer. I'm a talented boy.

The top of Patrick's Street will be the venue to unleash this new gift of mine, right where it meets with the Grand Parade. These are the two main streets in Cork city, the ones with cobbled paths and endless clothes shops, pubs and shoe stores either side of the wide, busy roads. As I said, it seems like all of Cork is here waiting to see a band. It's then when the Tina Turner songs strikes up, a cue to the crowd that something is about to happen.

"I call you when I need you, my heart's on fire!"

Fireworks! Explosions! Smoke machine!

"You come to me, come to me wild and wild!"

More fireworks! Bigger explosions! Too much smoke!

Enter flying in like I've been sent from heaven: ME!

Obviously people don't know who I am as I fly on stage and glide through the air, but, despite this, I have extreme confidence, like a hardened performer going through some last minute preparation. Nail my landing. Release the wires from my back. Give the crowd a nod and a wink. Tap my finger on the microphone to get people's attention. It does that awful loud piercing, ringing, whirring noise. I hold my hand up in apology as people grab their ears and look at me annoyed. Bad start.

My introduction isn't very long, just a "Hey everyone, I'm going to play some songs. Enjoy." Run through the song list in my head as I tune my guitar. I think I'll start with *Train in Vain* by The Clash. Warm them up. Start strumming softly, the infectious low guitar riff pricking people's ears. Dun-den, diddly den-den, dun-den, diddly den-den. Build it up, build it up, build it up. Crowd won't know what's going on.

"Who's this?"

"What's he doing up there?"

"Is that Hayes?" my big-headed buddy Vinnie from school will say when he sees me on stage. "What are ya doing, boy? You've never done anything like this before in your life!"

"Well, I did actually sing in a school choir on TV before. Remember? My Gran said I looked very fat on screen? No? OK.

Anyway, being a performer has always been a hidden talent of mine. Now it's time to show the world. Hope you're ready." Wink.

No reaction.

Probably need to work on my small talk with the crowd. First gig and all though so I let it slide. Everyone's bewildered. Confused. Lost. However. Before they know it they're swaying, getting into it. This song sounds familiar even though they've never heard it before (remember, I've wiped all memory of it from their minds). Toes tapping. Heads nodding. Hearts beating. I have their attention. They get it. In, on, they're along for the ride! Now I'm jamming. Guitar riff looping over and over. I'm ready. It's time. Open my mouth to sing. And then...

Two things usually happen at this point of my daydreams, the part where I'm just about to actually do the main activity. One: I start getting cold on my bed. Ireland. November. Bleak. Freezing weather. Wicked winds. Bare trees. Darker months, which is when I do most of my daydreaming. About five in the evening and I just got home from school. Going to be fully pitch black outside soon. Tired after my long day of daydreaming in school. Can't take a proper nap. My Mum's downstairs cooking up a storm so dinner will be ready in half an hour. Nothing good on TV. Which is why I go daydream in my bedroom upstairs instead. But now I'm cold. My Dad lit a fire half an hour ago but the radiator in my room isn't warm from it yet. Feet are starting to sting from the lack of heat. This leads to number two...

Start rocking my body slightly to warm myself up. Not so much that I snap out of the daydream or anything. Just enough to get a bit of heat going. Rocking is usually happening around the mid-drift region, both my hips doing all the work. Face in the pillow. Feet dangling off the bottom of the bed. Hips pumping. Up and down. Up. Down. Riding. Heating me up. Also getting me a bit hot and bothered. Not sure what's going on - still only about fourteen years old - but I think I like it. Feels like I like it. Yes. I like it.

Thoughts now dart across my mind. Is God watching? Might someone walk in? Did I lock my door? And if so, did I do it subtly? Otherwise my older brother Darren could be outside listening in, hearing the muffled noise of me making the sound of a strummed guitar. Calm down, calm down. No need to hide. Not doing anything wrong, just lying here. Keeping warm. Moving my hips. Dreaming my dreams. I'll just do it some more. Body. Mind. Dreaming. Rocking. Rolling. And, I think I'm pumping my bed. As if it's a girl. Not fully sure. Thoughts start to get muddled. But I really do like it. And I'm no longer bored.

Now another daydream pops into my head, this one about a girl named Emma who lives nearby. Big lips. Huge boobs. Think she likes me. Bit older though so not sure if I have a chance. Still, I like those boobs. And now the bed is her, I think? Not sure. Where was I, about to sing? Right. Must try to get back to that daydream. Focus.

OK. I'm back in the first daydream. Except the gig is over already. Seems I missed the on-stage rocking and have skipped straight to what happens afterwards back stage. Hey girls. Hey adulation. Respect. Fortune. Stardom! Time to get this after party going - And then Darren walks into my bedroom,

"What are you doing to your bed, ya weirdo?"

"Nothing, shut up, I'm not pumping it. Get out, *leave us alone*!"

At this point Darren and I usually wrestle and fight which is slightly awkward considering what I've just been doing. And then we hear our names being called by our Mum. Dinner is ready. Daydreams are over.

Anyway, the point is I think that's my first memory of wanting to be a star. Also one of the first memories I have for wanting to have sex. Great daydreaming, really. No wonder I continued to have that one/pump the bed for the next few months. Made sure to lock my door from then on though. Didn't want anyone else disturbing my singing and strumming. Fun times growing up in Ireland. Shoes. Off. Pump. On!

CHAPTER 2
BALLS

My first clear memory ever is of balls hitting me in the face. I think I'm four. And they're balls of ice. Pelting down. Pummeling me. Hailstones, as they're called. Peppering from the heavens. Gluing me rigid on the road close to where I used to live in Carrigaline, one of many single street towns in County Cork. Got lost on the way home from wherever I was before this memory began. Late for dinner. Ran through a high-grassed field. Darting through the wispy grass. Started raining. So I started running. Liked that part. Didn't care about getting wet. Just scampering for dear life. Eyes closed, mouth open, tongue out. Drinking up life. Delighted.

Until the first ice-ball hit me. Felt like a potato. Rat. Right in the forehead. Rat-a-tat-tat. More potatoes bouncing off my cheeks. Nose. Forehead. Eyes. Battered. Full on. Maybe I was being stoned for being late. Avalanche of apples hailing down on me. End of the world style thunderstorm. Stopped running. Unable to move. Closed my eyes. Gritted my teeth. And peed my pants. Like a little ape. Some relief. Gave me warmth. But now I'm in pain. Can't see. Lost. Discombobulated. Rain, ice and balls are coming down too fast, too hard, too many. Leave out a wail,

"HEELLLLP - MUUUUMMMYYYYYYY!"

As if on cue, out of the dark mist a heroic figure appears. Batman, Catwoman, Wonder Woman - My Mum. She came to find me. She came to save me. She's here. Scoops me up. Wraps her jacket around me. Carries me home. Takes me into the kitchen. My Dad grabs a towel. Superman. He knows what to do. Dries off my head as I stand there crying. Peeing. Frightened. But it's OK. I'm home now. Everything's going to be all right.

Not sure what happened after that. Memories are muddled from an early age. Let's hope I wasn't actually fifteen when this happened. When I close my eyes now all I see are random flashes. Too many memories mixed with too much booze. I remember car rides. Sitting in the back seat. Watching the emerald green world go by. Drawing on the fogged up window with my finger. Cartoon faces. I remember going to the beach. Running around in circles with my older brother Darren. Wearing a jacket when it went from sunny to raining. Eating banana sandwiches my Mum made us. Playing soccer with my Dad. Climbing rocks. Playing make believe. Being an adventurer.

I remember watching cartoons on Saturday morning. He-Man, Batman, ThunderCats. The brown carpet. The glass kitchen table. The polished oak coffee table in the front room. Eating Coco Puffs cereal in my soccer pyjamas. Drinking the chocolate milk left over in the bowl. Wrestling Darren. Playing on a little rocking horse toy we had. Falling back asleep.

I remember moving from one house to another close by. Both were in Carrigaline. I remember there were lots of green areas. High grassed fields to explore. Oak trees to climb. Front gardens to run through. I remember being outdoors a lot even though the weather was all over the place.

I remember going to play-school close by, kindergarten as they say in America. I remember yellow walls and plastic purple chairs. I remember being sad when my Mum dropped me off the first morning but liking it as the day went on. I remember running into my Dad's arms later that night. I remember loving being carried places. Held aloft in my parents' arms. Like they were holding up a trophy. Golden child. The chosen one.

I don't remember too many girls being around when I was small. Schools in Ireland were segregated so like most other boys I grew up having no clue how to talk to girls. It's true. No clue. Only girls I really knew growing up were my cousins, Niamh and Gillian. Rarely saw either of them though, maybe two or three times a year. My first memory of a girl who wasn't related to me was when my brother started hanging around with one who lived by us, Laura. Small, short brown hair, freckled face. We were only young, four or five maybe, but I remember Laura annoyed me. Darren was my friend. Now he was hanging out with her. Cycling their bikes together. Playing with toys. Running around the back garden. That's stuff Darren and I did together, God damnit!

In an attempt to communicate my annoyance I decided I would pretend to kick Laura like I might a soccer ball. Only pretend, I wouldn't actually do it. Looked out the kitchen window and saw them both in the back garden, playing in the sun. Here's my chance. Out I go. Start kicking the air like I'm Karate Kid. Go up to Laura and pretend to kick her. Unfortunately she walked towards me as I did this, so my pretend kick turned into a real kick. Thump. Into the stomach. She cried. I ran. Darren shouted. I got in trouble. And that was the first time a girl told me she didn't like me. We moved house soon after.

I remember driving by our new house as it was being built in Rochestown, a parish nearer to Cork City. Lots of new houses were being built. Watched our one go from nothing to a four bedroomed house. Red slated roof, white pebbled walls, brown window frames. Home. I remember running inside to the hallway and straight up the stairs. Tried to pick my Mum and Dad's bedroom as my own, biggest of the lot and had its own bathroom. No joy so went for the biggest of the three other bedrooms instead. I was a wise ten year old, I knew what I was doing. Somehow got away with it, Darren didn't object. How he would rue that choice.

I remember sitting on soccer balls in the back garden waiting for the grass to grow. Short shorts. Blue buckled shoes. White and green wooly jumpers. Cartoon t-shirts. Kicking my foot off the ground to make sure my Mum tied my laces tight enough. Standing still while my Dad put my jacket on me. Having gloves on strings that went inside of my jacket sleeves. Being done. Getting ready. Giving my Dad high fives. Running off through the dining room like an airplane. Playing with little rubber pink ping pong balls. Throwing them off the sitting room wall and carrying them in my pocket. Reading books in the front room. Enid Blyton. Roald Dahl. *The Twits. Matilda. The Famous Five* and *The Secret Seven*. Loving *The Faraway Tree* book series about an enormous magical tree that reached above the clouds filled with fairies, pixies and fantasy. Cycling bikes and eating ham sandwiches.

I remember sitting on my Nana and Granddad Hayes' laps down in Passage West, a port town where my Dad grew up. Loved going down to their tall, narrow Victorian terraced house. Somehow their back garden was about four stories up, higher than the roof. Had to climb lots of steep, narrow steps to get up there. My Granddad was usually sitting on a sun chair and my Nana would be trimming flowers. I remember them always being happy. Joking around. Two chancers.

Loved spending the night there. Drinking warm milk in the morning. My brother and I going for walks down the road with my Nana and Granddad. Running through an abandoned tunnel. Slowly walking down to the pier. Learning how to skim stones across the water. Whizzing skinny, flinty stones for ten skips at a time. Finding oysters and mussels stuck to the pier walls. Sampling a few straight out of the salty sea when my Nana wasn't looking. Empty reaching them back up. Kicking water at Darren. Getting my foot soaking wet. Granddad carrying me home. In the afternoon watching Japanese cartoon movies my Dad rented on video for us. Nana filling us up with glasses of Tanora, a special tangerine flavoured fizzy drink only available in Cork.

Never really flew anywhere when I was young. Holidays were always to places where we could drive to more or less, either somewhere in Ireland or else we'd take the ferry to the Isle of Man or Wales. Despite the boring car journeys to the destination, I always enjoyed those holidays. Learnt to swim in a massive tropical style resort pool on one of the holidays at Butlins, a family resort. Ate a lot of chocolate ice cream on another.

One time when we stayed at a B&B on a farm in Clare the farmer showed us how to milk a cow. Squirted milk straight from the cow into my face. Only young but I remember laughing at that. Everyone else in the stable did too. Milk dripping down my chin. So that was great a day in the hay. Also learnt how to ride a horse and jump fences that holiday, along with eat copious amounts of scones and homemade blackberry jam. Fresh as the cow's milk, those jam-covered scones were.

Another time in Wales a car crashed into ours, and drove off. Can't remember exactly where we were then. Pretty sure my Mum got very upset when it happened though so maybe my brain blocked that memory out. Good work, brain, repress those memories.

I definitely remember the car rides there and back being the worst part of any holiday. When you're young a two-hour car journey can feel like a four-day hike through the desert. Sitting in the back seat, bored out of your mind. Too young to really care about music. Car sick if you try to read a book. Tough life really.

Two hours was probably the longest I could take before freaking out about the journey. This was how long it took to drive from where we lived in Cork to my Nana and Granddad's abode in Tipperary, where my Mum grew up. We used to go stay there a lot when I was young, especially before my sister Sarah was born. My Dad would drive while my Mum would supply us with music and food, and my brother Darren and I would spend the journey poking and provoking one another. Like being covered with warm creamy milk in the face, it was a *real* hoot.

About halfway through the journey Darren and I would think we were close to dying from being on the road so long,

"Are we there yet, are we there, should we turn around and go home? I'm dying. I need water. No, cold water."

We'd be told to pipe down and my Dad would drive on. About twenty minutes before we arrived I'd fall asleep. Darren would follow suit. Both our heads would droop and flail around in the back seat, eventually bopping each other awake when the car went around one winding corner and then swung back around another. We'd wake up thinking the other head-butted on purpose and a flailing of the arms would ensue. We'd be told to cop on or God help us, and then we'd arrive at our grandparent's house. It was always an unreal relief arriving, mostly because we could use the bathroom and disperse of all the water we drank en route. I remember one time I peed for fifteen minutes straight. My little ponder pipe felt like a bulging water main about to explode. Bladder. Burst. Off.

My grandparent's farm was in an area called Grange, a place in the middle of nowhere. The nearest village up the road had a small, white, thatched roof house that was also a shop/post office/petrol station all rolled into one. This was the life and soul of the place really. There was also a red public telephone box from the forties that somehow still worked and two pubs, both right across the road from one another. That was it.

Everywhere else as far as the eye could see was lush countryside. Rolling green fields speckled with white sheep and spotted cows all over the place, thick forests and pinewoods along with the odd medieval crumbling castle here and there. Picture picturesque. Unless it was raining. Then all you saw was grey clouds and fuddy ducking mirt tracks.

Loved seeing my Nana and Granddad. Their house was a whitewashed farmhouse bungalow. Always greeted us with smiles and treats. Nana Ryan would make us brown bread and marmalade to eat while my Granddad would tell us to go around the back and knock on his bedroom window. He was old and spent most days in bed but when we knocked on the window from the outside he always got up and handed us out either money or chocolate bars, along with the winking warning,

"Don't tell your mother."

"We won't, we swear!"

Darren and I would slip the money into our socks and then race off across the field to eat the sweets and chocolate, ruining our appetite. Few minutes later we'd be called for dinner and have to race back through the field again. One of us would attempt to take a short cut and end up falling in a pile of nettles near where the cows drank from a trough or else we might rip our clothes as we tried to run through the thorny blackberry bushes that grew right outside their house. Whoever took the fall would let out a cry of pain and run even harder back to our Mum so she could heal us. Until she saw sweet wrappers in our hands and knew we wouldn't be hungry now for dinner. We'd claim we still were, we just had one sweet but my Mum knew.

Instead Darren and I would fight over who got the cool couch bed seat that was in the kitchen/living room area by the TV and who had to sit on a less comfortable wooden kitchen chair. Kitchen was small, quaint, well kept, tight and mighty. Oil burning furnace stove pumping out heat. Dinner would be served, a fine feast of potatoes, ham, turkey, peas, carrots, turnip, Brussels sprouts, and gravy. I'd pick at some turkey while gagging over the smell of the sprouts as my Mum and Nana would shoo each other to sit down and let them be the one to serve the food. In the end they'd both serve the table and everyone would tuck in, my Dad peeling potatoes by the bucket load and Darren suddenly enjoying Brussels sprouts just to annoy me.

After dinner we'd have dessert of fresh strawberries that my Nana grew, served with creamy vanilla ice cream. Some food always tasted better when my Nana served them, strawberries and ice cream and brown bread and marmalade being my two favourite combos. Then I'd help my Dad with the wash-up until he told me it was fine, I was just getting the floor wet. Darren and I would go off outside, running down the grassy country lane that led to a forest, trying to see who could make better mooing sounds at the cows.

Some days we'd all put on old clothes and wellies and go into the forest, running around and jumping in puddles and mud, running wild and free. Darren and I would jump in anyway, my Mum and Dad would choose the safer, drier, firm pathways. It was some laugh, except when it went from roasting sun to bucketing rain, an unfortunate and sudden occurrence of Irish weather, leaving us all soaked and miserable by the time we got back to the farm. At least my Nana always had some soup and sandwiches to warm us back up. After lunch Darren and myself would play soccer in the front yard, using two of the big red gates of the outhouses as goals, while my Dad fixed the door in my Nana's garage and my Mum picked some fresh rhubarb from the garden for dessert that night.

My Mum and Dad would sleep in my Mum's old room while Darren and I shared a fold out bed in the sitting room. We'd kick and punch each other over who got more space and who was hogging the blankets so rarely did we get a good night's sleep. My brother had bad eczema for a while as well so he'd spend entire nights scratching his legs and fidgeting like a dog in heat next to me, drove me up the wall. Scratching the itch. Some people can be so rude.

Sometimes we'd go visit our cousins Colin, Kevin and Niamh who lived nearby, about forty minutes away. Our aunt Margaret, my Mum's older sister and my godmother, and our uncle Frank would always be delighted to see us. (My Mum's younger sister Sheila lived in Greece, and her older brother Martin lived in Cork too.)

Darren and I loved hanging out with Colin, Kevin and Niamh. We'd usually play soccer in the big field out the back or else play Commodore 64 up in their bedroom. Niamh would usually be on the swings that they had in the back garden watching us playing soccer or else we'd all play board games together, Guess Who being a popular one at the time. I sometimes took bad hoppers off the swings but I had a good laugh on them until I did.

One of the downsides of my Nana and Granddad's house was that they only had two TV stations. Kind of got boring at times. Here though, at my cousins, a guy used to call around every week and rent videos out of the back of his car so they were always well stocked up with plenty of movies. Niamh was the same age as me but Colin and Kevin were older and picked over-eighteen movies. Both were big fans of Jean Claude Van Damme. Pretty sure I've seen *Double Impact* at least twenty times. Also pretty sure one of these videos allowed me to see naked women for the first time. Sharon Stone I think. Or maybe it was the three-boobed alien lady in *Total Recall*. Can't remember who was first. Set high standards for life though either way. Good ol' video boobs.

They had a dog as well, Alf, a small cocker spaniel. Myself and Darren hadn't really had much experience with cats or dogs so while we pretended to really like Alf, we were both a bit afraid of him, constantly thinking, *What if he bites us?* "Dogs can smell fear so just don't be afraid of him and you'll be fine," we were always told, the worst and dumbest advice ever. Just don't be afraid of what you're afraid of and then you'll be fine. *Obviously*!

One day when we visited my cousins were out at their friend Brian's house and Niamh was at her friend Pa Ryan's abode. That left Darren and I a bit lost as to what to do. Wasn't the same without them here to play with us. Not sure how but we ended up having a game of chasing with each other, running in and around the house. When Alf saw us running he joined in, scampering behind us. This scared the living daylights out of Darren and myself, so we ran faster. All we saw was a barking dog with his teeth showing chasing us down. He wanted to kill us.

So we ran and ran and ran, looping around the house, scared for our lives. We were nine and ten at the time. Boundless energy so we just kept on running, maybe for about thirty minutes non-stop. Both of us kept shouting back and forth, scared and stupid, trying to figure out how to stop Alf from catching, devouring and mangling us. By now I think we were both in tears. Colin and Kevin arrived home just as Darren and I ran into the house, planning on trying to lock the door behind us. We ran in the open front door, through the kitchen and headed for the sliding door patio that led into the back garden. Darren was in front, closely followed by me, then Alf. I remember hearing Colin shout out,

"Just stop running, Alf is only running because ye are!"

Just stop running so Alf can jump up and eat us? Again, worst advice ever.

"NO... WE CAN'T... PLEASE... HELP! MAKE HIM STOP... MAKEHIMSTOP!!"

Turned to look over my shoulder. Alf was right behind me. Oh Jesus. As I turn to face forward again all I hear is *SMASH!* Down Darren goes like a ton of bricks. Ran straight into the closed sliding door thinking it was open. Smashed himself face first into the clear glass door. I wish I could say this was the first time Darren had done this but I can't. Definitely the worst time though. Loud ripple as the glass cracked and shattered, then a roar from Darren as he felt the blood on his face. I had stopped in time so I was fine, clearly saw the door was closed. Alf jumped up into my arms and licked my face with delight. He had finally caught us. My cousins were right after all - Alf *was* just playing with us. Well what do you know?

Doctors were called as Darren was carried into the living room and laid on the couch. My parents kept me out of the room as the doctor on duty tried to stitch Darren's smashed face and cheeks back together. In the end he was fine, the scars healed nicely and are now gone on the surface. For the longest time after that though neither of us felt too comfortable around dogs.

(My Dad also bought us a little toy dog when we were really young that used to bark and do flips. I liked it but Darren used to jump on the couch afraid of it for some reason. I think that's where the initial fear of dogs came from. This incident didn't help the situation.)

The drive home back to Cork that night took ages. My Dad had to drive extra slowly as Darren was in a lot of discomfort. What should have been a two-hour journey took about four hours. Some balls, particularly for me, stuck in the backseat having to listen to Darren all the time. On the upside, my cousins and I still have a chuckle about it to this day and really, isn't that what memories are all about?

Chapter 3
Art Malaraky

As far as being creative goes my earliest memory is of painting houses when I was about six-years-old. Not actual real houses where I'm a child labourer, more the amazing, mundane paintings kids all over the world do on a daily basis. Grab a sheet of paper. Out with the paintbrush. Squeeze big bulbous blobs of red, yellow, green and blue paint into the pastel. Mix them around. Dib dab dob. And. Swoosh.

Run the brush along the bottom of the page. We have our ground. Base. Land. A start. Rinse the brush in water. Wipe it on the edge of the jam jar. Paint dab again. Two swift strokes up. The walls. Another short line across the top. Foundations of the roof. Quick refill on the paint. Connect the roof triangle on top. Paint the yellow sun in the top right corner (this is where I really shone). And. Done. Another masterpiece.

"Mum. Muuuuuuuuummmmmm. MUM! Look what I made - *Art*."

I think this all started in Cub Scouts. As far as I can remember I enjoyed the Cubs for the most part. I think. Grand place to go sit on hard, creaky wooden benches in the old, bare church hall with intense religious paintings looking down at you, wearing khaki shorts and shirt, and a weird bright red scarf tie with that odd, gold-coloured fake metal knot to clasp it together and slide up my neck. Itchy, blue, wooly socks too.

Can't remember what we actually did besides painting pictures. Couple of treasure hunts. Lot of rules. Recited lines. I think we had a sleep over one night at the church hall but I can't remember why. I do know it felt a bit creepy at the time. Group of young boys - most who I didn't know - sleeping in this cold hall in a church being watched over by grown men. Seemed a bit odd. Or maybe I just didn't like sleeping on cold wooden floors.

Anyway, that was the place where my foray into expressing myself through art started. Up to that point I had merely been consuming. Reading books in school and at home by the bucket load. Roald Dahl, Enid Blyton, *The Hobbit*, all the classics. Watched all the best movies too. *E.T. The Neverending Story. Short Circuit.* Japanese cartoons. All sorts.

Now though, it was time to get involved. Drawing houses. Eggs. Attempt to paint a flower. As good as Van Gogh? Oh no. Never too good at flowers. Or people's faces. Nor hands. Always far better when I was allowed to make up the shape of things really. I was quite good at colouring in though. You know, the drawings that are already drawn and you have to colour it in by numbers. Unreal at that. Neat. Careful. Tidy. I excelled. Made sure to stay rigidly within the lines. Colour, shade, pencil. I had it down to a tee. Even started winning best in show for those efforts. Don't think they were called best in show, more like "Very good Mark, you win today's colouring in competition". The medals I took home to my proud parents. Beaming!

It's funny how you look for recognition when you make art of any kind. Every single boy in Cubs would say the exact same thing after they finished their painting or colouring attempts: "Mine is crap but geez, yours is very good. Really good. Mine is crap though, isn't it? Huh? What do you think? Mine. Crap. Right?" Then you would wait for the other person to give the obligatory: "No way, yours is really good, brilliant. My one is the crap one, right, mine is crap, I can't draw at all, right? What do you think?" This would continue back and forth until somebody said "Yeah, mine is way better now that you mention it." One of us had to end that tiring conversation. Plus, I did win a medal for mine.

Only once did another boy call me out on it. A year older than me, my brother's age. When I turned to Darren to give him the usual 'mine's crap, yours is great, what do you think of mine' line, this other boy - Ruairi 'The Rhino' - called my bluff.

"You're only saying that so that we say no it's not, yours is better than ours. So stupid. Why do you do it, why does everyone do it?"

Because I'm weak and need the approval of others? And now I will forever be seeking this outside approval? Foundations rocked. Truth. Dagger. Right to my core. I think I let out a whimpering "No I don't, what are you on about? Mine is crap, look, I'll prove it." And then I ripped up the beautiful and *immaculately* coloured in masterpiece right there in front of everyone. Immediate disqualification for a medal on the night but I had to prove my point that I didn't need anyone's approval, right? I made the correct decision. Yes? Or no? Who cares, ha ha. Ahem.

Pretty sure my colouring talents were put to rest that night. My Mum couldn't explain it. Few weeks earlier she had bought me a beautiful painting of an old vintage car sitting outside a manor house with a majestic garden to the side. This was meant to be my pet project, I was even going to do it in watercolours. *Watercolours*!

My Mum had gone all out for me. Every Friday evening she would move the kitchen table to the side and lay out a black bin bag on the white kitchen floor, just for me and my work in progress. I would be whisked off to Amsterdam in my mind, imagining myself as a young Van Gogh, deep in thought and concentration as I worked on my soon to be globally recognised masterpiece. Fun Friday nights under the kitchen lights.

Well, until that angry little rhino boy called my bluff and gave out to me for seeking approval. So now I was just going to give it all up and let the beautiful piece forever remain half finished? Correct. Yes. *Exactly*.

Not that I was going to fully give up on art. Soon I would be enrolled in after-school art classes. Here, however, I was back trying to draw my hand or a sunset, maybe even once attempt some flowers in a vase. That awful generic gibber that can frustrate the life out of any abstract artist slash rigid colourer. My passion was gone. Felt like a sheep trying to all draw the same apple. Frustrated me beyond belief. Could see what I wanted to draw in my mind. Just never came out like that when I tried though.

The worst case of that was at my Nana and Granddad's farm in Tipperary one afternoon. My parents and my brother were going out for a walk and asked if I wanted to come or stay. Nay nay, I'm going to stay here to colour and draw. So they left and I did that.

Drew a boat with my pencil. Finished up and realised it was not a very good boat. Started to annoy me. I had seen Darren do the same earlier on that day. His drawing was good. Why can't I just draw what I see in my head? Why is this so crap? Why won't my hand do what my head is thinking?! Without knowing it I started jabbing the pencil down on the piece of paper on the table. Stupid art. Jab. Stupid drawing. Jab. Stupid boat. JAB. Stupid brain JAB. Stupid ME! JAB JAB JAB!!! Three quick jabs, a fit of rage and a sharp pencil. Not a good combination. Rammed the pencil down in blind rage. Stabbed myself by mistake. Kept jabbing a few more times before I realised what happened,

"STUPIDARRRGGGHHHOWWWWW. My finger, MY FINGER! My hand. Stupid other hand - Why did you do that???"

My Mum arrived back from the walk to see me nursing my bloody, lead-filled finger. What happened, she asked. I don't know, I offered. Embarrassed. Worried. Freaked. Am I a psycho? No, I'm cool, right? Cool kids aren't psychos. Although, am I cool? Jesus, I don't know. Maybe this is just the closest I could get to Van Gogh? His ear, my finger?

Couldn't explain myself. The pencil slipped. I was annoyed. Frustrated. Angry. I don't know, Mum. It just happened. I didn't mean for it. But it did. An accident. Weird accident. I won't do it again. Waved my bloody finger in the air like a wand and gave my best attempt at a queasy smile. See, all better. I'm cool!

With that I retired my art and colouring malarky. At least I had the medals to remember the glory days. Doodles in class was all I was good for after that stabbing incident. Told my Dad I wanted to play soccer instead. Hurling. Golf. Anything. Something. Just throw me a ball! Art off. Sports on!

Now whenever someone asks me "Any good at art?" I just say, "Yeaaah. Won a lot of competitions when I was younger." The truth. Technically. An artful dagger. An artful dodger.

Chapter 4
Boy Boobs

So I'm at the kitchen table, I'm seven and I'm savouring a bowl of what would soon be my form of crack – Breakfast cereal. My Mum is in the sitting room next door, minding my new sister Sarah. She's just been born. I came back from school today to see her at home for the first time. It was mighty. This tiny little ball of a baby all wrapped up in a pink blanket in a cot in my sitting room. Blond hair and blue eyes. Not sure who she looks like.

I know I look like my Mum. Same colour eyes and hair. My Mum has dark brown, shoulder length hair curled up at the ends. She kind of a looks like an Irish version of Jackie Kennedy mixed with the Mum in the American TV show *That 70s Show*. Small, sound, mighty Mum.

Sarah starts yawning at me so I yawn back at her and she smiles at me. Then I try to watch TV but my Mum said I couldn't because it would be too loud and Sarah might need to sleep. So it's going to be like that, is it Mum? Chosen sides already.

Now instead of watching TV on the couch in the sitting room, I'm in my kitchen. Munching cereal. In walks my Dad, just home from a long day at work. He kind of looks like Michael J. Fox's

Dad in *Family Ties* (minus the beard) mixed with Father Ted Crilly from the Irish sitcom *Father Ted*, what with his greying hair, lean build and friendly face. First question he asks me,

"Any soccer news, Mark?"

"Not sure Dad, don't think so."

This was always our greeting after school. If ever there was some soccer news - a transfer of note, the draw for Ireland's World Cup group, things like that - I took great pride in breaking the information to my Dad first. Today, dead.

No news is good news though, right?

"I have some news for you, Mark."

"Tell me!"

"Guess…"

"Blue? Batman! I don't know."

I was never a good guesser.

"Here's a clue…"

My Dad starts swinging his left leg and rotates his hips.

"What's that?"

"Guess…"

"Are you hurt?"

"No, come on, guess. It's something to do with sports."

What's he on about? Whatever motion that is, it doesn't look sporty. I wonder if he's losing it?

"Don't know Dad. Are you swinging your leg like a golf club?"

"No, why would I swing my leg like a golf club? This is a golfing clue."

My Dad then does an excellent golf swing as if he's taking a tee shot.

"Oh yeah, that's a good one."

"Guess again, you must get it now."

My Dad starts doing the leg swinging, hip rotating motion once more. Adds in a peau peau noise for every swing, as if he was a sniper of some sort. Really throws me off. Mind stuck in a rut.

"I think it's golf."

My Dad gives up.

"Not golf. It's soccer. I'm kicking a soccer ball, see?"

"Oh, now I get it. Ha, good one Dad! Why are you kicking a pretend ball?"

"You said you wanted to join a team."

"I did?"

"Was it you or your brother?"

Well if Darren said he wanted to join a team then I definitely said it too,

"I said it before him! Am I joining one?"

"You are. This Sunday, are you free?"

Hmmm, Sunday, Sunday, what have I going on Sunday? I'm seven, so nothing. Yeah, I'm free.

"Brilliant, can't wait!"

And so began my foray into the competitive world of soccer. The team was called Tramore Athletic. They trained at the secondary school that my Dad used to go to, Scoil Crios Ri. Behind the main school building there was a pitch. Not really a pristine soccer pitch like I'd see in movies and on TV that the children in America get to practice on. More like an irregularly shaped field with patches of grass and dirt. Kind of looked like it had been freshly ploughed by wild horses. Perfect place to go play.

Darren couldn't go that day so I went alone (what eight-year-old has plans he can't change, maybe a birthday party?). Not too happy about going solo but I couldn't let my Dad down. Drove me to the school on a cold, overcast, damp Sunday morning in

September. In lieu of changing rooms, the car park was where we were to get ready. Tut. What kind of set-up is this?

I'm wearing tiny white shorts, itchy white wooly socks and a blue Everton jersey, the team my Dad - and I by default - supported. How I rue that choice. I think we've won one trophy in all the years I supported them. My brother went with Liverpool, Everton's local and fierce rivals. Not sure how he got away with that but it was an apt choice, fueled some good rivalry.

Anyway, it's cold. I'm in shorts. I know no one. I want to go home already.

"Just go out and see what it's like," my Dad tells me, "I'll wait here for you."

"OK. I'll just go have a look. I'm not going to change into my new boots yet though, in case it's not on. I'll go in my slippers and come back if I like it."

Out of the car I hop. The car park is also the schoolyard so there are bike racks in a weary looking shed and a rusty basketball hoop that no one uses. Salute some other boys who are in the shed with an awkward nod of the head. Field is surrounded by a crumbling stonewall. Run through a gap in it, out on to the field and almost trip on a divot. Say nothing, jog on.

Coaches in shiny green shellsuits are setting up soccer drills everywhere. Boys of all ages milling around, from seven to fifteen. I might be the youngest here. Watch some of the older boys doing tricks and passing the ball to each other. They look cool. I wish I was their age. I wonder if I can play on that team? As I'm deep in nonsense thought, one of the boys miscontrols the ball and it shoots off in my direction.

"Hey boy, kick that ball over, will ya? Pass it back."

"Who, meeee?" I point to myself.

"Just kick it back."

"OK!"

This is brilliant. I'm with the cool guys already. Run to go kick the ball back. As I do I see that it's not the kind of ball I usually play with in my back garden. The ones I usually play with are light plastic balls of air that a butterfly could kick with ease if it had legs. This looks like a lumpy medicine ball, a big heavy bag of leather filled with soup cans. I wonder if I can kick it? Too late now, I'm running and just about to… Whack!

The ball doesn't even move. My foot stays rooted to the leather while the rest of me flies over the ball. Land in a heap. Waves of pain crash over me. Eyes water up. Feels likes I just kicked a lump of cement. Lightning rod of pain shoots through my entire body. Owwwwww. OWWWWWWWW. Play it cool, my brain shouts at me. Boys don't cry.

As cool as I can muster, I roll over on the grass towards the ball. Pick it up and heave it feebly in their direction. Hear them laughing as I roll the other way and lay with my face in the grass. Turn my head to the side and see they're all giving me thumbs up, thanks. Give them two thumbs up in return, arms stretched out in front of me. Looks like I'm some sorted of stupid Superman lying face down on the grass. Pick myself up and hobble back to the car park. Why oh why did I kick that big boys' ball with just my slippers on? Felt like kicking a brick in my bare feet. Think I broke my foot. About to pass out. Can't make a scene in front of all these people. Must keep up appearances.

Shuffle back through the gap in the wall. Brave face as I walk past the shed. Hold onto the basketball pole for a second. Regroup. Go again. Walk. Don't cry. Quick. Haul myself back inside the car dragging my entire limp, left leg behind me like a golf bag attached to my body. My Dad looks beyond excited,

"How did it go? Should I get your boots out of the back for yo-"

"DAAAAAAAADDDD, IWANTTOGO – sniff - HOOOME."

"What happened??"

"There was... Sob... Big boys... Sobsniffsob... Big boys balls... I want to go home."

After I got home and lay down on the couch in my sitting room for an hour or so with my ankle iced up, I explained exactly what happened. Don't think my wailing was the reaction my Dad expected, hoped for more. Looked worried that that would be it for soccer and me, over before it could even begin. Little did we know that in the future I would go on to love playing it, compete in all sorts of competitions around the world and win all kinds of trophies. At the time we weren't aware of this though.

"Think you'll try again next week and see if you like it with Darren there?"

Tried my best to cheer him up,

"OK so Dad, one more go. I think I will like it."

Attempted to swing my bandaged left foot and rotate my hips while lying on the couch eating my bowl of cereal. It was then I saw the look of hopeful pity on my Dad's face, one that told me he was now pinning all hopes of Darren being the soccer player in the family. At least I had my cereal. Peau peau.

As it happens I didn't go to soccer training again for a few weeks. Picked up another foot injury, both ankles this time. I blame Darren. Maybe I started it. Not sure. Later that week we were watching TV but nothing good was on. Mind started wandering.

"Here Darren."

"Yeah?"

"Ever jump off the roof?"

"All the time."

"The big one?"

"The big one is too high."

"I'm going to jump off that."

"No you're not."

"Yeah I am, I'm going to right now."

"Well I'm going to do it first."

With that I ran out of the sitting room, up the stairs, climbed out of Darren's bedroom window on to the lower roof section, raced up the smaller, slanted, red tiled roof while holding on to the white pebbled wall on the side of the house, hoisted myself up on to the main roof two stories up, then ran and just jumped off without really thinking. I should've probably stopped to consider what I was doing perhaps but I might have bottled it and Darren would've pipped me to doing it first.

That jump was not really a wise call for many reasons, the main one being I was wearing soft velvet slippers instead of runners. The lack of a rubber sole meant that when I planted the landing on the garden below, all the shock from my flabby body was absorbed directly through my feet. Striking flash of pain shot through me. Stomach turning. Sick sensation rippled up from the soles of my feet and spread throughout my body like waves of terror. Oh dear Jesus, what have I done? Stood crouched for a few seconds looking like an Olympian that just nailed the pummel horse landing, before slowly keeling forward, looking like an idiot falling face first into a bed of roses.

Darren, watching from his bedroom window, quickly distanced himself from the crime scene, as you would. Closed the window as soft as he could, crept back downstairs to the sitting room and started watching TV again like nothing happened. When my Mum asked if she knew where I was, he simply replied "Not sure." The proper answer would've been "He's outside crawling towards a bush to hide so you won't see him, wondering if he might have paralyzed himself" but that would've got us both in trouble.

Couldn't walk properly for two weeks after that. Still though, it was worth it. The shock my soles went through turned Darren off ever attempting such a jump. So I won. And, apparently I looked kind of like Batman when I jumped, with my black dressing gown fanning out like a cape around me. Well worth the pain.

On the downside, the lying around and doing nothing so I could rest my swollen ankles was probably when I started to up my cereal intake from a few bowls to a box a day. Eat that boredom away. Still, no pain, no gain, isn't that what fat people in denial say?

Thank God I did actually start playing soccer regularly. Combat this newfound love for breakfast cereal. Munch it all day long if I could. And I did. Coco Puffs, Frosties, Cornflakes, I liked them all. Special K was always a favourite though. Maybe because it had the word 'Special' in it. My seven-year-old mind assumed it must be better than all the rest. Or was it that my Mum's name is Kathleen so the letter 'K' got thumbs up in my mind? Not sure.

Both of my grandmothers, or Nana Ryan and Nana Hayes as I call them, used to have it in their houses too so I always enjoyed that aspect of the cereal as well. They used to let me douse copious spoons of sugar on top of each bowl and allowed as many refills as I liked. I was a chubby child for a while, now that I think back. Obviously I had no clue at the time that I was actually chubby, but I definitely grew out before I managed to grow up. Still not fully grown up, some might say.

After school I would love to just sit in my kitchen and eat bowl after bowl while watching cartoons on the small black Sony kitchen television. Finish the first bowl. See some sugary milk coating the bottom. Top it up with cereal. Bit too much cereal. Needs more milk now. Might as well just make this another full bowl. Eat. Repeat. Eat. Repeat.

As I got older the cartoons became TV shows, *Baywatch*, *McGuyver*, *Knots Landing*. Anything really. Just as long as I had cereal at hand I was happy. Eventually I started making my way through a couple of boxes of it in one sitting. My Mum would come home from the weekly shopping on a Friday and I'd have polished off a box of cornflakes by the time all the food was put away. It eventually got to the point where my Mum held a mini intervention in my kitchen on a Friday night,

"Mark, are you eating too much cereal?"

"No way Mum," I replied while shoveling another heap of Frosties into my mouth, the current flavor of the month. "Only my third bowl this evening, the next will be my last. Probably."

I remember my Mum delicately phrasing the next part.

"It's just, some people have asked me if you are maybe eating more than you should be."

That caught my attention. No longer watching *Top of the Pops*. Something's up. Ears go a bit red. Slowly take another spoon of sugar coated, weight-gain, grain of delight. Lap up the milk from my bowl and hide behind it before bracing myself,

"What do you mean? Who said that?"

"Just some people. Not in a bad way. They just thought you looked a bit heavier when they saw you last."

"Whatpeople? Whatdoyoumean? No I'm not."

"OK Mark, I was just asking."

What are earth is mother talking about, I wondered. Is she losing it? Probably. Just finish this bowl and give her a thumbs up. Keep her spirits high while she obviously goes senile.

As I stood up to go rinse my favourite speckled white cereal bowl and put it in the dishwasher, the top button on my summer shorts popped off. Maybe I jerked my body. Maybe my shorts had shrunk? Not sure. Thought it was funny though.

"Ha ha, Mum, see that? It just popped right off!"

"I think you might have had enough cereal for tonight Mark, don't you?"

It was then that I saw my reflection in the darkened kitchen window. Realised I was sucking in my belly. Wheezed out a slow, deep, full of cereal breath. Aaahhh-oh. Now I get it. I'm fat. Oh Jesus. That's what my Mum was trying to tell me. Ears go redder. Face follows. My Mum is turning on the dishwasher so doesn't see me realise this. All she hears is,

"Sorry, I won't eat any more cereal, I'll stop. I get it."

Ran off to my bedroom and looked at myself in the full-length mirror. Don't look too fat. Took my top off. Start holding in my breath. Caught myself, I'm doing it again! Realised this was something I'd been doing for a while. Fooling. Tricking. Bluffing. Some ape. Trying to hide my flabby belly. Hoping it might distract from my fleshy nipples. I always wondered if mine were big or simply fat ones. Did I have boy boobs?

Now I knew. Although seeing as I used to wrap my towel around my whole body and not just my waist when I got out of the shower makes me think I knew all along. Maybe this was why I also sucked in my face when I looked in the mirror. Hide my big, squirrel, nut-storing cheeks. That's it: No more cereal. Ever!

Well, in moderation, of course.

Next week I was back playing soccer. Needed the exercise. Haven't looked back since. Farewell, boy boobs, see you when I'm old and fat.

Chapter 5
Is She Scottish?

Looking back at it, my parents put me up for all kinds of after school activities when I was growing up. Sports was a given. Soccer, hurling, Gaelic football, pitch and putt, table tennis, swimming, badminton, indoor, outdoor, mental, physical, the whole shebang. Art. Reading. Maths competitions. Anything on offer. Always dropping me off to a sports field, library or community hall, then collecting me an hour or two later. Some parents. Whizzing around, making sure I got the most out of life. Also helped to get me out of the house, a bit of relax time for them no doubt.

Tried my hand at musical activities for a while but never really got fully bitten by the musical bug, despite my rock star daydreams. Played a bit of tin whistle in school, good enough too. Couldn't beat the true sound blowing out when your fingers and breath all aligned with the holes on the whistle "A highdilly didilly didilly do, hey hup the garden how she grow." Some kind of song like that. Stopped playing the whistle for some reason, can't remember fully. Maybe I saw a music video on MTV with Slash playing the guitar and thought *What the funk am I doing with this whistle?*

I did also play the piano for a while. Santa gave me a small Casio keyboard for Christmas one year. I loved that keyboard, especially the one song that was already prerecorded on it, Wham's *Wake Me Up Before You Go Go*. Used to impress everybody by subtly pressing that Demo button and then pretending to play along. When my delighted aunts and uncles heard me go, an encore was always called for but I feigned tiredness,

"That one took a lot out of me, maybe later."

There was never a later.

After a few months I kind of lost interest. Clearly I wasn't a prodigy so teaching myself didn't happen, no matter how many How To books I read. Couldn't even read the music notes. So, my Mum said she would find a teacher for my brother Darren and I. Give piano a proper whirl. I think I was about ten. Still had time to become a prodigy. One of the teachers in my school recommended a lady named Lisa to my Mum. Apparently she was a wizard at the piano. My Mum signed Darren and myself up. Piano. On!

The day of our first lesson Darren went to Lisa's house right after school. He would be there for three to four and my lesson was four to five. I remember on the drive to Lisa's house for my turn my Mum was making weird small talk. Looking back at it now I realise she was trying to prepare me for something but at the time I was oblivious.

"What's Lisa like, Mum, will I like her?"

"She's very nice, lovely lady. She does speak a bit different to you though."

"Huh? What do you mean? Does she have an accent?"

"Well no, not exactly but it's just…"

"Is she Scottish? I can't understand Scottish people, I bet she's Scottish, that's a strong accent isn't it?"

"Well, emm, you'll see. This is her house, send Darren out when you go in."

"OK, see you at five o'clock, I'll taaalkk to yaaa layterrr."

Ten-year-old me had a terrible Scottish accent. Knocked on the front door and an old woman answered. Looked like a granny. Lisa's older than I imagined.

"Are you Mark?"

"Hi. I am. Is this the right house?"

"Yes, come in. Lisa is almost finished with your brother. You can wait here and watch cartoons. Would you like a drink?"

"Yes please!"

Sat and waited in the living room, eating crisps and drinking fizzy orange, watching *Top Cat*. Big fan of the piano lesson so far. About five minutes later I heard Darren outside the door, saying goodbye. Popped his head into the living room.

"Your turn."

"What's it like?"

"Good. Did Mum tell you about Lisa?"

"Yeah, she's Scottish, Mum's outside waiting."

Looks at me weird. Off he went, in I go. Led through the darkly lit kitchen to the converted garage where the piano and Lisa are waiting for me. Smells like they're having pork chops for dinner, I think we are too actually, better stop eating all these crisps. Hear the sound of the piano playing as I walk in, sounds amazing, some classical number,

"That sounds ama-"

Lisa stands up and greets me with a smile and a handshake. I stand and stare, then try to act normal. Look at the piano. Black, an upright I think. Look around the room. Dartboard on the wall over there, freezer in the corner over there. Lawnmower looks nice. Couple of toolboxes next to it. Dusty looking brown couch beside the piano. Very nice. Finish up the visual tour of the garage. Shove a fistful of crisps in my mouth to keep myself busy. Anything to hide the fact that I'm trying to figure out if Lisa has Down Syndrome.

Bad as it may sound, I was never really used to being around people who were disabled in any way, mentally or physically. There was a deaf school next to my primary school so I did see plenty of deaf people but it was always from a distance. Now though, in this rundown converted garage, I'm pretty sure I'm about to meet a disabled person for the first time. I think she is anyway,

"Hi Mark, nice to meet you."

"Hello… Hi… Hello Lisa. Are you… You're not - Are you Scottish?"

"Scottish? No, I'm from Cork. Same as you."

"Oh yeah."

"Come in and sit down."

"OK, I'm sorry."

"Why are you sorry?"

"I just… I don't know… how to play the piano."

"Well that's why you're here to learn!"

Swallowed my mouthful of crisps and sat down at the piano. Lisa didn't seem too dissimilar to me really, just spoke a bit different, as if there was cotton wool in her cheeks. Looked normal too. Curly red hair, around my height but in her mid-twenties, wearing a purple wooly jumper and blue jeans. Her glasses with the really thick lenses were the only giveaway. Only minor things really but they were kind of huge to my tiny mind, at the start at least.

Avoided the elephant woman I created in the room and got around to the lesson. I did feel my ears glow red when I couldn't fully understand something she said, somehow my fault for not listening well. Kind of enjoyed the lesson overall, when it sounded good I loved it but when I messed up I hated it, myself and everything in between like nothing else. Very healthy creative reaction.

Kept up the lessons for about six months. Lisa was a good teacher and really nice but I started to find their house a bit dreary after a while. Always seemed to be eating pork chops, the smell never changed. I also thought I would be learning how to play cooler music than what was on the lesson menu, some European dance music for example. Instead Lisa told me I should start with the basics and move up to that. After mastering scales we moved on to some classics like *Greensleeves*. After I really *nailed* that song I assumed the next step would be dance music followed by performances on the TV show *Top of the Pops* soon after. Alas, Lisa felt I should stick with classics for the time being. My interest soon waned.

I think Lisa realised she was losing me at Christmas time so she changed it up for a special treat. Instead of a normal lesson I would be given a bag of crisps, a chocolate bar and a big glass of Fanta while I listened to her play all my favourite songs for an hour. Couldn't say no either way (my preferred option would've been to go home early) so I just nodded my head along,

"Sounds great."

Unfortunately, I only knew two songs off the top of my head, *Get Ready For This* and *No Limit*, both by the Dutch Eurodance band 2Unlimited who were huge at the time. Lisa had never heard of them. She knew plenty of Mozart though, so that's what was on the menu. I tried my best to listen along but pretty soon I was fast asleep on the couch in her garage, dreaming of cheesy Eurodance music.

Woke up when I spilt the full glass of orange all over my grey school pants, leaving a dark wet patch on my crotch area. Looked like I wet myself in my sleep. Despite my pleas of innocence Lisa told me it was OK, lots of boys wet themselves.

As it happened I had a bit of a problem growing up with wetting myself in my sleep. Got to the point where I was way too old to be doing it. Just loved my bed, my pyjamas, being warm. Would've gotten cold if I got up to use the bathroom in the middle of the night. So I used to just lay there. And wait. Until it happened. Again. More sheets ruined.

Anyway, the fact that this was not the case now made me more adamant to make Lisa see the truth. Deliriously so. Swore on every religion available that that wasn't what happened but I could see she didn't believe me. By the end I was trying to lick my pants to prove it was only fizzy orange. Now it was Lisa's turn to look at me like maybe I was a bit different. Needless to say, I never went back again.

One extracurricular activity I was enjoying a lot more was the soccer team myself and Darren played for, Tramore Athletic. The main man in the club was Der O' Callaghan. About forty, looked a bit like Robert DeNiro, looked after all the underage teams. Owned a pizza shop too, Zico's. Gave us free slices and chips after the games. Some man.

Can't remember too much of the games but the trips we went on still stand out in my mind. I remember this one day trip in particular when I was twelve where the whole club went to a holiday place called Trabolgan. This was a water-park, sports adventure land, all-in-one fun family resort about an hour from where I lived, like a faded, smaller, worn down Irish version of Disneyland without any of the rides. Team bonding exercise or something like that.

I remember in the deep end of the swimming pool they had a wave-making machine. You'd swim around and ride the waves. Kind of deep. Darren and the older boys on the team a year above me were doing it so I wanted a go too. Swam down and waited for the waves to begin.

First wave caught me by surprise. Way bigger than I expected. Swallowed a bucket of water. Struggled to get my breath back. Everyone else was doing their own thing so no one noticed me flailing, panicking and drowning. "Darren… Dorney… Chockie – Help!" Finally caught the attention of a guy Bobby O' Toole, this pleasant brute of a boy built like a tank with the head of a hippo, who manages to drag me off to the side.

As I lay there puking up pool water and gasping for air, a small, plain, pale skinned, brown haired girl around my age came over to us.

"My friend likes your friend," she says to Bobby in a thick Scottish accent. "Will he get off with her?"

Before I could say no and ask her if she supports Rangers or Celtic, Bobby says yes. Did he not know I'd never kissed a girl before? I could barely breath and just came close to drowning. I'm not ready for this. Nervous as funk. Plus, and most importantly, I don't even know what the girl looks like. What if she's a Rangers fan? Catholics. Protestants. Frowned upon.

"Which girl is it?" Bobby asks, still acting as my spokesman.

The friend points over to another brown haired girl standing about twenty feet away. Tall, toned, tanned, long hair past her hubullas, nice lips, looks good in her black bikini. Kind of reminds me of my neighbour who lives around the corner from me that I fancy, Katie. Brown hair. Big lips, big eyes, like the main girl in the TV show *Boy Meets World*. At the time I had no clue what my feelings for her meant, I just knew that I was eager to impress and wanted to hang around with her. Unfortunately, things had soured. Kind of my fault.

One day I joined her after a game of soccer while she was out with her new baby brother Dougie in his baby-stroller. Took turns pushing the pram as we strolled around. This is the life, I thought when it was back to my turn. Dougie seemed to enjoy my pushing technique a lot. Push, weeee. Push, weeee. Push, we- Oh Jesus. Pushed too hard. Pram hit a tiny pebble on the road. Front wheels buckled. Whole thing toppled over. Baby brother flies out. Hits the ground. Face first. Starts wailing. Scrapes. Cuts. Bruises. Nothing *too* serious, but after that Katie and her whole family stopped talking to me. So that was nice.

Anyway, this girl in the black bikini could be Katie's replacement. On looks alone I like her. Give her a wave, a thumbs up and a wave again, then collapse on my back and spit out the rest of the water still coming up from my lungs. Bobby arranges a time and a place with the friend where we should meet for this kiss: Monkey bars by the five-a-side pitch next to the indoor hall in one hour. Sorted.

Well, one thing leads to another and before you know it myself, Bobby and two other friends Keith and Stephen (two small, blond haired, mousey looking twins) lose track of time while playing crazy golf. Bobby lost track of time anyway. I was watching the clock tick every minute away, hoping he would forget. Not sure why I was so nervous. Would I get in trouble if I was caught? By who, I don't know. There was definitely apprehension though. Half an hour after the time arranged for the kiss, Bobby remembers. Tells Keith and Stephen. I smack my forehead,

"How did we forget?! Well, too late now. Damn. Sugar. Rats."

"No way boy, we can still try. Come on, she looked up for it!"

"But you didn't even find out if she's a Celtic fan or not? What if she supports Rangers? I can't kiss a Protestant girl, can I?"

Bobby tells me to shut up. Of course I can. He is well up for me kissing this girl for some reason. Keith and Stephen agree with him. I do too. Off we go to the monkey bars. Arrive. No one in sight. Wait for twenty minutes. Still nobody around. Looks like I missed out. Dose.

"Time to head back I'd say, our bus is leaving soon."

On the walk back I go on about how I'm gutted she wasn't there. Really looking forward to kissing her. Man, I missed out. Jokingly say how we should pretend to everyone that I did actually kiss her if anyone asks. They all look at me like I'm a weirdo: "No."

"Just joking lads, not serious about that, ha ha."

I was dead serious.

Get back to the car park where the bus is waiting. Three teams worth of soccer players all hanging around outside it. Five soccer managers as well: Der, Ken, Dave, George and Mick. All legends. All laughing. It's then I spot the girl and her friend. Bobby does too. Oh no.

"There she is Marky boy, you can still do it!"

As the group sees me they all cheer. They must know what's going on. My feet and hands start sweating. I wave back. The tall girl starts walking towards me. This is all very surreal. Bobby, Keith and Stephen keep walking. I stand as the girl reaches me. She smiles and laughs. I laugh and snort. She tells me her name. She is Scottish. My mind goes blank. Forget her name. Ask her where she wants to go. She doesn't know. I say how about here, pointing to a cluster of bare trees next to us. We walk into the middle of the trees. Still in full view of the soccer team but down a bit at least.

I don't know what's going on. She seems to have more of a clue. I follow her lead. Eyes. Shut. Heads. Tilt. Embrace. Tongues going at it. Slow. Then fast. I'm not breathing. Eyes shut closed. This feels nice. Hear everyone cheering. Next minute I feel something hit the side of my head. A funking stone. Ow. Look around. See a guy Shane from my soccer team shouting out "Go on Hayser!" Apparently throwing a stone at my head was his way of saying well done. Bit of blood. I say to the girl maybe we should go back. Emerge out of the trees. I make a dramatic wipe of my mouth with my sleeve, a 'look at me lads, I'm covered in salvia!' Soccer team cheers. I pump the air. Girl goes off with her friend for dinner. We all get on the bus. And then we go home. Me worried the entire time that my parents might find out and I might get in trouble for some reason.

Great first kiss really, although I never found out if she was a Rangers or Celtic fan. Say nothing.

Chapter 6
Simply The Best

I think I was twelve before I even became fully aware that there were Irish people who were black. Not black Irish as the American term goes (Irish people with dark features like dark hair and brown eyes) but actual black Irish people.

This realisation came about at a quiz one day. Quizzes are huge in Ireland. People love them. Community get-togethers. School fundraisers. Pub piss-ups. Christmas parties. Weddings. Funerals. Irish folk can't beat a good quiz. Big fan of the trivial trivia.

"Name the second longest river in the world?"

"What country is Maputo the capital of?"

"What year did the Irish soccer team first compete in the European Championship?"

That kind of thing. Some laugh. Before smartphones ruined it all.

I used to do a load of quizzes growing up. Besides being a proud man with an elegant soul who loves golf, my Dad has always been a big quiz head. Always the quizmaster when his school held a quiz fundraiser. Also volunteered as the school's soccer coach so it was a good balance. He worked in the north side of the city in a school a tad bit rougher than mine so the soccer side definitely helped make him a fan favourite with the students. Promoted to principal after a few years so he enjoyed working there as well. Personally I think the fact he was the quizmaster helped this along but say nothing.

My Dad prepared for upcoming quizzes like a master chess player deciding tactics before a big tournament. Studiously pouring over encyclopedias at home, standing in the dining room, books strewn across the dark mahogany table, pen behind the ear, ruffling his salt and pepper hair, mulling and debating which question would be just right - not too easy but not unfairly hard. This is where I honed my quizzical skills. David Hayes, the wizard like quiz professor, popping random facts and spits of knowledge at me. Soaked it all up. Let the gibber flow!

Represented my school at national tournaments and the likes, usually on a team of four - Me and three other nerds. Karl, Raymond and Donald. I never really considered myself a full on nerd. First of all we didn't really use the term nerd much when I was growing up. Secondly I didn't think I looked like one. The other guys on the school quiz team did in my eyes: Karl, skinny and tall with thick glasses and a love of playing air guitar while spouting Greek maths theorems; Raymond, chubby red-face, curly ginger hair, non-stop quoting Star Wars, and; Donald, a pale, sick looking weasel of a lad, forever dressed up as Spock from Star Trek.

I, on the other hand, considered myself just a boy with dark brown hair as bushy as a squirrel's tail who happened to do his homework and be good at school (and also lived in a blissful bubble of self-denial). Considering that I did compete in maths competitions for my school as well - Saturday afternoons spent doing sums, subtraction, addition, division and so on - I see now I can no longer really fool myself about my former life. Although I did play various sports a lot so that convinced me I was half-and-half really. Soccer, Gaelic football, hurling, those kinds of sports. Not chess, backgammon and fantasy world role-playing. Nerdy on the inside, sporty on the outside. I was a chocolate bar slogan.

Anyway, one day at a school quiz an odd question came up that none of us had ever heard before,

"Name four brothers who've played soccer for Ireland."

Sport. My strong suit, apparently. None of the other three had a clue about it, so all eyes turned to me. Raspy, whispered voices let loose,

"Come on, Hayes, do you know it? We need this one. You said you liked soccer. WHAT IS IT?"

"Calm down, give me a second, Raymond, I'll get it."

Hmm. Four brothers? Who the funk could they be? My Dad never asked me this one and he knew all the best sports trivia. Brothers, brothers, brothers? McCarthy? O'Toole? O'Malley? No. No. No. Oh no. I don't know. This will not please the nerd group.

"Ehh, I don't know."

"You what?? What do you mean you don't know?! Statistically you should know this!"

"I don't know. I don't have a clue. Never heard this question before."

"By the son of Vulcan, you better make a guess."

"OK. The McCarthy brothers."

"Are you sure?"

"Yes, Spock, I'm sure. That's my guess. Next question."

We raced through the next nine with ease. This quiz was already sown up. The others weren't happy but I didn't care. I just wanted to know the answer. Handed up our sheet. Engaged in awkward ten-year-old small talk. Waited for the answer. The teacher in charge took the mike and listed out the answers.

"Number one: Name four brothers who have played soccer for Ireland: Paul McGrath, Terry Phelan, Chris Hughton and Phil Babb. Number two: What Greek God was known for his…"

The teacher tailed off. I tried to compute. Huh? None of them are related. That's wrong.

"Hey guys, that soccer question must be wrong, that answer makes no sense. This quiz is stupid. I'm going to go say something."

Up I go to the teacher in charge, Mr. Cotter, an old bald guy with a thick brown mustache, decked out in a red tracksuit that went well with his whiskey coloured nose and cheeks.

"Sorry sir, the first answer is wrong. They're not brothers."

"The first one… Oh, they are brothers. It's a trick question. They're all black. Black. Brothers. Get it? Now back to your seat or I'll dock you a point."

Get it? Get *what*? That that's wrong and you smell of stale booze? That I get. The answer I don't.

"Tut."

When I got home my Dad asked if they had any good questions. Any new ones he could use in his next quiz?

"Yeah, I do actually: Name four brothers who have played soccer for Ireland?"

Seemed he already knew the answer. Asked me how I knew that. Told me not to tell my mother that question. Or really say it to anyone. Only then did I get it. It was kind of bad. Or was it? Not sure. All I knew is that I was clueless about black people.

As far as races go, Irish people are pretty white. Pretty and white, says you. Ah stop, says I. When I was growing up there were no black people in Ireland, none that I ever saw anyway. Foreign concept really, kind of like Russian folk, Chinese people or ghosts. Only recently did I learn about Frederick Douglass, the great black

American abolitionist who came to Ireland in 1845 and gained support for his fight against slavery. He even gave a talk in Cork and was nicknamed 'The Black O'Connell' after the great Irish abolitionist and liberator, Daniel O'Connell. No one told me any of this growing up.

Nay. The first black man I remember was the one I saw in a porn magazine somebody had one day after school. Didn't know what everyone was huddled around looking at so I popped my head in between two boys' shoulders and took a peek. I must've missed the good stuff because all I saw was a page of ads full of naked women and bubbles saying *Phone this number! Hot times guaranteed! Call me now, big boy!* In the bottom right hand corner of the page I remember seeing the back of two naked women on their knees looking up at a naked black man holding what looked like a horse's leg. Slowly read the caption… *'Enlarge your pe-'* Jesus. That's not a leg. And now I knew what 'hung like a horse' meant.

Next black person I saw was on TV. Pretty sure it was Danny Glover in Lethal Weapon "I'm too old for this s**t!" I was at my cousins' house in Tipperary watching one their non-PG videos. All the cursing would've made it off limits if I tried to watch it at home. Shortly after that I saw Eddie Murphy in Beverly Hills Cop "Trust me!" This was on TV over Christmas on an Irish station. Sneaked a watch of it in the kitchen on my own late one night while pretending to get some cereal for supper.

For a while I thought all black Americans were funny policemen. Didn't want to be racist or look stupid by asking any questions so I remained blissfully ignorant. I remember seeing some black English TV presenters as well. One guy presented a children's show, one with a lot of puppets. They were all different colours too so it didn't seem to out of the norm for the show. I was young. Dumb. Naive. Unaware.

The first time I met a black person was when I was thirteen. My team Tramore were playing a team called Mallow, a country town full of farmers. I played centre back and their only striker was a boy named Stanley. When I saw him my eyes shot open wide. Black as the colour with big, bright, white teeth and a huge friendly smile. Pure surprise. Not expecting this from a team full of country folk. It'd be different if they were from the city, slightly more cosmopolitan I would've thought. Even stranger, when he said hi to me, his accent was an even thicker Irish one than mine. Heavy Cork slant hung on every word.

"How are ya *biy*, best of luck day, *alright*."

"Oh yeah, thanks, you too, brother."

Gave me a weird look followed by a dazzling smile and a deep hearty laugh. High fived me then walked away laughing. Stanley was *sound*. Barely met him but already we were friendly. Look at me go! I think I was extra nice to him to make sure I definitely wasn't racist in any way. If he tackled me late, I shrugged it off with a "that's fine" and a head nod. He seemed to be one of the happiest people I ever met so wasn't hard to get on with as it was, even if I did just meet him. Not that he scored or anything. Couldn't be *that* nice to him.

Next black person I met was a girl named Mairead who used to be on the same bus home as me from school sometimes. Mairead was a big, strong girl, bit of a mix between Serena Williams and Tina Turner. My Dad was a fan of Tina Turner's music at the time actually now I think of it. I remember the song *Simply The Best* being played over and over again on our record player at home. As an ode I used to sing a few bars of the song to Mairead when I'd see her,

"Dun dun dunnn dun, better than all the rest, better than anyone, you're simply the best!"

She got a great kick out of my warbling. I think she fancied me a lot actually, always gave me a big smile and would offer me a seat on her sturdy lap whenever the bus was full. We were always friendly to each other so sometimes I'd accept. Things soured though. Tupac Shakur was big in Ireland at the time as well so I attempted to bond with her over rap music. My constant repeating of lyrics offended her in the end.

"Yo yo yo, what up my… Em… Mairead, what up west *siiide*?!" Maybe I wasn't saying "what up" correctly. Not sure. She seemed to stop taking the same bus as me after a while. Only nodded an awkward hello if ever I saw her around Douglas village as well. Tut. I messed up. Should've stuck to singing. My Tina Turner impression really is the best.

Chapter 7
The Booze Brothers

The summer of '96 was a mixed bag really for Ireland. On the one hand, we won the Eurovision Song Contest, a singing competition between all the countries in Europe. Each country sings a song and then all the other countries vote for their favourite song, giving points from one to twelve. The songs are typically awful, as in *awful*, but people seem to love it. Somehow it's been going strong since 1956. Ireland has actually won it seven times making it the most successful country ever to grace the Eurovision stage. If you win you host the competition the next year though, which can cost a chunk I do believe. Maybe that's why one year a puppet called Dustin the Turkey was chosen as our singing representative. Our economy couldn't handle another win.

On the downside for the summer of '96 there was a lot of trouble up in Northern Ireland, what with the Protestants and Catholics fighting it out. I wasn't too aware of this at the time though, mostly as Cork is way down in the south of Ireland, away from it all. Sure it was on the six o'clock news every night, reports about bombings or gunshots, but the news was something my parents and older people watched. I was never really a fan of the news, not the stuff they opened with anything. It was always too serious for my liking. I was much more into irreverent fun.

The summer of '96 was a big year for me as well. It marked the first time I ever went to a school disco AND the first time I ever had a booze. I was thirteen going on fourteen and my first drink was a Donkey's Bollocks (bollocks being another term for balls). Only really pretended to drink it mind you, didn't actually swig it back. Some seeped in though I'm sure, so it still counts.

In case you didn't know, a Donkey's Bollocks is a homemade concoction of whatever you could fit in an empty Coca-Cola bottle without your parents noticing that their drinks cabinet had been tampered with. Whiskey, scotch, brandy, vodka, rum and sometimes even a bit of poitín, a potent, mythical drink somehow made from potatoes which was kind of illegal and apparently could kill you if you drank more than a capful, an Irish version of moonshine. Either have the mixture straight or else top up the bottle with a small bit of coke. Quite the horrendous feast, more or less the liquid equivalent of a donkey's bulbous balls.

It was a wet, warm and windy summer's night when I first tasted a Donkey's Bollocks. I remember it well. I was standing on a footpath covered with sludgy mud looking leaves on the side of a country road, waiting in line outside an old, haunted looking monastery. This is where our school discos were held, in with the monks. The aim of the school disco was to see how many girls you could kiss. This was one of our first chances to mingle with the opposite sex now that we were at the age where we started to fancy them.

I had kissed a few girls before so I kind of knew what I was doing in that department. There was the hot, tall brunette I kissed on a soccer day out at the leisure centre earlier in the year. Then there was a girl who my friends at school set me up with. She wasn't my ideal candidate, kind of reminded me of how an aunt looks because of her perm style haircut (I was watching a lot of Baywatch at the time so that had changed my perspective on what I liked in a woman). Didn't want to be known as a frigid though. It was a pleasant, sloppy kiss, even if I did keep my eyes open the entire time by mistake. After that there was… I think they were the only two girls I kissed up to that point actually. Moving on.

The place was called the Rochestown Monastery and the name of the disco was Roco, which was held every Friday night. Roco was known as the best school disco at the time, mostly down to the good ratio of girls who attended. Tall, small, fat, skinny, blondes, brunettes, handful of red heads, most of them dressed in shorts dresses while some of the less classier ones went with skimpy mini skirts and tiny boob tubes. Roco was the place to be.

The monastery was old, first built in 1884. It had a large white spikey gate with a long winding driveway that lead up to a Roman Catholic church, the main grey-stoned monastery with lots of smaller buildings running off it, a once grand pink school building which now looked battered from the ongoing fight with the weather and a vast grounds that included a lake, well manicured gardens filled with deep forest green bushes and sweet smelling red roses, purple hyacinths and white lilies (my Mum and Dad were keen gardeners), along with a dense wooded area and a well-kept graveyard.

The disco was held in around the back of the monastery in the big gothic looking hall about the size of a full basketball court. The hall looked like the inside of a church just without all the pews. Fit a couple hundred people I'd say. DJ located up on the altar playing music. Disco balls shimmered off the stained glass church windows that depicted the crucifixion of Christ or catching the glint in the Virgin Mary's eye in the stable. It felt cool.

There was also a sweet shop off by a side entrance so you could go fill up on sugar to keep you buzzing along. Black Jacks (chewy liquorice flavoured sweets that used to have a Golly Wog boy on the wrapper), Fruit Salads (chewy raspberry and pineapple flavoured sweets) Roy of the Rover bars (chewy Pineapple flavoured bars), Wham bars (toffee flavoured delights) chocolate Mars bars, sweet cigarettes, sugarcoated cola bottles, fizzy drinks and crisps. Buzz. On.

Outside by the cloak room there was a narrow strip of grass and gravel that ran between the hall and the main monastery. This is where we went to get air, hang out and even have a sneaky cigarette. Security guards were everywhere so it was hard getting away with anything. Nobody wanted to get kicked out. At least having all those security guards resulted in the low number of fights. Pretty sure most of the guards were monks too.

Back to the Donkey. So my buddies and I are outside in the queue waiting for the gates to open. Sweating already. Not sure why. Feel lost. What do I do? I'm confused. One of my older friends Jim, who's about fifteen at the time, hands me the plastic bottle with the Donkey's Bollocks.

"Take a smell off that."

Sniff. Mank. Smells like a wet rusty nail.

"Doesn't smell too bad. Reminds me of when my Mum bakes a Christmas cake."

In Ireland Christmas cake batter is lined with a splash of whiskey.

"Take a proper smell, you didn't even put it near your nose."

"I did, I swear."

"You didn't. Take a smell."

Sniiiiiiiiffffffffffffff.

"*Jesus*, that's disgusting! How can you drink that?"

"It's not too bad once you get used to it. Want a drink?"

"I'm OK, thanks though."

"Are you sure you don't want a drink? I think Darren had one."

"He did? All right so, let me have a go."

This was the way with Darren and myself growing up. Seeing as he was a year older than me, if he did something I would follow suit soon after. If Darren jumped off a bridge, I'd sail off a few minutes after him. Up to this point in life I rarely did something before Darren had done it, especially anything that was frowned upon, what with the fear of being grounded by my parents if caught. I think the fact it was his birthday that night was the reason I was allowed go to the disco in the first place. He had a newly bought turquoise Fred Perry shirt on while I was wearing my new white Fred Perry shirt. I was a big copycat back in those days, monkey see, monkey duu.

Odd thing was we didn't really look alike. Darren had that blond hair, blue eyes, All-American look while I looked more like bushy brown haired Spanish boy. Darren also had a dimple-cheeked smile that the girls seemed to like whereas I had more of a confused/mysterious look as if I was always trying to remember whether or not I was wearing underwear.

Anyway, now that I knew Darren has taken a drink from Jim's concoction, I'm up for one. If I was caught I could always say, "But Darren did it too." I take the bottle back from Jim. Inhale another whiff of it. Almost makes me sick.

"Stop smelling it willya!"

"Oh yeah, OK, here goes."

Didn't actually want to taste it but seeing as this was the first school disco I'd ever gone to, I felt I should be cool and fit in. Put the coke bottle to my closed lips and hold it there for a few seconds. Pretending to take deep gulps, sound effects included.

Lips couldn't be shut tighter if I tried. The Donkey's Bollocks starts dripping down my chin like the juices from a tasty burger, just that this burger is raw and tastes like paint stripper. Pull the bottle away, slobbering my lips like I just took my first sip of water after returning from a stint in the Sahara.

"Thanks, that was good."

"You didn't even drink it!"

"I did, what are you on about?"

Hand the bottle back. Turn my head and spit on the ground. Jesus. Mank. Wipe my mouth with my sleeve. Taste it burning on my lips. That was *disgusting*.

"Whatcha think?"

"Not bad, thought it'd be worse."

"It'll put hairs on your chest, Marky boy!"

"I have one already I think."

Only my first time going to a disco but Darren had filled me in beforehand. At the start of the night, various groups of boys would huddle on one side with groups of girls huddled on the other. DJ might play a song someone knew and the groups of boys would start dancing and jumping like apes. Groups of girls would slowly be dancing and having fun with themselves. Few songs later, the groups would disperse into smaller groups. A boy from one group might approach a girl from a different group. His job would be to find out if her friend liked his friend.

"Will your friend Mary get off with my friend Colm?"

"Colm? I don't know. Let me find out."

She'd go back and suss it out. Sometimes it'd be just a simple shake her head: No. Other times the girls would mull and discuss. The boy would go off and tell his friend they're figuring it out. If and when a girl liked a guy they would then awkwardly meet up against a wall or out on the dance floor. Might be small talk but most of the time they'd just start kissing, 'getting off' with each other as we say in Ireland. I know in America that means something else. Innocent here though. Needless to say, it was *great* fun.

Some of the really cool guys would get off with seven or eight different girls in one night. The night of the Donkey's Bollocks Darren was only with one girl but apparently she was the hottest there so he stuck with her. I managed to kiss two girls. Happy enough with that.

First girl I was set up with was a surprise ambush. Her friends just pushed her towards me as mine did the same. Kind of nervous but the thought of the booze in me gave me some false confidence so I danced on. She was tall and skinny, not too well endowed breast wise but had long, golden brown, Mediterranean style hair and big plumped up juicy lips so I didn't back away. Looked good in the dark night light.

We danced for a few seconds with our hands awkwardly on each other's waists, stepping up and down on the same spot. The moonlight streaming in the open windows felt like a spotlight was on us. She took out her chewing gum, stuck it behind her ear, closed her eyes, tilted her head, and opened her mouth. Sign for me to do the same. Thumbs up to my buddies looking on. Lick of the lips. Still burning from the Bollocks. And - Let's dance! Kiss for a song, like two awkward horses trying to eat the heads off each other. Pull back. Smile. Nod. Let go. Never see each other again.

The second girl was waiting up against a wall for me. I had seen her outside by the sweet shop and thought she was hot. Tall, straight blond hair and a huge set of hubullas which were well shown off in her tight, short black dress. Gave the nod yes when her friend asked my friend Rob if I would get off with her. Over I go with Nirvana's *Teen Spirit* playing on the speakers. She shouts something inaudible at me. Laugh and shout back "*Yeah!*" Realise then she had told me her name, Samantha. Eyes close. Lips lock. Kiss. On.

We had barely been at it a minute when I felt a whack across the back of my head. What the funk? Turn around and see an old, grey haired guy in a tattered brown cardigan, rain pants and wellies. Who's this farmer pointing a torch at me?

"NO KISSING ALLOWED."

"Did you just hit me with that torch?"

"You should know better too, Samantha!" he says, shining the torch in her face.

"Leave us alone!" she screams back.

"Yeah, just leave us alone, man."

"Don't you f**king tell me what to do you little f**ker. Get your f**king hands off my f**king daughter."

"Your what now?"

Whack!

Another crack of the torch.

It was at this point when I was kindly asked to leave the disco. Grabs me by the ear. Punts me out the door. Only five minutes left until the dance was over but still, I felt grave injustice. Kick up a confused fuss at the gate but not too much, just in case he knew my Mum or Dad. Nothing much I could do but just wait outside for all my friends to come out. Group gathered around me as I leant up against the monastery wall, one leg bent, both hands in my pockets, spitting out through my liquor-laced teeth.

"Did you get kicked out?"

"Yeah."

"What did you do?"

"Just getting off with a girl. Her old man hit me with a torch."

"Daycent."

As in decent.

"I know."

Grabbed a chewing gum from Darren before our Mum collected us by the front gate. Hopped in the backseat of the car, paranoid I somehow stunk of whiskey, brandy and vodka even though it had been almost four hours since I pretended to drink.

"How was it, Darren? Did you like it, Mark?"

"Yeaaah, it was grand I suppose."

It was unreal. The donkey's bollocks!

After graduating from pretending to drink at school discos, I was soon pretending to drink on Saturday afternoons. This was the ideal day and time seeing as you could leave the house early in the morning and not have to be home for dinner until six. Gave you plenty of time to drink, have fun, sober up, and get home in time for Mass.

When you started off day drinking in Ireland almost everyone drank cider. Scrumpy Jack was the most popular option at the time. Tasted like Cidona, a non-alcoholic fizzy apple drink that's ridiculously popular in Ireland. Scrumpy Jack was also cheap as chips. Couldn't go wrong.

Beginners would get one can, those a bit used to it might go for two, hardcore went for three and the real nutters might have four. First time I ever went, I started off with none. Hadn't planned on going drinking. I was just off cycling my bike around town when I bumped into my brother and four others - Tony, Paul, John, Colm and Jamie. They were all either fourteen or fifteen, a year or two older than me. Spotted them hanging around outside a corner shop in Douglas called Daily's, a newsagents that also had an off-licence (otherwise known as an offie, or liquor store as they say in America).

"Hi boys, where are ye off to?" I ask while cycling my bike around in a circle.

"Nowhere," replies Darren "You should go home."

"Why are ye hanging around here, are ye going drinking?"

"No. Don't say that to Mum either."

"I won't, I'm not stupid like."

"You are."

"No I'm not, shut up Darren. Paul, are ye going drinking?"

"Yeah, keep it down."

"I will, don't worry."

"Are you coming?"

"Ehh… I'm meant to be playing a World Cup soccer tournament in a minute with Ricky, Mick, Brian and a few other lads."

"Fair enough."

"Fiiine, I'll come watch for a minute so sure."

They were all waiting for Jim to sort out the booze. Seeing as everyone was too young to get served, Jim was chosen to go hang around outside Daily's and wait for the right person to come along who could go in and get the booze. Wait. Wait. Wait. Jackpot. Usually a guy that just turned eighteen who was either trying to be cool and/or sound to younger folk. In return you'd have to give him money to buy cigarettes for himself. Great bartering system.

A few minutes after I joined the rest of the gang, Jim arrives back from Daily's with a bag of cans. Hops on his bike and we're off. Follow along as they cycle across the small bridge leading into the woods nearby, The Mangela. No clue why it was given such a horrible sounding name. Maybe it was because boys and girls would go there to mangle each other, as in kiss. Not sure.

The Mangela was a pleasant wooded area with lush green grass, winding footpath, bendy river, babbling brook, wooden footbridge and even a small waterfall, all enclosed with lots and lots of trees - Willow, birch, sycamore, horse chestnut, oak, the works! Picturesque kind of place, one that we would soon ruin.

Over the hill we cycle, through the trees, across the bridge, past the brook and pull up alongside the waterfall. It would be here where the boozing accorded. Few girls where already there just sitting around. One of them is Jim's girlfriend and the rest are her friends. All older than me so I never spoke to any of them before. Almost everyone, guys and girls included, is wearing tracksuit pants and either a soccer jersey or a t-shirt. All the girls looked a bit grungy. Not a huge fan of any of them.

Jim was funny with girls. In my eyes he never really seemed to care what they looked like. Maybe he was operating at a higher level than the rest of us, going for the personality route. Not I. In my eyes none were that good looking, not my type anyway (I preferred ridiculously good-looking now I was hooked on Baywatch).

It's a sunny day but still pretty windy and cold, the good, old head wrecking Irish way. While they all open a can and cheers each other, I hang around by the bridge, attempting to do wheelies. After sussing out that there are no parents around, I make my way over.

"So this is what you do? Just sit around and drink?"

Shoulders shrug. Yeah.

"Want a drink?" Paul asks me.

"Nah, thanks though. What does it taste like?"

"Here."

Tony hands me a cold, golden can of Scrumpy Jack.

"Don't drink it Mark."

"Just let him drink it if he wants, Darren. Open it and have a go."

Crack open the can. Look around to make sure my Mum or Dad haven't magically appeared in any of the bushes. Take the tiniest of sips. Slurp. Reminds me of Cidona all right.

"Cheers Tony."

Hand him back the can. Now I'm in. One of the gang. Giddy up. Nod an awkward hello at the girls. Maybe one or two aren't bad looking after all. Hop back on my bike before an awkward conversation can be started. Start doing wheelies again. Ten minutes later I take another sip. Rest of them have finished one can each already. Seem to be a bit tipsy. Convince myself I might be too.

John then gives me half a full can, says I can finish it if I want. Now I'm fully in. Now I've my own can. Now I'm fully in. Nurse it like there's no tomorrow. The amount of times I would almost put it to my lips and then put it back down as I joined in the conversation. Eventually I took another mouthful as I walked off to pretend to go to the bathroom by the bridge. Spit the mouthful of cider into the grassy bank of the river. Pour the can onto the ground. Didn't want to get it too drunk or anything. Fill it back up with water from the river and head back to the group.

Now I'm in fine fettle. No more booze to worry about drinking. The big danger was getting sick if you'd too much too quickly. No need to worry about that anymore. Just stand there in the circle, drinking manky river water from my can. *Far* smarter option. This is the life!

By now the rest of them are drunk. Paul asks if I am too,

"Yeah I've been chugging this can back sure, almost full when I got it. Pretty drunk alright. This is some laugh, isn't it?!"

Clusters of the group start wandering off. Few of the lads go off with a few of the girls to cavort while the rest of us go run around the forest. Drunk and free! Or, at least pretend to be. Blame the drink for doing stupid things like jump in puddles and whack each other with branches. Well, pretending to almost do them.

As it does in Ireland it soon started pouring rain, despite being sunny for a couple of hours before. Pouring as in *bucketing*. Everyone bolts for the trees above the waterfall to get cover. This was one of those pours that had no intention of giving up though. Our fun in the sun is over.

Two options really: Stay hiding here in the woods. Or. Make a run for it to our bikes and just go home. Almost six o'clock anyway. Let's just go home.

We kind of had to climb up a steep hill to get to the trees. This was now basically a mud pit with all the rain. Nobody else except for me really copped on to this. All ran straight down the hill to the bikes while I chose to take the path the long way around and just walk down. All lost their footing within seconds. Slid down the mudslide into the waterfall. Everyone thought it was the funniest thing ever until they realised that going home covered in mud might get them caught drinking. They didn't really care though. They were drunk.

I, on the other hand, was not. So I did care. And didn't want to be caught. I'd be grounded for weeks, stuck in my room while everyone was out playing. That thought freaked me out a bit. Decided I was definitely going home. No more hanging around in the rain. Darren was coming with me too. He was hungry, covered head to toe in muck and slurring his words. Liability.

We start cycling on the slick wet roads back home to Rochestown, battling through the torrential rain and chewing copious amounts of gum to get rid of the smell of cider off our breath (river water in my case). Just as we round the last corner before our house the chain on my bike falls off. Whack my shin off the wheel as the bike goes wonky and almost take a hopper.

"Hang on!" I yell out to Darren, "My chain fell off."

"I'll meet you at home" he yells back. "Too wet... If Mum asks we weren't together!"

"OK so!"

Kneel down and fix the oily chain, watching Darren drunkenly zigzag his muddy way home on the bike. Few minutes later I follow him down the driveway. Put my bike in the shed out the back and quietly make my way in the back door of the house. Whip off my wet shoes and pants and put them in the washing basket. Check my breath. If I can just get to my room without seeing my Mum or Dad, I'll be fine. Open the kitchen door - Stopped in my tracks by my Mum. Oh Jesus. She doesn't look too happy. And I'm not wearing pants.

"Were you out with Darren?"

"Ehh, no. I was playing soccer out in the backfield. Why?"

"He's upstairs getting sick all over himself."

"Huh? He is?"

"Yes, sitting on the toilet getting sick onto his knees."

"Why would he do that?"

"He was out drinking with God knows who, covered in mud too."

"Drinking? Coca-cola or what?"

"No no, it doesn't matter. Your dinner is ready if you're hungry?"

"Yeah, *starving*. I've only had water and an apple all day."

Needless to say, this would become our brotherly act. From then on every time we went drinking together I always made sure my chain fell off or my lace became undone right before we went into the house. Let the sacrificial lamb head in first, then follow along and eat both our dinners. Sneaky. As. Funk.

Not sure if Darren ever knew about taking the bullet for both of us. I'd like to think so but I don't think he had a clue. I'm a great younger brother in fairness. Sometimes I'd be far drunker than Darren too. Lying on my bed staring at the ceiling and wondering about life. Doing my best to avoid getting the dreaded spins while I listened through the bedroom wall as my Mum or Dad gave out to my drunken brother in the room next door after finding more drink stashed away in his sock drawer.

"I was minding it for a friend, I swear!"

Sure he was.

"Is he drunk again?" I'd ask my parents in the kitchen later, rolling my eyes. "Tut." Shake of my head. "What's he like?"

Chapter 8
Masters of Myth

Ireland is a great place to go if you ever want to hear some made up facts. We are masters of the myth. Forever hearing them from various friends and acquaintances when I was growing up, although at the time I was clueless and believed them all. Usually these tales were told on the cold, thirty-minute walk home from school, a renowned time to tell stories to one another before the days of electronic gadgets to keep us occupied,

"The guy who lives in that house is a *giant*."

"What kind of giant?" I'd reply in wonder.

"You know those two sisters are lesbian witches?"

"What's a lesbian?" I'd ask confused.

"Stay away from that house, the man who lives there is the devil."

"*Really*? The *actual* devil lives on my street??" Half afraid, half in awe. "I knew we had a nice house."

The older you got the less you believed the fantasy world stuff. Eventually you came to realise they were all spoof and no longer needed to ask your Mum,

"Stephen said that if I went down that manhole I'd end up in Australia, is that true?"

Around the age of fourteen and fifteen you entered into a new stage of myth-based, fact-checking-less, lies. These involved girls or sex. What you should and shouldn't do.

"Girls love when you lick their ear and rub their leg anti-clockwise."

"They do?"

"Yeah, has to be at the same time though. It was in FHM magazine."

"I never read that page."

"You were probably too busy going at yourself looking at your one half naked."

"No I wasn't!"

That was another myth I remember well, one which involved what happened if you - for want of a better phrase or two - fiddled your own flute, pondered your own pipe, tooted your own horn, if you know what I mean. I preferred to call it a Tommy Tank, deriving somehow from the cartoon *Thomas the Tank Engine*. Tank. Sounds like a certain word. You get it. I hope. I'll stop.

Anyway, according to local legend if you did this act too much it left you blind (so you must shut your eyes if you do it) and with one abnormally big arm (your good hand, the one you used for writing).

"So some people need glasses because they do it to themselves too much?"

"Yeah, it's because all of the squinting or something, I don't know. It was in the paper though."

"The paper? No way!"

"Yeah, that's why Mitty wears glasses. Ever see the size of his right arm?"

The buddy in question – let's call him Mitty, Walter Mitty - did have terrible eyesight. His glasses were like two jam jars on his face, magnified his tiny, squinty eyes to look huge. He also had a rock hard bulging bicep on his right arm whereas his left arm looked like a weak string of spaghetti. Two and two… The myth grew. Gave weight to the theory. Whenever Mitty disappeared from the group out of the blue, we all knew what he was up to,

"Where's Mitty?"

"Tommy Tank."

"*Again?*"

In reality Mitty had some sort of weak bladder problem but we didn't find this out for a few years. Mitty had a few problems going for him. He was also the only fourteen-year-old I knew who was balding. Patchy, black hair running thin. He was kind of skinny-fat as well which made him look a bit sketchy for some reason. Bony face, scrawny torso and stick legs with a paunchy belly. Not that that was related to the myth but the whole slightly paedophilic look didn't help.

Another problem of Mitty's was that he was the world's biggest liar. Non-stop spouting out lies. Every day he'd supply a new snippet of spoof.

"You know that girl who we see on the bus with the pink hair, older one? Did ya hear she was pregnant but then did something with a coat hanger and now she's not?"

"Ah stop."

"Seriously boy, I swear, ask anyone."

Seeing as Mitty had already spread the rumour around to everyone and anyone with an ear, we were never too sure if it was definitely made-up or not. Always that slight slither of doubt that kept us guessing and eventually, half believing it.

"Was it a wooden coat hanger, I wonder?"

"I don't know the exact details but you know how she got pregnant?"

"No but go on…"

"She walked on the circle design on the ground by the church, the one with the cross in it."

"And that's how she got pregnant?"

"Yeah, it's bad luck to do that after sex. My Mum told me that too."

As usual Mitty would end the story with "don't tell anyone though". Never could even if I wanted to seeing as Mitty would have already told everyone, repeating the inside tidbit to our entire world. Eventually his lies were integrated to become factual knowledge we kept on mental files for everyone.

An area of expertise for Mitty was on how strong people were and how they had won fights. This guy beat that guy with a secret, Bruce Lee kicking move that he learnt from watching *Enter the Dragon* while that guy beat this guy with a hurley (kind of like a hockey stick) over the head. Always fun to listen to the different ways all these unknown people leathered the living daylights out of each other. Each fighting tale would always end with the same warning,

"Remember: Never fight a pikey."

"Why's that?" I asked the first time he said it.

"They never give up. The fight doesn't stop until one of ye is knocked out or dead."

"Jesus Christ. You're lying?"

"Trust me. They're vicious, boy."

In case you don't know a pikey is another term for a traveler, which is another term for a knacker, also known as a pieball, which stemmed from the term gypsy and has roots in the word turnpike. They live in caravans and travel around usually by horse, fighting and drinking, robbing stuff and trying to sell it back to you, probably half inbred, always looking to be treated equally while pickpocketing you at the same time. They're not all bad, but most aren't too good.

Pikeys always wore cream or grey wooly jumpers, blue jeans covered in muck, with black boots or runners, also covered in muck. Their eyes were slightly Asian looking for some reason, as if they had a squint going on a lot. Must have been big Tommy Tankers. Perhaps that explained their rosy pink cheeks but that might also have been from being outside and running away from the police all the time.

Lot of the stuff they said sounded exactly like the word 'hubulla'. Every sentence ended with 'boss' too. Later in life I would mimic this 'hubulla, hey boss' language as a joke, which would then ironically stick in my vocabulary. But this would be all in the future.

Back then I was fourteen and listening to Mitty far too much while also trying to stay away from pikeys as much as I could. The first pikey tale I ever heard from someone besides Mitty was when my uncle Frank told my Mum and Dad about the pikeys who stole a work trailer out of his front yard. They then came back two days later and tried to sell it back to him without realizing where they stole it from originally. When Frank saw it was his trailer the pikeys made a run for it. Jumped in their van and drove off with the stolen trailer still attached to their van. Frank rang the police who got on the case straight away. Within ten minutes they had located the pikeys driving through the Tipperary countryside, making their way towards Dublin. One of the guards rang Frank from the police car to confirm the licence plate on the trailer,

"Yeah," said Frank, "That's them all right."

"Bad news I'm afraid, we can't do much about this one."

"What do you mean? They stole my trailer, get it back from them."

"They're part of the Barry clan, a dangerous lot. If we arrest them it'll cause fierce retaliations against us."

Jesus, I thought, even the police are afraid of the pikeys. Mitty was right.

Not long after hearing this tale I had my first run-in with some. More of a runaway, really. My buddy Sean and I were walking home from the cinema, cutting through the car park of Douglas Court, a shopping centre by my house. It was a glorious Sunday afternoon and we were on our way home for our roast dinners, having just seen *Lock, Stock and Two Smoking Barrels* in the cinema, a movie quite similar to *Snatch*. Two of us walking along, seeing who could do a better Jamaican impression of the phrase,

"Chill, it's only Winston, maaaan."

Out of nowhere we hear,

"Hey, come 'ere."

Look up. See two boys our age walking towards us in the deserted car park.

"Are they talking to us?"

"Don't know, say nothing, they're pikeys."

"Oh Jesus."

Head down. Make a diagonal detour to the far side of the car park.

"Come over 'ere hubulla."

"Who, me?"

"Yea, gis alook. What's the time?"

Oh no. Mitty had warned us about this line: "If they ask for the time it means they want to rob your watch."

Looked down at the Casio watch my Dad had given me for my birthday. I love this watch. They're not getting it. Taller, brown haired, dirtier looking pikey makes a beeline for us.

"Hey boss, don't fuocking move, give me your watchubulla."

"My watch? No. The time is almost five though."

"Give it here or I'll stab ya," says the small red haired one with big gold earrings.

Look down and see the little pocketknife he pulled out of his pocket. Sean and myself look at each other. Minds read. Both know what to do: RUN! Start sprinting for dear life. The two pikeys aren't expecting it, slow to cop on. We sprint past them and through the car park. Pretend to go left at the crossroads sections with a shimmy of our shoulders then dart right up the hill that leads to the main road. The pikeys gave up chasing us after ten yards but we didn't know this. Just ran and ran and ran like two Forrest Gumps until we got home. I even ran past my house and hid in the trees at the bottom of my street, just to make sure they weren't following me on horses. Peer out of the leaves: All clear. Pikey free. Get home in time for dinner. Phew. Close call.

About a month later I'm in the city centre with my buddy Noel. Just came out of a sports shop by the bus station having bought a new pair of football boots for myself. Instead of lugging them around town with me I left them at the shop. Go back and collect them later on my way home. Head off to go play pool with the five pounds change I have left after buying the boots. Strolling along the banks of the River Lee, we spot a group of about ten pikeys cross the road in front of us. Even though we are on a main street that's usually busy, it's really quiet on our side. As it does when you predict something bad is about to happen, dread fills my bowels. Noel and I both know: They're crossing for us.

"Don't do anything stupid, play it cool," Noel says under his breath.

"OK," I whisper, double-checking I wasn't wearing my watch.

By now the group of pikeys are blocking the path in front of us. Only about twelve- or thirteen-years old, which meant they were a year or two younger than us. Made the whole thing worse. One of the taller pikeys with a slender, pale, rat like face whips out a knife and asks us for the time. Not again.

"Ehh, not too sure."

Entire gang pulls a knife of some sort out of their pocket. Felt like we were in Oliver Twist.

"No watches?"

"Sorry, not today."

"What else do ye have, boss?"

"Don't have anything."

"Empty your pockets."

Noel shows his pockets. Empty. Weird. He must have something. I follow suit. Try to hide the five pounds in my hand discreetly but one of the little weasel-faced pikeys spots it,

"Give us that yeh queer or I'll cut ya open."

Hand over the money. Clenched my bowels. Feel the knife pressed against my jacket.

"Go home and cry to yer Mammies."

"Will do."

Off they go to spend my money. Myself and Noel do a quick U-turn. Jump on the next bus home to Rochestown.

"At least I have my boots," I kept saying as we trundled home in the old rattling bus.

"Yeah, sweet."

We were both embarrassed but also kind of relieved. At least we didn't get hurt. Not the end of the pikey affair though, these things come in threes and all. Few weeks later I'm back in Douglas, walking to the cinema with Mitty. Same car park, again on a Sunday. Schoolboy error. The pikeys are relentless. Out of nowhere, we sense two guys walking behind us. Straight away we hear their pikey accents.

"Hey boss, nice white jeans."

"Thanks?" Not sure if he was complimenting me or not.

"Did your Mammy get them for you?" says the other.

"She did actually, Christmas present."

"I don't like the look of you."

Oh Jesus. This sounds like they want to fight. These two are older than us as well, maybe seventeen and eighteen. Not going to end well. Never fight a pikey, remember? Mitty, what do we do? Mitty? MITTY?! My looks at Mitty are ignored. He's just walking normal, saying nothing. I look again at him and scream with my eyes: What's the plan, *run*?? No response. In fact, Mitty's eyes are now shut. What's he doing?

Out of the corner of my eye I see the reflection of the pikeys in a shop window. One is tiny and jumping up and down like a monkey, gold ring laden knuckles scraping off the ground. The other is taller and looks like a sneaky, rat-faced fighter, a nasty piece of work. Keeps pushing his tiny little friend into the back of me, seeing if I'll react. After two pushes I turn around to tell him stop. As I do, the taller one shouts out

"DO YOU LIKE 7-UP, DO YA?"

Before I know it a plastic bottle is thrown in my face. Grenade attack. BOOM! As this happens the small monkey one runs onto a seat, jumps into the air in front of me and throws a Bruce Lee style punch with his dirty monkey paw. POW! Bottle of 7-UP SMASHES me on the side of the head as I feel a dunk of his filthy little fist catch my eye socket. Neither hurt but the ambush throws me off. Duck and weave and go to fight back but the little ape has already run off. Taller rat runs past us, spitting into Mitty's face as he does. Sprints off waving a knife in the air, laughing like a mad man.

I'm in a bit of shock, confused and lost. Are we fighting? Did we just fight? What just happened? Look at Mitty who still hasn't said a word. Takes off his glasses. Wipes them clean. It's then I see he's wet his pants. Weak bladder. Before I can say anything he turns to me, shaking his head,

"Typical pikeys. What did I tell you: They always run away."

As I stood there rubbing my face, glad that at least the affair didn't turn into some sort of bloody battle to the death, I realised a valuable lesson: Some people are pikeys and others are just complete and utter spoofs. Both are kind of dangerous. And both need to be dodged. Good. To. Know.

As it happened I picked up some sort of stomach bug the day after that pikey run-in. Kept getting sick, couldn't keep anything down, not even water. On the other end, I couldn't do a poo. All out my mouth. All lodged in the back passage. This continued on for a good week, got so bad I was getting sick my stomach lining. Had to spend a week in hospital and everything, doctors couldn't figure out what was wrong with me. Just kept giving me various different syrupy medicines. None worked.

Eventually, even the very thought of taking more syrup medicine started making me sick. Projectile vomiting around the hospital room. Felt bad for the other people sharing the room, except for the old naked guy on the bed next to me who kept releasing his bowels at every chance he got. He had the opposite illness of me and used to almost rub it in my face. I remember waking up one time in the middle of the night to see him lying there naked and asleep on the bed next to me, doing a river of poo off the side of the bed. That haunted me for a while.

Anyway, after a week in the hospital the puking stopped and I got to go home. They never did find out what was wrong with me though. It took another few weeks before I was pooing normally again but at least all that time on the bowl gave me good time to ponder, something I still enjoy to this day. Looking back at it now, I half wonder if instead of "scaring the shit out of me", those pikeys scared the poo into me. I wonder. I really do.

Chapter 9
Fight Club For Men

High school. Secondary school. Tomato. Potato. In Ireland classes usually went from nine in the morning to half three in the afternoon except on Wednesdays when we got a half-day. Out the door at half twelve. Every week. Oh yeah. Free birds!

When I tell this to American folk their first comment is "Half twelve means twelve thirty?" Then their eyes bulge and heads pop off at the thought (similar reaction to when they first hear my flute filled, lilting Irish accent).

"Aw maaan, I wish I went to school there growing up, my life would've been so much better!"

They then proceed to tell me about the crappy, brand new BMW car they drove in high school, show me photos of the girls in their class (many of whom would at least go on to try out for Playboy), and wrap up by telling me about this one time where they went on a date with their teacher. It was OK though, nothing weird seeing as they were mature and the teacher was only eleven years older than them at the time. "Only eleven years? What's age but a number, huh?"

Clearly American schools had their perks. And Irish schools had half-days on Wednesdays. We also had uncomfortable school uniforms, all boys' schools and corporal punishment, so the half-day balanced things out really.

Anyway, one thing about all these free Wednesdays - six years worth - was knowing what to do to fill them up. At first the freedom was elating. Young. Dumb. Free! Let's go sit on a wall. Kick a ball off the wall. Or just kick the wall. Five hours of this and off home you went for dinner. Great day spent by the wall. Let's all meet here again next week!

Eventually the wall moved on, replaced by cycling around the housing estates on our bikes. Pointlessly cycling around the place doing wheelies, looking for curbs to jump over. Building ramps. Take hoppers. All that fun stuff. My Dad bought my brother Darren and I new mountain bikes one year for Christmas. I was fifteen. Darren's bike was grey and blue with the name RIDER on the main chassis while mine was green and black with the name TERMINATOR. Don't think I ever loved an inanimate object more in my life. Made me look cool, what with its big chunky tires and shiny green crossbar. People always complimented me on it. This bike brought far more value to my life than I ever could on my own.

On the downside, it did seem to be out to terminate me. Even though I was good at bicycle tricks something always seemed to go wrong. Thought I lost a testicle one day. Did a big ramp jump over a mound of mud into a skip filled with soft foam. Made it over the mud with ease yet somehow landed just short of the skip. Bike first, balls seconds. Could barely walk for a week. Bloody mouth and loose tooth on top. Had to give it a go though. Chance on.

One of my best tricks was being able to cycle with no hands then almost fully stand upright on the saddle. I say *almost* fully seeing as the closest time I came to pulling it off my front wheel clipped a tiny pebble, snared viciously to the right, throwing me off over to the left like a piece of discarded meat. Hit the pavement hard. Left me with a suspected dislocated shoulder. Blacked out for a bit too so can't definitely be sure if I ever made it to standing up fully upright on the saddle. I think I did though.

Terminator took a hit for the worse after that fall. My Dad had to bring it to the repair shop to fix the bent front wheel, snapped breaks and faulty saddle. Promised that I'd take care of it when it came out of the shop. Even told my friends, "I can't mess up my bike again, no more tricks, OK?" Laid down the law. All rolled their eyes and cycled off.

My buddy Paul had found a new route where we never cycled before so went to go check it out. Few hilly fields across from where we lived had recently been bought to build houses on. No clue how any houses were going to be built on it seeing as it was basically a steep hill, but at least the builders created all these cool tracks for us to race around. Few hours go by. Realise I'm bursting for the bathroom. Not something I could really jump off and do up against the wall. I needed to go home to make the deposit, if you know what I mean. One part of the field was ridiculously sheer, almost like a cliff. Also the fastest way home. Told the others I'd be back, must go TCB.

"Huh?"

"Take care of business."

Took off over the sheer side of the hill. All I heard was Darren say,

"Be wide, that's too steep you idiot!!"

Before I know it I'm scuttling head first down a vertical drop. Oh sweet Jesus. Way dodgier than I thought. Going too fast. I'm not going to be able to stop when I reach the bottom, just going to go straight into the busy main road, head on into all the traffic. Oh Jesus, oh Jesus, oh Jesus. Start to move the wheel side to side to slow myself down. Doesn't work, just makes me wobble like I'm on a tight rope. Now I'm going to take a hopper. Can't afford to lose a testicle. What the funk do I do?

"NOOOOOO!"

Cry out to no one in particular. Paul shouts something back from the top of the hill. Something about pulling the brakes. *Pull the brakes?* Won't that be dodge?! Might snap them at this speed. My Dad will kill me if I mess them up again already. Everyone is now shouting at me to be careful. Halfway down the cliff. Cars are beeping and whizzing by on the main road below. I'll die if I hit that road. Pull the funking brakes. Just let them snap.

"PULL THE FRONT BRAKES!"

I do as I hear. Yank hard. Front wheel stops dead in its tracks. The whole back of the bike and me lift up into the air. I'm clinging onto the front handlebar for dear life. Somersault forward. Land hard on my head on a stony, dry surface. Bounce forward. Still holding on. End up back on the bike. Did a full flip. Some trick. Except I didn't stop. Feel blood pouring from my mouth, pain rushing through my head. Still holding the breaks. Let go then yank hard on them again. Another somersault forward. Sail through the air, letting go of the bike this time. It flies off into the traffic. Hits the road and slides forward while I land face first in a bush by the bottom of the cliff. Look up to see a big eighteen-wheeler truck drag my bike along the street, sparks flying into the air. Holy Jesus - The Terminator! I think it's been terminated.

The truck releases the bike a hundred yards down the street, letting it zip off and smash into a wall. Haul myself to my feet, feeling my wet socks from what I almost hope is blood and not urine. Jacket is ripped, cuts on my face, hole in my jeans. Not good. The Terminator is a mangled mess too. Snapped wires. Bent wheel. Saddle missing. Looks like someone went at it with an axe. At least the back wheel works?

Look back up to the top of the hill. Everyone's shouting the same thing:

"WHY DID YOU DO THAT?!"

"YOU SAID PULL THE FRONT BRAKES!!"

"*DON'T* PULL THE FRONT BRAKES!"

"Oh. Right. I thought you said…"

Doesn't matter. They all go back to doing wheelies. I need the bathroom now more than ever. Grab the Terminator and carry it home like a fallen soldier, Forrest Gump carrying Bubba through the Vietnam Jungle. When I get done in the bathroom and go back outside my Dad is standing over the crumpled metal mess.

"What happened? I just got it fixed."

"I don't know what happened, Dad. Weirdest thing. Cycling along and must've hit a pebble. Blacked out. Woke up. Bike was like this."

"Well, as long as you're OK."

"I think so. It was a bad fall. Those pebbles. Can we go get the Terminator fixed again?"

"No."

"No?"

"No."

So that was the end of my biking days. Probably safer for my testicles at least.

Sports were next for killing time on Wednesdays, usually soccer, soccer and more soccer. We did climb trees a lot too now that I think of it. Spent a lot of time surveying which were the best trees to climb. Building swings on them. See who could climb the highest tree. Most dangerous. Followed by the dumbest.

Once we got bored with just climbing a tree and sitting there for hours on end, we started tree jumping. This involved leaping from the top of one really high tree over to the top of a tree next to it. Nice and safe. Eighty to a hundred feet in the air. Branches stabbing you in your face as you hoped for dear life you managed to hang on to a thick one and not fall to your death below. When one buddy John took a nasty fall and broke his arm, we kind of looked for something else to do. At least he had a lot of branches to soften the blow as he fell like a sack of potatoes. Lucky boy.

The next activity on the Wednesday menu was fighting. Watching from a safe distance as other guys would fight each other in the woods near our school. Sweet Jesus. Those fights were brutal. Fifteen-year-olds can be highly cruel. Uniform wearing boys stuck in school all week with no girls around. Our energy and frustration had to go somewhere. This was our Fight Club.

The woods were like a cauldron, a Roman coliseum. Different levels of walkways, paths, trees and nooks where people would gather in anticipation. All looking down to the cleared area below that had a few tree stumps as benches and a stream running alongside. Very picturesque, like an old oil painting you might see on your Gran's wall, just that this one was filled with lots of pasty, spotty, jacked-up Irish boys in school uniforms raring for blood. Tension rife in the air.

One boy would step forward into the middle of the clearing and preside over matters, almost like a wedding in church.

"We are gathered here today for the fight of Spud McGee and Bogman."

I always thought Bogman was a great nickname. Who's going to mess with Bogman? Sound guy too. Just liked a fight.

"Are they both here today? Does anyone object to this fight? Can we have the ring, please?"

A circle would form in the clearing. Bogman and Spud McGee would appear from the crowds. Bogman was built like a boxer, looked like a young Sylvester Stalone. Always the one to say he didn't really want to fight. Just heard what the other guy said about him, would ask if it was true? Spud McGee was built like a weasel - tall, lanky and bony, with ginger hair, covered in freckles and a big hook nose. No wonder he was always angry. He would always have other little weasels and snakes in his ear behind him.

"Don't listen to Bogman, only luring you in. Punch him boy, get the first dig in."

Spud, obviously a pretender to the crown, would tell Bogman he heard him saying stuff about him too. Bogman would say he never said that, must be your friends making it up. Weasels and snakes would hiss and squeal,

"Is he calling you a liar? Just fight him."

Bogman might say again that he wasn't really up for fighting, just don't keep saying that stuff about him. He'd turn and go to leave the circle of doom, as we shall now call it. Fight's over. They sorted it out with words. Time to go home.

Oh no. Crowd gets restless. *We paid money to see a fight*, people would scream inside their heads. *What's this?*

"Fight. Fight. FIGHT!"

With Bogman's back turned, Spud McGee sees his cowardly opening. The roar of the boys makes him loopy. Fatal mistake. In a fit of pumped up adrenaline, Spud runs for Bogman, swinging an open-handed bitch slap. Bogman's already one step ahead though, anticipates the snakey move. Ducks. Swivels. Swings. Catches Spud with a lightning, Mike Tyson style upper cut to the jaw. Spud is shocked and confused; "*I thought I threw a punch*" swirling through his brain. He gets another left hook from Bogman to the face. Spud lets out a terrified yelp. Holds his nose. Blood spurts.

Crimson flows. Spud freaks. Flails his arms. Bogman seizes his chance. One-two, left-right, right-left, boom, boom, BOOM! Fight's over. Spud McGee is down, his uniform now a red, bloody mess. Bogman has won.

The referee, our priest from earlier, jumps in.

"All right, that's enough, he's done."

Spud's weasels and snakes are no longer there to help. Just his one long-suffering, best friend, Patrick, who told him not to do it. Patrick was more of a nerd than a fighter but him and Spud were neighbours so they had that bond. The weasels and snakes have now joined Bogman's side of the circle, trying to be best friends over there instead. Fickle game, after-school fights with fifteen-year olds.

Usually either more fights would be on the bill, or they'd suddenly appear, fueled by the raw emotion of what just happened. Another frustrated angry growling boy would claim a guy he didn't like for no real reason. In Ireland the term 'I claim ya boy' means 'I challenge you to a fight my good man!' The term 'I'll bate ya' means 'I will beat you and win', not to be confused with the term 'I'll masturbate ya.' Similar enough.

I'd always make sure to maintain a distance from the clearing. This was a place where rules and etiquette were out the door. People would challenge you to a fight for no reason.

"I don't like how you look when you look at me."

"Huh? You want to fight me over that? Are you funking insane?"

"What the f*ck did you just say to me, f*ggot?"

"Ah come on now, no need for names. I kissed a girl last week too so your argument is a bit invalid."

Thankfully I knew just enough right people who thought I was sound to get away with not having to fight in one of these gladiator type settings. I was able to make people laugh just enough if the situation ever got too sticky. Good at mocking and banter. Two well-worn crutches.

My main ally at the time was Bobby O' Toole from my soccer team. Big guy built like a tank who seemed quiet when I first met him on the soccer team. Only when he transferred over to my school did I discover he had a reputation as being an animal fighter. Absolute beast. Could beat any boy our age in a fight - and those a year above us - with ease. Feared. Took a shining to me for some reason.

When Bobby started going to the same school as me he began phoning me every Sunday night. This was before mobile phones so he would always call my house on the landline. This was also the line the Internet was used for so it was pretty clogged most of the time, only able to perform one duty at a time. Landline was the hub of communication. I think initially Bobby called me to make sure he had all the right homework done before class on Monday. Already in trouble for fighting in school so wanted to keep up on the homework side of things. I was the boy he turned to, being the smartest (only) person he really knew in school. Soon though, these phone calls turned into long meandering chats about the weekends we had. This despite the fact I saw him at school every day and on Saturday at a soccer game. Didn't matter though, Sunday night calls happened as if we hadn't spoken in months.

Bobby would tell me about the fights he always seemed to accidentally get into while I'd tell him about all the trees I climbed and the funny squirrels I saw. After an hour of this I would tire and try my best to wrap things up. Busy boy, homework to do, television shows to watch. An episode of *Mr. Bean* would be coming on soon. Unfortunately I had not yet learnt the skill of being able to wrap up a conversation. Instead of saying "Goodbye, must go," whenever a pause opened up, I'd go with the endless offer of "Any other stuff happen?" Forever hoped for a "No" response but this was never the case. Instead more stories about girls we might like and the chances of them liking us back.

After an hour and a half to two hours, Bobby would always be the one to bring the conversation to an abrupt end, usually when I was mid-sentence,

"So this squirrel just stared me down, right in the eyes and I said to him-"

"Hayes, better let you go boy, g'luck!"

Beep. Phone dead. Conversation over. Culled, as if I was the one keeping him on for ages. Some weeks I wondered if I was boring him to death. Maybe if I drone on it'll stop the weekly calls. Nay. Come the following Sunday evening the phone would ring again at seven o'clock. On the upside, at least he taught me how to wrap up a phone call.

After Bobby hung up Darren's girlfriend Chiara would call looking for him. From an early age Darren developed his trend of getting long-term girlfriends. First there was Cara, then Ciara, followed by Chiara who is now his wife. Rumour has it that I would stay on the phone pretending to be Darren, what with my phone conversation flowing so well after my training with Bobby. Just chat away to Chiara for the next hour or so. Apparently around this time Chiara really fell for Darren. She knew he was going to be the one. And now they're married. Only rumours though, purely hypothetical. Not like Darren paid me to talk on his behalf.

Anyway, back to Wednesday afternoon fight club in the woods. After the main event either another fight would be on the cards or else the fights would be over and it's time to go home. If there were any more fights on they were rarely of better value than the first though, dropped in stature. Usually you might have a weasel claim a softly spoken giant who did no harm to anyone and was actually as strong as an ox. I'll let you guess who wins. At times I might leave as the commotion of the first fight is wrapping up. Avoid traffic and the possibility of being claimed. Get home in time for dinner where my Mum or Dad might ask,

"What did you do all day?"

"Ah, just hung out by the wall, kicked the ball around, you know. Any more gravy for the potatoes, please?"

There were other ways to pass these free Wednesday days. Maybe you go hang out at a shopping centre. Good place to see girls. Bad place for guys claiming you for no reason. Maybe you go into town and play pool at a place called The Vic, an old Victorian red-bricked building where all the cool kids hung out. Arcades in the front, pool tables at the back, snooker tables upstairs. Whole place was dark, bar the lights from the arcade machines and the circles of light over each pool table. Always liked dark places like this for some reason. Good place to admire girls as well. Brown haired, blonde haired, few red heads. All sorts really, tall, small, skinny, chubby. All in their school uniform, hiking up their skirts a few extra inches. Mostly white girls though, there was a lack of variation back in those days.

The Vic was also a bad place for guys claiming you for no reason. Even worse, these were guys from different schools. Unknown quantities. God only knows who was a bluffer and who would beat you to a bloody pulp. Still though, at least my pool playing techniques became well honed. I was lucky enough to avoid hassle mostly from playing soccer with my team Tramore. Either from having teammates like Bogman and Bobby O' Toole, or playing against guys like that, I got on well with enough fighters to make sure I never really got into a squirmish. Fight off. Pool on.

Clearly there were lots of fun ways to spend a Wednesday afternoon. Fighting. Playing pool. Playing soccer. Eyeing up girls. Almost losing testicles. Great hoot. However, more often than not because of the weather, none of these options would be available. When there's torrential rain outside, you're just not that pushed in going back out into for the sake of the above. Already got soaked walking home from school. Waiting for the bus to go back out somewhere meant another douse of rain. No bus shelter either, just a pole on the side of the road with a bus sign so you'd have to hide under a tree near pole to dry and stay dry. This usually led to the bus not seeing you and not stopping. Dose. Day ruined. Time to take off my uniform, rid myself of those itchy pants, take a shower and watch TV.

Our TV options were limited. Daytime talk shows. At least they were American talk shows though. Not just the classy affair that was Oprah either. Nay, I'm talking the "good" stuff (as in awful). Sally Jessie Raphael. Jenny Jones. Ricki Lake. Sometimes, if we were really lucky, Jerry Springer might be played. This was a whole new world for us. This was America. Are they all like that? That place is *mental*. And look at the women! What are they wearing? Are they strippers? Whures? Forgive me God, I know I shouldn't be watching but did you just hear what she did with her husband's brother when she was pregnant? And the husband knew about it and he doesn't even mind?! What is this foreign land? America is *unreal*. Jessie! Sally! Jerry, Jerry! Fight, fight, FIGHT!

One way or another it seems Wednesdays were fighting days when I was growing up. Even happened on the days when I might get really bored and wonder what my hair might look like blond. Not going to bleach it or dye it, my Mum will kill me. Not yet anyway. I'll just try some home brew fixes. What could I put in my hair that would make it blond? In front of the bathroom mirror I would go. Wonder if I can give myself hair like Jerry Springer.

Check under the sink for possible tools to help. Hmmm, baby powder? Let's give that a whirl. Wet my hair with water. Comb it back. Put some powder in my hand. And. Apply. Hmmm. Looks dumb. Or maybe I just didn't do enough. More powder. More applying. Even worse. Now a thick doughy feel to my hair. Pasty, almost like a glue. Still not blond. Just horrible browny grey looking. And my head smells like a baby's ass.

Maybe I'm just using the wrong substance. Powder isn't strong enough or white enough. How about I try this Sudocreme instead? Like a white form of Vaseline. Yeah, I'll just smother that on my head. Lather up my wet powder head with thick white cream. One handful and I realise I've made a horrible mistake. This is not going to work. Blond just doesn't suit me, particularly not this horrendous shade of manky brown white. Great work.

Around now is usually the point when my brother would come into the bathroom, see me, laugh at my head and ask what I was doing?

"What are you doing? I'm in the bathroom, get out!"

We would then either get in a wrestling match as I pushed him out the door or else he would leave laughing and I'd be left alone looking at my pitiful head in the mirror, beating myself up.

"What *are* you doing? Look at the state of yourself. Go have a shower, clean up you dope."

Maybe give myself a slap in the face for good measure. Keep myself in check, Wednesdays being fight club for men and all. Good laugh all the same. Way better than going on a date with your teacher. Weirdos.

Although saying that, overweight, half-naked American women calling each other whores on television versus young Irish boys in school uniforms leathering lumps out of each other in a woods – We're not so different really.

CHAPTER 10
JUNIOR CERT NIGHT

For such a wet, cold, murky country we eat some amount of ice cream in Ireland. Even in winter we're slurping away on Fat Frogs, Calypsos or Magnums, whatever the hottest ice cream is at that moment. We don't really care. Just let us enjoy our Mr. Freeze.

Seeing as we don't really have seasons, ice cream was never a seasonal food only eaten in summer as a refreshing way to cool down. It was never that hot and sunny in the summer, or ever really. That's the biggest problem with Ireland: The weather. We have many problems I know but the weather is like an umbrella under which all the others fall. Imagine if it rained four or five days a week, almost every week of every year. Well, welcome to Ireland.

When the weather report is always "it's going to be a lovely, sunny, miserable, overcast, cloudy, wet, warm, Baltic day with a slight to good chance of hailstones" it's hard to know when one season actually begins and the other ends. Just one long wet, muggy miserable day rolled into the next. Even when it's considered a good day out, you still get some rain. And every other season on top. Blustering winds for a while. Bitterly cold too. Stormy and gloomy come next. Humidity kicks in. Followed by another torrential downpour. The sun peeks out of hiding for a bit. And then a lovely sun shower springs out of the heavens.

This is all only on your walk home from school, four seasons in twenty-four minutes. Schizophrenic climate toying with your emotions. Flaky, psychotic, demented weather. Always keeping me in the lurch, keeping me on edge, needling me in the head. Tossing. Turning. Turmoil. How am I meant to know what to wear when I leave the house?! You're hot, you're cold, you're wet, you've sweat - It's awful. No wonder Irish people bottle up their emotions; we don't know what to feel with the ever-changing weather. Am I happy, sad, annoyed, hopeful, depressed? What am I? I don't know! I'm damp, damn it! Just give me a wet drink too.

Obviously all this rain gives us miles and miles of lush green fields and forests and rainbows and streams a babbling and woods a whistling and leprechauns a leaping around their pots o' gold. But. It also gives us perennial heartache over the lack of sunny days. They say summer in Ireland is a Thursday in July. The fact that the place is so mighty when the sun comes out *almost* makes it worse. A glimpse of what could be. And yet, that hope makes it just about tolerable too. Perfect country when it happens.

The first sign people keep an eye out for is the fabled 'red light at night, shepherd's delight'. If the sun sets and leaves the sky glowing red, people start getting giddy because - Here comes the sun!

"Tomorrow's going to be sunny, tomorrow there will be no rain! We must buy shorts and flip-flops and sunscreen and everyone go to the beach, OK? The entire population of Ireland must take work off tomorrow and clog up the beaches. Pubs: Create a beer garden of some sort, this is it, this is our big chance. SUMMER IS FINALLY HERE!!!"

Everyone is in a great mood, which is odd for some hardcore cynical folk. Ice cream sales are through the roof. Life is grand.

"Jeez, Ireland would be some place if it was this sunny all the time, huh?"

"You're telling me boy. Now schlap some tanning oil on my back, willa?"

One fear of every big occasion in Ireland is that the rain will ruin it. Weddings. Graduations. Birthday parties. All hanging on a knife's edge. I remember the first time this affected me: I'm fifteen. It's a Wednesday. Second week of September. And tonight is going to be the biggest night of my life so far: Junior Cert night.

The biggest nights of your life growing up in Ireland are when you get the results for various exams you do. In third year you do the Junior Certificate, which are summer exams. These determine what level you are going to go on in school for the next three years. Honours (higher), Ordinary (medium), or Foundation (lower level when you use fingers and toes to count yet you still get the answer wrong). How book smart are you, basically.

Final school exams are three years later in sixth year when you do your Leaving Certificate. How well you do in those determine what you can apply for in university. Your whole life is determined with a few exams really. Are you going to end up as a fish farmer scrapping your way through life stinking of fish or will you be the Lord of the Land living the high life on the manor?

We've just started fourth year. Easiest year of the lot in school, bit of a breather until you start studying again in fifth year. Our exam results are due out at midday. Tick, tock, thick, thock. Concerned about what I got. Concerned about the weather. Constantly looking out the window, watching the seasons change before my eyes every few minutes. Anxious. Mulling. Wondering. Daydreaming. I wonder what Pamela Anderson is up to in

Baywatch today? Wish I was in Malibu, chilling in the sun, bouncing around the beach. Instead I'm stuck here. Praying that it won't rain. Itchy. Need to get out of this uniform. Need to get out of this place.

Clock strikes for midday, dunnnng. Hear my name boomed out over the intercom "Hayes, Mark Hayes". Run to the front office. Get a head rush. Dizzy. Take a breath. Rip open my brown envelope. Scan the pink and yellow slip. A, A, B, A, C, A, B, A, A. *YES!* Wuu huu! Got it. Who cares about the Bs and C in French, History and Latin. People will only hear about all the As. Focus on the good stuff. Honours. On!

Compare results with friends and competitors. Most are happy. Rob, Vinnie, Derek, Aido, Loner and Barry all got what they were after. Paudie won't tell me what he got, seems a bit annoyed but that he's like that even when happy. Few people aren't happy at all. This guy Lorcan is fuming. Thinks he was cheated out of good results. Sure you were, you idiot.

Not a fan of Lorcan. Moved to Cork last year from Dublin, lives around the corner from me now. Big, black haired galoot with a long Pinocchio nose. Tried to be friendly with him when he first arrived until we got in a fight playing soccer one day. Only a friendly game in the green in our park but he started mocking Darren about the scar he had from running into the glass door before, even though Darren wasn't even there. Kept mocking him. Asked me what I was going to do about it if I didn't like it so I punched the dope twice. Once in his big nose and the other in his right eye. Always walked around like he was the big man because he was bigger than everyone and from Dublin but the punches shut him up. Ran away crying to his Mum then came back ten minutes later wearing a bicycle helmet. Tried to fight me while wearing it thinking it was protection. I punched him in the other eye though and he ran off screaming and holding his face again. Eejit.

Made sure to read my results out loud again so he could hear me, then continue on with my consoling, congratulating, scheming. Time to go celebrate. Booze on!

That night a huge underage disco was being held in what was the most renowned nightclub ever to exist in Cork City, Sir Henry's. At the time I didn't know too much about the place, bar the fact it was a cool club where all the good-looking girls were going that night. I passed the place a few times but to me it just looked like an old, worn down, grey bricked, four story Victorian building behind the library in Cork. There wasn't even a sign on the door to get in. The short history of it is that Sir Henry's was - and still is - an institution in Cork. Even though it no longer exists today, people still talk about it like a mythical warrior in the Fenian times,

"Oh, you should've seen her back in my day. Ten stories and seven wide if she were an inch. You'll never get how good that place was, *never*. You just don't know what it was like. We were free. You'll never get it, Marky boy."

"Well maybe if you explained it better then I would."

The legendary status was also helped by the fact that the likes of Nirvana had once played there, opening for Sonic Youth. Not sure how they ended up there really but then again Michael Jackson also played a gig in Cork once upon a time so maybe it was the place to be.

Anyway, Sir Henry's was where everyone was going to celebrate the results, our own underage nirvana for the night. Boys and girls from every school in Cork. Not just us fourth years who got our results either, fifth years went out that night too. Might have a chance meeting some older women. Although I was meant to meet this one girl I had kissed already a few times, Geraldine. Not the greatest fan of her name but she was beautiful looking. Blond hair always tied up in a ponytail with a pink hair tie, same height as me, slim with big looking boobs (just a mirage, padded bra, tut). Somehow always tanned, dressed to show off her body and wore make-up that made her look older than fifteen, more like a girl who went out clubbing.

We met playing pool in the Vic. People couldn't believe she liked me so much seeing as the general consensus was that she was the best looking girl in there which in turn made her one of the best looking in all of Cork. My friends also couldn't believe when I was slightly turned off her after seeing her run. She was trying to avoid getting wet from the rain outside the pool hall so sprinted away up the road for shelter. Reminded me of a mix between an ostrich with her neck bobbing and a chicken with her arms held like wings to her side. Just a small thing but seemed to stick with me. My issue with being turned off over finicky reasons started from an early age.

Still, she was hot and sound enough. Although she liked to flirt with other guys as well so my interest waned even more, which in turn made her like me even more. I'd play it by ear if we would hook up or not. Either way tonight was going to be unreal. Young. Free. Alive!

Race home from school. Gold results ticket in hand, Willy Wonka style. Bit worried that it's kind of cloudy out but not too concerned. The weatherman said on the news last night that it would be a dry Junior Cert night. He said those words *exactly* so I trust him. Show my Mum and my Dad my results. Delighted for me. Wuu huu. I'm delighted they're delighted. Made them less strict about me going out that night. Never been to a disco in town before so both warned me about not doing anything stupid.

"I know I know, I'm not my brother."

Darren would be coming out that night too so having him there made it seem safer as well. I wouldn't get into any trouble then surely. Although maybe I was seen as the more responsible one despite being a year younger, seeing as Darren had been caught a few times drunk already at that stage. He had just come out of a lengthy grounding stint. Both of us promise to behave. Just out to have fun.

"You don't need to drink to have fun you know that, don't ye?"

"We do Mum. I've no interest, I don't think I'd like the taste at all!"

This part was true. Not a fan of the Scrumpy Jack cider I'd been drinking a can of during the summer now and again. Moved on to trying a girl's watered down strawberry vodka concoction one day. Preferred it but had to be careful with vodka, I was told. Apparently that stuff got you really drunk so I never drank more than a few mouthfuls. Saying that, strawberry vodka was on the menu for me tonight. Quicker and easier to drink than the cans. All about getting to the fun faster.

Eat my dinner of potatoes, chicken, carrots and my Mum's homemade turkey-flavoured gravy. Loved that dinner. I would drink that gravy like cups of tea if society didn't frown on such a thing, tut. Check the kitchen clock. Five bells. Time to get ready. Race upstairs. Hop in the ridiculously hot shower, as I liked to have it. Follow this with getting annoyed and frustrated at my roasting red shower head and unmanageable hair, all fluffed and puffed with far too much shampoo and conditioner. Spend the next thirty minutes applying gel and combing the beast meticulously.

At the time Irish boys cared a lot about their hair looking just right. Although maybe not all as much as psychotic as myself. My hairstyle was a centre crease that kind of looked like Alfalfa from Little Rascals. This involved me combing my hair slick back, then parting it in a razor thin centre crease right down the middle. Next, I would form a fringe by running my hands through the front of my hair until I got just enough of it to stand up and fall over on both sides, like two little hills with a river running straight between them. Back and sides would then be re-combed and flattened down to perfection. My wet gel head would dry naturally or with the slight aid of a hair dryer. Check the mirror to see how well it pleased me. Repeat process over and over until just right. Then, *and only then*, would I be ready to go.

Check my watch. Quarter to six. Darren bangs on the bathroom door.

"Are you ready? You've been in there ages again, come on!"

"Yeah, calm down, I'm coming."

Open the door. He's waiting outside, fully ready.

"Your hair only looks *beautiful*," he says while ruffling it, knowing full well this would infuriate me.

"WHAT ARE YOU *DOING*?!"

Freak out and wrestle him to the ground, both of us rolling around the blue pile carpeted landing. We're both in our best outfits. Me in my white Fred Perry shirt and navy blue jeans, him in his turquoise blue shirt and navy blue jeans. Don't want to get our perfectly ironed shirts creased or crumpled yet this was almost always the way - A wrestling match minutes before we had to leave the house. Just as we hear our Mum coming up the stairs we break apart. I manage to flick him hard in the side of the head before getting back into the bathroom and locking the door.

"UUUUUUGGGGH" at myself in the bathroom mirror as I comb my mangled up hair again for the umpteenth time. It had looked so good too - Idiot!

Another knock at the door,

"GET AWAY YOU DOPE!"

"*Mark*, no need for that language."

"Sorry Mum, I thought you were Darren."

"Are you ready? I can give you a spin if you want."

"No it's fine thanks, we're going to walk."

"OK but it's raining out."

"*What?* Really? Ah no *way*!"

Open the bathroom window and stick my hand out. It is raining, of course it is. Only lightly but still, rain is rain and wet is wet. Dark clouds look dodge too. Decide to accept the generous lift offer from my Mum. Asks us if we want to be dropped right into the city centre.

"No, just to Douglas please Mum, everyone's meeting there."

"I thought the disco is in town?"

Suspicious already. Douglas is where all our friends arranged to meet up to go drinking first. Why would we only take a lift there and not into town?

"We must collect our tickets for the disco, a guy in Douglas has them."

"Oh, right."

Good spoofing. Lift on. Get dropped off at the shopping centre in Douglas. Wave my Mum goodbye. Wait until she's out of sight before Darren and I agree not to talk to each other again for the night.

"Fine so."

"Yeah, fine."

Go meet our friends at a place called the Slabs. These were four huge slabs of dull grey concrete that were in a field next to the shopping centre car park. Never sure what was in the mysterious slabs of concrete, each one was about five feet high, twenty feet wide and thirty feet long. Gave us a place to sit and drink at least.

Already a good number of people gathered there. Seems like more groups of friends had the same idea as our group, which consists of friends that live close to me. You had your core group of close friends, those who lived closest, then friends from school and soccer but that was it really. Where else were you going to meet people? We're all more or less dressed the same, just different colour shirts underneath our black jackets. Presume I'll see my school buddies in Sir Henry's at some point although people seemed to be humming and hawing when I asked what they were up doing. I'll worry about that later.

My main concern now is trying not to be annoyed by the rain but it's tough. Ruining my hair. Vain boy. At least Paudie is annoyed by the rain too. Funny chap. Small and built like a wiry boxer, always with a scowl on his freckled face. Good laugh as well though, even if he does looked pained when he laughs. His ginger hair is shorter than my style, more of a flat top but he has a spikey fringe that the rain will flatten if wet. Both of us stand and mutter complaints to each other about the weather trying to ruin our night already.

Our hefty buddy John arrives happy as Larry along with a big bag of booze for us all (he has a pudgy shaved head so doesn't care about the rain). We each gave him ten pounds earlier in the week to sort out booze for us. Rub our hands together like we're old men. Everyone else is drinking cans while Paudie and I are having a naggin of the strawberry vodka, a naggin being a small plastic 200ml bottle, same as a hip flask in America. John hands out the booze to everyone, gives Paudie and I four small bottles of coke with two bigger bottles of vodka.

"What's this?"

"They didn't have any of that strawberry crap, got you this instead."

"But this is a double-naggin of vodka."

"What are you on about boy, it's way better than the other stuff."

Not expecting this twist. The strawberry stuff I could handle. Vodka and coke I only tried once before. Not a fan. Too late now though, all I had. Double-naggin isn't fully twice the size of a regular naggin, but it's pretty close. Tip out half the coke in each bottle and pour half of the double-naggin into each one. Mix it together. Carefully open the cap and let the fizz out. Take a whiff and wince. *Ughatha Christ Almighty.* Smells like turpentine. Paudie takes a slug from one of his bottles.

"Not too bad."

I take a slug of mine,

"Yea*ugh*. Ssssss. SSSSSS."

For some reason I start hissing like a cat. Try to get rid of the taste. Almost puke in my mouth. Jesus, this is manky. Still, after a drink or two I get used to it. Not nice but tolerable if I don't drink too much. John, Darren and our other buddies are getting through their three or four cans fairly quickly. Still drizzling and we're all slowly getting wetter and wetter. Horrible. Miserable. Mank. Rain is once again trying to spoil our fun. Almost seven o'clock. Plan is to get into town before half seven, or else the queues outside Sir Henry's will be massive and we mightn't get in. Everyone starts drinking up faster. Paudie and I are struggling with our drinks. The rest finish their cans just as the heavens open up and it starts *bucketing* out of the sky.

"Run!"

"Rain!"

"Drink!"

"Quick!"

Everyone else runs for the bus stop. I've just finished my first bottle. Feeling queasy. Just me and Paudie left drinking. I think he's on his second bottle already. Balls. In the confusion of the rain and people yelling to hurry up, I open my second bottle and chug it in one go. Hold my nose to avoid getting the smell or taste of vodka. By now the rain is gushing. We're getting soaked. My perfect hair! Paul shouts at me,

"Come on, let's go!"

"I'm finished, run!"

We both peg it. Sprint through the car park into the warm, humid Douglas Court shopping centre. Hit by the smells from all the small shops and stalls right by the sliding doors as we enter. Pet shop. Fish shop. Bakery. Good mixed with bad. Focus on with the warm sugary cake smells wafting out. The fish stall with the horrendous fish smells takes over. My senses seem to be magnified, hyper-aware. Perhaps the drink has awaken me, reinvigorated my numbed soul! Or else I'm just drunk. Notice a sign at the fruit and vegetable shop 'BEST POTATOES IN CORK'. Ha! Says who? No time to ask. Got to keep on running. Don't want to miss the bus. Sprint on. Like a young Bilbo Naggins running carefree through the shire. Come on Paudie!

Out the exit on the far side of the shopping centre, back into the cold rain, past the cinema on our left and down along the dark wet grey streets towards the bus stop. Get there in time to see a bus pull away.

"Ah nooo, wait!"

Everyone else made the bus except for us two. Disaster. At least we're sheltered in the bus stop. Both freezing, huddled in our soaking wet black jackets.

"Where's your bottle?" Paudie asks me.

"I drank it all."
"*Both of them?*"
"Yeah, did you?"
"No."
Pulls a full bottle out of his pocket.
"Do you want it? I've had enough?"
"No, you have to drink it. I drank all of mine!"
"Can't, it's too much. Why did you drink both so quickly?"
"I didn't want to get my hair any wetter."
"You could've just put it in your pocket."
"Well IschknowthatnowdontIJesus."
"Are you drunk?"
"Ha ha, I don't know. Here, Paudie, it'schJunior Schert night!"
"Yeah I know. Calm down, the bus is coming."

Drink has started to hit me. Bus. Driver. Fare. Pay. Laugh at nothing. Don't care about my hair. Maybe I am drunk. Best night ever. Although. Bus ride. Stuffy. Packed. Swaying. Feel sick. Sit down. Shut up. Say nothing. Arrive in town. Everyone piles off the bus right outside the library.

"Balls. Look at the queue."

Hundreds if not thousands of boys and girls are already lined up. Queue slithering like a snake all the way down the street, wrapping itself around the corner.

"Jesus, we'll never get in."

"We will, look, there are the boys."

See Darren and the rest huddled together in the queue. Paudie and I mosey our way over to the metal barrier separating them and us. Pretend to just be saluting the lads. Look around. All clear. No security in sight. I go first and try to hop the waist high, skinny metal barrier. Not sure how exactly but instead of climbing straight over I somehow hop up standing on top on the metal bar. Holding

Paudie's shoulder I hoist myself up fully and look at the crowd of people queuing either side. With a burst of determination I raise my hand into the air and shout,

"JUNIOR CERT NIGHT!"

The crowd cheers. I start pumping my fist, letting out a Braveheart style war cry,

"YEAAAAHHH!"

And then,

"NOOOOO!"

Foot slips. Me, the barrier and a bunch of people fall to the floor. Nasty fall but I'm laughing my head off, lying in a puddle. The crowd spills out over the barrier, causing a heave and a rush for the front door. Security floods in and tries to keep queue hoppers from skipping ahead. In the commotion Paul and I end up inside the queue but a bit down from the rest of the lads. How bad, at least we skipped past all the rest of the suckers. Chumps!

Now we're slowly shuffling along, talking to people in the queue around us. Paudie is kind of drunk, I'm really drunk. Dark. Cold. Wet. Blurry. By the time we get around the corner and up to the main door, I'm absolutely hammered. Drink has fully kicked in. Paudie has his arm around my shoulder. Holding me straight. I'm laughing, burping, talking gibberish. All our buddies get in ahead of us. Paudie pokes me in the ribs.

"Sober up a bit, we have to get in."

"Don't worry, we will. Although if one of us doesn't the other should go in anyway, OK."

I'm definitely doing that for my sake, somehow convinced Paudie is the really drunk one. About six people away from the door he warns me one more time to act sober.

"Calm down, I am. Let me do the talking."

I can barely walk but somehow I manage to make it to the front door. See a few burly men in black jackets, huffing into their hands to keep warm. Hello, bouncers. They don't seem to be too fussed but I hear them ask Paudie if we've been drinking,

"No, no way, don't like the taste," I tell them.

Foxy haired bouncer eyes us up. Shrugs his shoulders. We're in? All I have to do is walk inside and the fun will begin. In front of me there's a closed door, an open door where I can see light coming from, with a stairs leading up to the club and then, next to that, a dark alleyway. On my first attempt I walk into the closed door, trying to almost climb up it. This wakes the bouncer up,

"Have you been drinking?"

"This is the greatests clubbs in Cork, do you know that?" I reply and then go to make my way inside the door of light. My body and legs are on a different page though. Miss the open door and walk down the dark alley. Realising my grievous error I try to turn and go back but my legs have left the building. Swivel and turn, flopping and falling in a heap on the ground. "You know what," I say to no one, "I might be drunk."

Hear Paudie plea my case for the bouncers to let me in. No joy. Comes over and asks if I'm all right.

"I am, I am, *I am I said*. You go in, you go in, go on you go in."

Paudie doesn't need me asking twice. Tells me to go get chips to sober up and try again. Gone. Gather myself up with the aid of the wall. Jeans are soaked from the puddle I fell into. Stand outside in the narrow, pitch-black alley with all the other too drunk people, just listening to the music, wondering what it's like. Rain is still coming down. All I see is a dark cobbled wall, deep bass thumping out from inside.

"Sounds unreal," I say to the bouncers. "Let me in. Please. Go on."

"We've warned you once."

"It's not my fault, the weatherman said it would be schunny!"

"Go away or we're calling the police."

That threat sets me straight. Wander off down the urine smelling alley. Confused. Drunk. Alone. This is meant to be the greatest night of my fifteen-year-old life. All my friends are inside. What am I going to do? Head back by the bus stop where we got off. Look around to survey my options. See a couple of dodgy looking pikey gangs hanging around. Look like they're up for fighting. Dodge on. Next minute I'm on a bus back to where I came. It's only half eight and I'm goosed. Get off the bus in Douglas. First thing I see is the big bright cinema in front of me. That's it: I'm going to go to the cinema on my own. The greatest night of all time.

Cinema is packed when I get in the door. At least it's warm here. Try to act sober as I queue up in the ticket line. See a few guys in my class. Huh, what? People go to the cinema on Junior Cert night? Never knew that was an option.

"Aido! Loner! Nobsy!"

"Hayser, where are you coming from?"

"Henry's. They kicked me out. Now I'm here."

"Yeah right - Really? Are you drunk?"

"No but maybe a bit, yeah. What are we going to see?"

"Saving Private Ryan."

"All right so."

They head off and I go get my ticket. Follow them inside the dark theatre. Can't see a thing. Start hissing out their names.

"*Aido... Loner... Nobsy... Where are ye?*"

Usher hushes me.

"Be quiet and find a seat, the movie has started."

"Shhh," I reply.

Plank myself down in the open seat right next to me. Give him a thumbs up so he leaves. Look up and try to focus on the screen. My head is bobbing and swaying everywhere trying to find the lads. The screen looks all blurry like it's in 3D but I'm not wearing 3D glasses. Ask the woman next to me if it's 3D. Shrugs me off. My world starts spinning. Oh no. Please not the spins. I'm too drunk to move. Movie is so loud. They're all fighting and killing on screen. They're on a boat. People are puking. Now they're in the water. On a beach? What's going on? Blinking hard. There's Tom. Someone dies. My mouth's watering. The sound of machine guns rattling through my head. This is too much. Can't handle it. Freaking out. Can't hold on. It's coming. Oh Jesus - BLAAARRRGH.

Next second I'm puking all over the back of the seat in front of me. I'd like to say I didn't get sick on the poor girl's hair in front of me, but I can't. Heaving like there's no tomorrow. The usher is back and has me picked up by the arms, carrying me down the aisles.

"Please don't let me see anyone I know, please don't let me see anyone I know," I keep mumbling to myself. Spot Lorcan laughing at me from his seat. Mouths the words at me "I'm telling your Mam on you." I try to shake the usher off so I can grab Lorcan and tell him not to but his grip is too strong. As I pass by the back row I hear,

"Hayser?"

"Lads! Someone got sick, this guy's an idiot, see ye outside."

Aido, Nobsy and Loner all give me a confused look. I thumbs up in return then the usher horses me out the door, like Uncle Phil throwing out Jazzy Jeff in *The Fresh Prince of Bel Air*. As I lie on the ground I apologise to the usher and ask if I can go back in. Refuses. Tells me to go get food and sober up. I tell him it's Junior

Cert night, the greatest night ever. Points me in the direction of McDonalds up the street. Away I go.

At least it's stopped raining as I make my way there. My senses are now all out of order. Don't know what's going on any more. Order some chicken nuggets and chips. Take them outside where it's quieter, too many happy families inside. Sit at the wet picnic tables outside, plop myself down in a big puddle. Starts to rain again. My McNuggets are floating around in their little container turned swimming pool. Really hits my spirits, looking in the window at all the sober dry people, all laughing and smiling. Dip my soggy floppy chips in the diluted curry sauce. Everything tastes like rain and cold tea. I'm done. This night is over. Can't hack it. Decide I'm going to just go home and explain to my parents what happened. They'll ground me for life but I don't know what else to do. Soaked. Freezing. Drunk. Feel sick. Never been caught drinking before. Proud of my record but that's over now. Time to hand myself in.

As if they read my mind, two older guys around twenty-years-old shout over at me from a sheltered table outside. One small, one tall. Both look kind of rough, like boxers, shaved heads, smoking cigarettes, wearing tattered grey and black bomber jackets.

"Is your Mam Mrs. Hayes?"

"Huh. Me?"

"Yeah you."

"Yeah, she is."

Decide not to mention that I call her Mum, not Mam.

"She taught me in school, she's cool, boy."

"Thanks," I reply with pride, taking it as a personal compliment as if I'm somehow responsible for this achievement.

"Shouldn't you be out for Junior Cert?" the other guy asks.

"I am. Meant to be in Henry's but they just kicked me out of the cinema, I don't know."

"Ha ha, are you serious?"

"Yeah, I'm going to go home, I'm too drunk."

"Whoa, I wouldn't do that boy. Do your Mam and Dad know you're drinking?"

"No, they'll kill me. They don't drink. I'm just going to tell them what happened though. I got good results today."

"Don't go home, trust me."

"Yeah, your Mum will freak, boy."

At least the other guy knows my Mum's right name.

"What else am I meant to do? I didn't know it would rain, the weatherman again on TV."

"What time is Henry's over?"

"Eleven. My Dad is collecting us outside after, he's going to know what happened when I'm not there."

"Go back into town so. Just eat more curry chips."

"Here's some chewing gum. You'll be fine by the time your Dad collects you, I promise."

"Do you want a lift?"

Look up at these two shaved head saviours. I'm going to trust them. Saving Private Hayes.

"All right so, thanks. Sound."

Before I know it they have me dropped back into town at the bus stop where my Dad is going to collect us all. I go to a chipper nearby. Stock up on more curry chips, a burger too. Makes me feel way better. Warm in the chipper as well, dries me out a small bit. At about five to eleven I go back to the bus stop. My buddies are already there, talking about the night,

"Way too busy, couldn't move."

"Hardly any hot girls too. Everyone got soaked from the rain."

"What a load of crap."

Happy enough when I overhear all of this. John spots me,

"Ha, look who it is, Marky boy!"

"Where were you? Did you get arrested?"

"No, weird night though."

Fill them in quickly, just as my Dad pulls up in his car.

"Shhh. Say nothing in the car obviously," Darren warns everyone.

Despite my night and the state of me, I still draw the short straw and have to go in the front seat while the rest pile in the back. Now I'm going to be the one fielding questions. Jump in. Paranoid. Mouth stuffed with chewing gum. Roll down my window to get rid of any smells.

"Mr. Hayes, had you a good night?" Paudie politely asks from the back seat.

"Not too bad, Paudie."

"What did you do, Mr. Hayes?"

"We ended up at the cinema."

"Oh very nice. What did you see?"

"The new Tom Hanks one."

Oh Jesus. Saving Private Ryan. The one I saw. Hot. Cold. Wet. Sweat. My body experiences the four seasons in one second.

"The cinema in Douglas?" I ask way too quickly, almost choking on all the chewing gum.

"No, the new one in town."

Oh thank Jesus.

"How was the disco?"

"Not too bad, Dad," I squeak back, barely able to breath from the lump of gum stuck in my throat, "Although the rain almost ruined it. Those weathermen, huh? Awful altogether."

Somehow I got away with it all. Lorcan kept his mouth shut. There were no reports in the newspaper about someone getting sick on a girl at the cinema. Geraldine was upset that I stood her up at the disco all right but this just made her like me even more. Started getting a bit too clingy for my liking, even if she was hot.

Worst part of the night might be the fact that I still can't watch Saving Private Ryan without feeling seasick. On the upside, at least the whole incident didn't turn me off booze or anything like that, thank God. Every cloud really does a silver lining.

CHAPTER 11
FASHION VICTIMS

"Is that girl Jane good looking? She looks all right."

"Nah, lot of make-up and just wears good clothes - Mutton dressed as lamb."

This was a great phrase I heard a lot when I was around the age of fifteen and girls were a main source of small talk amongst my friends. At the time we used it to describe a girl who dressed herself well, giving the illusion of appearing better looking than she actually might be. Later in life we would call these girls transformers - looks great at night, not a pretty sight in the morning. I'm sure Irish girls had similar names for us guys, probably the same.

I, for one, would prefer to think of myself as having been a lamb dressed as mutton. That's to say I'm not really sure if I had much of a fashion sense growing up. In fact, I don't think you could say many Irish people do, did or ever really will. We're kind of sheep in that aspect, although at least I was a slightly off skew-er kind of lamb. Not that I haven't had a few fashion blunders in my day.

First there was my great sports jacket mistake back when I was ten. An important milestone in an Irish boy's childhood is his Confirmation, the day when children in sixth class of primary school are given money by their family and relations in exchange for staying faithful to the Catholic Church. Something like that. We were unknowingly signed up for lots of stuff in school. I remember it was just after we were all made join the Pioneers, where I swore and pledged I'd stay off drink until I was eighteen. Potentially follow in my Dad and Grandad's steps and become a teetotaler for life. That went well.

Anyway, for my big Confirmation day I was given the luxury of picking out my own outfit. This was huge. Up to that point in my life my Mum had more or less chosen all of my clothes for me. This would be the first time I got to stamp my own flair on my look. The key was to try and pick things that you might wear again, not just one-off items worn on the day. Have to be suitable for church wear and maybe Sunday dinner wear, or even some every day clothes if you could manage it. Fine juggling act.

Needless to say, I chose rather well. Plain navy boat shoes that were popular at the time. Bright white socks. Sandy-brown cord jeans. Oversized wine shirt that I reasoned I would grow into. Diamond, flowery green waistcoat that looked like the design of a hotel carpet. Matching green dickie bow. Purple boutonnière (a male corsage). And, a bright red, suede sports jacket, shoulder pads included. Dapper Dan on!

Seeing as it all came under budget, I was free to make this mistake. Live and learn. My Mum did her best to get me to reconsider the sports jacket though.

"I'm just not sure if you'll ever wear it again Mark, it'll sit in your closet and be a waste."

"No way Mum, I'll wear this *all* the time. I'm going to look so cool."

Pleased as punch as I looked at myself in the mirror, imagining how I would spend my summer wearing this playing soccer, climbing trees, cycling my bike - It would go everywhere with me! Most stylish boy in town. I think I must have been reading *Matilda* at the time. Whatever way Roald Dahl described Matilda's Dad as being a used car salesman wearing his sports jacket to work sounded to me like a cool look. I want to look like that. He must drive the coolest cars ever too. I want to be cool like that. How right I would not be.

The day of my Confirmation I wore the jacket to the church but found it uncomfortable after ten minutes so I took it off. The shoulder pads were a bit odd too now that I was wearing it out in public for the first time. Made my body look like an upside down triangle, like those soft cheese Dairylea Triangles that were popular at the time. None of the other boys were wearing jackets like this either. Hmmm. Was I ahead of the trend? Do I look cool? Or does this jacket just make me look both sleazy and cheesy?

Saw my Mum's concerned face when we got home and I still wasn't wearing it. Smiled and put it back on as I went outside to play soccer with my brother before we all went to dinner. Felt like I was in a strait jacket trying to run in it. Too restricting to play sport in, what kind of a sports jacket was this? Also, I told myself, I don't want to ruin it by getting grass stains or anything on it. Better take it off. I'll just put it in my closet where it will be safe.

And that was the end of that. Never. Worn. Again.

That wasn't the last time I wore shoulder pads though. My next fashion statement had them too: Turtlenecks. That same summer I remember being in my parent's bedroom looking for something or another (probably just snooping) when I came upon a bag of clothes. Looked like it was going to be donated to charity. Better not be throwing away my sports jacket! Opened the bag and rooted inside. On top was a black turtleneck. *Never seen my Dad wear this*, I thought, *I think I might like to wear it myself.*

Again, I'm convinced I was reading a book about cat burglars at the time and they must've been described as all wearing black turtlenecks and black berets. How cool and stealth are they? I want to be like that! Could barely contain my excitement as I whipped off my soccer jersey and put on the turtleneck. Bit of a tight squeeze but it's nice. Shoulder pads make me look buff too. Heard my Mum call me for dinner. Strolled into the kitchen wearing my new bold fashion statement, trying to play it cool in front of the rest of my family.

"Dad, mind if I wear your jumper?"

Busy carving up a slab of ham, he gave me a confused look and shrugged his shoulders: OK. It was then my Mum informed me,

"That's my jumper. You can wear if that's what you like though."

This was my Mum's? I'm wearing women's clothes?

"Actually, now I think of it your Nana gave that to me."

This is Nana's jumper? *I'm wearing granny clothes?* Oh Jesus: I'm a Granvestite.

Oddly enough this knowledge didn't stop me from wearing the turtleneck more. Nor did the mocking my brother gave me about it. Didn't care. I liked the look, made me sophisticated looking, in my mind anyway. The shoulder pads did get a bit of a weird reaction when I first wore it out of the house so they had to be cut off. Sad to see them go, but again, they did give me that upside down triangular look so maybe it was for the best. Either way, for the next few years turtlenecks would be my go to item whenever I had to dress smartly for anything. Well, turtle necks and that bloody oversized wine shirt that I still haven't fully grown into. I've narrow, woman-like shoulders, apparently.

Pretty sure the reason for the lack of fashion knowledge was a result of having to wear school uniforms five days a week. (I also think this might be the reason a typical Irish guy's sense of style when he's in his twenties or thirties is probably five to ten years behind the rest of the fashion conscious world.)

During our school days we were forever wearing the same outfit. Each school had a different uniform. Typically a grey pants with a grey or white shirt, a green, grey, navy or black itchy wooly jumper, all coupled with some sort of stripy tie. Mine was a navy jumper, grey pants and white or grey shirt. Over and over. All we wore for five days a week, six years in a row at school. Very little variation really. Friday and Saturday nights. Sunday dinners out. Christmas parties. That was about it for dressing up.

The rest of the time it was school uniform, followed by sports wear. Tracksuits were and have always been huge in Ireland. Comfort and style. Sometimes I would wear my red Adidas tracksuit pants with a black and white striped Juventus soccer club jersey. Other times my shiny white Fred Perry tracksuit pants with a turquoise Lazio jersey. My favourite was probably my full Borussia Dortmund tracksuit, my favourite German soccer team. Black with dashes of luminous yellow lines, coupled with a purple and blue striped Barcelona jersey. How I liked to clash those colours. And support all the best soccer teams in Europe. Fake soccer jerseys were all the rage. Your coolness amongst your friends was based on how real your fake one looked. Collars always worn up too.

Runners were cyclical. For a while you only ever wore white ones. Then the population went through a stage where only black runners seemed to be allowed. After a couple of years this fad faded away and white runners became the only acceptable social norm once more. Whatever everyone else in school was wearing at the time really, although school shoes were technically all you were allowed to wear with your school uniform.

Usually you'd get at least a year's worth out of each school uniform before the wear and tear kicked in. Same went for shoes but at least you could slightly have some unique flair here, stand out a little. For the first three years I went with whatever everyone else was wearing, Clarks, a bland brand if ever I saw one. Plain, black shoes with thin, black laces. Second year everyone moved on to Doc Martens those cumbersome German shoes with the thick PVC air-cushioned sole that were popular on America TV shows at the time. I think I remember seeing them on *Sweet Valley High*. Oh, Elizabeth and Jessica Wakefield, those beautiful long blond haired, blue eyed twins on the show about a high school in the San Fernando Valley in L.A. How I yearned for ye, watching every day after school back in cold, wet Cork. And now I'm rambling. Where was I again? Oh yeah, German shoes.

Doc Martens kind of had a punk metal, biker look to them. Usually people got black. Not me though, I went with blue. First step out of my shell. Heavy. Uncomfortable. Cumbersome. They were seen as cool though and that in turn made *me* cool, or so I told my Mum.

Next year came a polar opposite trend, Dubarry, a traditional Irish brand in existence since 1937. They got their name from a Madame du Barry, the main mistress of King Louis XV of France back in the 1700s. Very fancy stuff altogether, like the shoes themselves, navy boat shoes that made us look like sailor boys, frilly curly laces and all. Posh it up for a bit.

As bad as they all were though, my worst fashion offence ever was the pair of shoes I bought next. Complete panic purchase. I was fifteen at the time, still in fourth year and very confident that my fashion style was right on the cutting edge of magnificent. That's what I told myself in my own fifteen-year-old head anyway, despite having a history of being delusion about my sense of fashion.

It was my first day of work at a clothes shop. Waiting outside on a bitter cold, wet Monday morning at nine bells. Shop had not yet opened so myself and few other workers were just hanging around, chitchatting, and pretending to kick imaginary footballs, that sort of thing. At one point I'm standing by the footpath, kicking the curb to keep my feet warm. Just as we see someone arrive to open up the shop, I kick the curb one last time and my right Dubarry sailor boy shoe bursts open like a split banana. The front section of the rubber sole flies backwards while the top of the boat shoe flies forward. I'm left standing there with my white sock sticking out of half a shoe. What the Jesus, how did that just happen?

Stand there scratching my head. Absentmindedly put my foot down into a puddle while looking around for the parts of my shoe that flew off. On cue it starts to rain so everyone runs inside the store.

As the rest meet and greet the shop manager, Tony, I try and put my shoe back together using hope and black magic. No joy. By the time it's my turn to introduce myself I'm being viewed with immense pity and embarrassment by all the shop employees who have arrived for work. *Can he not afford a proper pair of shoes?* I see etched across all of their faces. *I wonder if he's a pikey?* Annoyed by my presumptions, I greet the manager with,

"Hi, I'm Mark. Just so you know my shoe was fine until just a minute ago. I don't know how it happened. I'm not poor."

He starts petting my hair like I'm an injured bird,

"Hey hey, come on, that's OK, shhh. We'll get you a new pair of shoes. And some socks too by the looks of it."

Stupid wet, dirty black, once white sock showing me up as well. Tut. Bad start. The assistant manager Connor, a tall flamboyant chap with a brown quiff flopping across his face, asks me what size shoe I am. Arrives back within a minute with a pair he found out the back. Opens the box and pulls them out. Full on pair of leprechaun shoes by the looks of it, almost made me want to sing a lyrically string of tooraloora gibber and dance a jig on the spot. Polished black, slip-on shoe with a broad, flat front and a big fake shiny silver buckle instead of laces. Oh sweet Jesus. These are horrendous. Hands me a well-worn, ragged looking pair of socks as well that they offer to customers when they're trying on shoes in the store. Delightful.

"Thanks, they look lovely. I'll make sure not to leave the shop with them on."

"You'll be fine I'd say, these will just be your payment now for the week."

Ah for funk's sake. They weren't obliged to pay us for the week's work but usually the places gave you something worthwhile at the end. Where was I supposed to summon fake enthusiasm if I knew all I was getting were these ridiculously uncomfortable leprechaun shoes? The minute our lunch break came about I went to the nearest payphone and rang my Mum,

"My shoe exploded. I need new shoes. This is a joke, the shop had to give me some, for God's sake, Mum."

"Calm down, calm down, we'll get you new shoes. Have a look around town and see if you find any nice ones."

After a tough day of observing how to put shirts on hangers, we were let go from work at four o'clock. Quickly ran up to a shoe shop up the road, Sapphire Shoe Store. For some reason a highly odd pair caught my eye. They were called New Rocks. Black leather boots. Big metal heel. Frankenstein style. They were what I imagine a skinhead, punk loving, Neo-Nazi would wear on his way to kicking some heads in.

I think I blame Bono for these shoes piquing my interest, as I'm sure I saw a photo of him in a Sunday magazine the day before wearing a similar looking pair. Bono wears this kind of shoe because he's quite a small guy. The huge metal heel gives him the lift he needs. At the time I was fifteen and beginning to spurt up, about six feet tall. These shoes added about four extra inches. Not only that but my feet were a size twelve (size thirteen in America). These things were like cinder blocks on my feet, looked like I was trying to walk around wearing empty milk bottle crates. Gangly. Awkward. Clopping. Could barely move. But still, for some reason, I wanted these shoes.

Checked the price: £100. Jesus, that's a chunk. Let's see what my Mum says to me. Get home. Describe the shoe. My Mum's face winces.

"Are you sure you want that kind?"

"Yes! Of course."

"Well if you want to put fifty pounds of your own money towards it, it's up to you."

"I still have birthday money left over, I'll do that. The shoes will last me a lifetime too, Mum. Finest German leather, the woman in the shop said to me, she was really sound."

Next morning I'm outside Sapphire Shoe Store early, longingly looking in the window, waiting for them to open. Plan is to buy the shoes, wear them down to work at the clothes shop, put the runners I'm wearing now into a plastic bag and then tell the manager Tony I don't need his leprechaun shoes or horrible socks. My payment will have to be something cool instead. Mighty plan!

Shop opens. Try on the New Rock shoes one more time. Hmm. Is my Mum right? Are these shoes impractical? No, all the girls here at the shop are telling me I look great, really cool, they wish their boyfriends were as adventurous as I am.

"Thanks girls, we can't all be like me though!"

Hook. Line. Sinker. Pay my money. Check my watch. Almost nine. Need to get to work on time. As I'm waiting at the counter I see another guy in the store pick up the shoes I just bought. Puts them down. Doesn't like them. Oh no. Are these not cool? Girl hands me back my receipt and a bag with the shoes in them. Thank her and step away a bit dazed. The immediate dread of buyer's remorse hits me in the gut. Why did I buy these shoes? They're just for school and my school pants won't even fit over them so now I'll have to cut the bottom of my pants to make a slit so they'll be wider why did I buy them?! Feel like wailing sirens on my feet. Big, metal cumbersome dopes. I need to try them on again, just to be sure.

Kick off my runners. Horse the cinder blocks back on. Look in the small crappy mirrors in the stupid shoe store. How can I see what they're really like with this mirror? For God's sake. Look around. No full lengths. Walk out by the front door. Spot a full length mirrored window next door. I'll check that. Quickly scamper out. Look at myself. Sweet Jesus, I look like a giraffe with cement blocks on his feet. What am I doing? I hate these boots. Back into the sales girl,

"Sorry, I know *just* bought these but I actually need to return them now straightaway for a refund."

"Excuse me?"

"Yeah, I don't like them, at all."

"Unfortunately I can't."

"Pardon?"

Points to a sign above the register: NO REFUNDS.

"But I just bought them."

"Sorry, that's the policy. Plus, you've already worn them out."

"I just stepped outside the door for a second!"

"Well that's still outside. Nothing I can do. Now if you excuse me, I have other customers."

"You can't do this, the customer is always right, *the customer is always right!*"

"Not this time. Your loss."

"I'll take you to the Small Claims Court, wait until the Ombudsman hears about this… *Your books don't even balance!*"

Everything I learnt in Business Class started flowing out of my mouth like gibber at this point. Made a bit of a scene. So much so, in fact, that Tony, the manager of the shop I was working at, had to go up later that day and apologise for me. Whole thing was a disaster. Even worse, I was also stuck with the leprechaun shoes. They were now mine, Tony told me in no uncertain terms. They would be my pay, end of story. And, I was informed, I wasn't allowed to wear runners or my new cinder block shoes to work. Neither deemed appropriate. Great stuff. Stuck in the shiny buckled brogs. Tremendous altogether.

Went home that night and tried to put a brave face on to my Mum. Attempted to pretend like I did like all my new horrendous shoes. She had no clue why I had so many pairs but I wore my new boots around the house with pride to prove what a great buy they were. Such a smart Marky boy, aren't I? Far more comfortable than any other shoes I've ever bought. Don't even need my slippers now I have these clunky insane clown shoes to wear.

Grasping at straws, I went to go ask my sister Sarah to see what she thought. Let's ask the seven-year-old for fashion advice. Knocked on her door and walked inside, for some reason half doing a tap dancing jig despite having the grace of Frankenstein, just as Sarah was leaving her bedroom. Kind of walked into her. My big metal soles, her small bare feet.

Like a sack of silent spuds, down she went in immense pain, still clutching her penguin teddy bear, Pengie, to her chest. Fell back against her bed, bounced off it, let out a cry and hit the floor with a sickening thud, her long blond hair forming a halo on the floor. Pengie rolling lifelessly across the floor coupled with Sarah screaming with gusto reminded me of a scene from an Alfred Hitchcock movie. I knew something was wrong.

Four hours later, after a lengthy trip to the hospital, it was confirmed that I had broken Sarah's toes with my shoes. My poor sister. Victim of my fashion.

Speaking of victims, I'm pretty sure the calamitous shoe incident scared me for life. Always have trouble choosing shoes ever since. Bernard Herrmann's theme song from *Vertigo* pops in my head when I need to make a choice. Especially during the time of the events of that wedding in San Francisco. Shoe shopping vertigo. Victims. Both.

On the upside, those Bono, New Rock boots have lasted a lifetime. Still floating around the shed in my back garden at home somewhere, fully intact, impregnable to aging.

At the time I also filed a case against the shoe shop with the Smalls Claims Court. Only took five months of me filling out endless forms before my case was heard. I lost. Case dismissed, within minutes. However, four years later, the shoe shop went out of business. So at least that made us even in my eyes.

Chapter 12
Wild Horses

Fourth year in school was really the first time you got to experience the outside world. Big step for fifteen-year-olds, one that they - parents, teachers, society - assumed we could handle. Up to that point everything you did or encountered was school or family related. Now though, on this kind of gap year period, we got to experience grown up activities. Such as the wonderful world of work. Oh what a joy.

At this stage of life work really only meant doing chores around the house. Clean your room. Tidy the shed. Hang out the washing. That kind of thing. Led to pocket money, which was my only source of income at the time. Only get paid when the work was done. Clean and tidy. Job done. Engrained in me ever sense. Might explain why even to this day I'm a ridiculous neat freak. Pristine bedroom. Looks like a hotel maid has gone to work on it every morning.

Anyway, back in fourth year we were going to do two weeks work experience. Our teachers gave us a list of suggestions as to where to try and get a job but we were all allowed to pick and choose where we went to work ourselves. Preferably something in the line of work we wanted to do when we grew up.

Surprisingly, despite being the wise old age of fifteen, I'd no clue what this might be. All I knew was that I now had spikey short-ish hair, I was getting taller by the day, and also a bit leaner than previous years. No longer as full a cereal face as before. In my mind I thought I looked like a brown hair Zach Morris from *Saved by the Bell*. In reality it was probably more like Screech. Not that any of this helped with my job search, obviously. Clearly I was not ready for the real world.

Some people in my school used work experience as a chance to get a part-time job in local hotels or pubs. Zero interest in that though so I followed the lead of what a few others in my class: Do nothing. My long-standing motto will pull me through "Ah I'll be grand!"

As a result I spent my first week of work experience working in a clothes shop called GQ, short for Gentlemen's Quarters. They happened to be looking for a fair few people so myself and three other buddies all went to work there. There was Ronnie, who kind of looked like the main character out of the cartoon *Hey Arnold* with his rugby ball shaped head and blond hair, Vinnie, who looked like a Lego man with his block shaped shaved head and square body, and Leo, a small Albino boy with a fiery temper. We were all in the same German class and so decided to try and find work together. All really wanted to be clothes sellers. Ahem. The thought of free clothes was probably the main attraction.

Plus, we started the hunt too late to find anywhere good. All the appealing places were gone. Fifteen-year-old gym teacher at the all girls' school sounded good. "Come on now girls, let's really get a deep leg stretch in before I teach ye all how to play soccer, deeeeep stretch!" All in their short-shorts and tight tops. Heaven!

First I tried Scoil Mhuire, renowned for having the best talent in Cork. Lot of nines with a handful of tens. Slim bodies, big boobs, short dresses. Posh. Pretty. Prudes. Hard nuts to crack, which made you want them more. Alas, no joy. Next, I turned to Ashton, the school with the second best talent. Odd ten, good mix of nines and eights. More Bohemian style. Filled with beautiful brunettes and mysterious foreigners. Again though, nay. How about Christ the King? Still kind of enough good talent. One or two nines, some eights, good few sevens. And, nope. Where else? Regina Mundi, the girls school closest to ours but with not that great talent? Jolly, friendly, rumbustious kind of girls. Huh? Not even *there*? Come on, give Marky boy a chance! Tut. Clothes shop it will have to be.

At least that was better than a shoe salesman, the back up option. Although we did all look a bit like Al Bundy in our shirt, tie and slacks work outfits when we showed up for our first day at work. GQ was a fancy, marquee store on Patrick's Street, the main street in Cork. Huge glass windows with well-dressed mannequins decked out in sharp outfits for men, suits or casual, cardigan over the shoulder look. Décor looked like the inside of GQ magazine, which was popular at the time. Jazz music and Frank Sinatra being played over the speakers. Polished bleached wood floor with staircases made out of brass, along with rows and rows of suits, shirts, jumpers, pants, jeans and shoes. Sharp, just like me.

GQ only needed two of us in the flagship store so it was a raffle between Vinnie, Ronnie, Leo, and myself to see who would stay. Leo and Vinnie literally both pulled the shorter straws and were sent off to different shops close by. Ronnie and I both felt like we won a prize of some sort by getting to stay at GQ. At least we could hang out together as opposed to being solo in one of the other shops. We were all messers and chancers in a sense but we definitely had more fun when there was another chancer around to mess with.

What we didn't realise was that the manager of GQ, Tony, was the worst by far to get stuck with. Old, grumpy, sweaty, small and clueless, he looked like a mix between a toad and a mole. Also had no time for me after my exploding shoe incident on my first morning that I mentioned before. After half an hour of getting asked to do janitorial work like "Scrub and hose the footpath outside the shop" and "Wash the windows and hoover the whole place" myself and Ronnie realised our job would be to dodge Tony and his cleaning requests as much as we could.

At least the assistant manager, Connor, was sound. Also the first real live gay person we had ever met. At first we weren't too sure but slowly we pieced the puzzle together. Tall and lithe with high cheekbones and darting eyes. Stylish, fancy hairstyle, shaved on the sides with a brown fringe that either flopped over his forehead or else was combed back, depending on the time of day. Wore lots of pink and purple shirts. Told us he was in his late twenties but clearly pushing forty, no matter how much moisturizer and lip balm he applied to his face and mouth in front of us. Flamboyant reactions whenever something annoyed or excited him,

"I asked for no sugar in my coffee, NO SUGAR, sugar. *Clearly* I'm sweet enough." Wink. Click. Twinkle.

Constantly talking with his flailing arms, hands that fluttered like butterflies. Tuts, eye-rolls and lip puckering every second minute. Loved to gossip. Spoke a lot about his Spanish boyfriend Jorge who might or might not be the love of his life. He wasn't too sure. It was really the boyfriend part that gave it away but just to be sure I enquired,

"Boyfriend as in your *friend* who's a boy or do you mean actual *boyfriend?*"

"Oh wouldn't you like to know. Are you asking or offering?"

"Pardon?"

"You guys should come to the bar around the corner with us sometime."

"What bar?"

"The Otherside."

"Never heard of it."

"Oh they'd like you guys there."

"Is it tough to get in?"

"How old are you? I better stop or I'll be locked up."

"Fifteen, I'll be sixteen next year."

"Oh my God, I'm going to hell! Shoo shoo, shouldn't you two be hoovering?"

Whatever Connor was talking about, it was always said in jest with a smile and a wink. Myself and Ronnie presumed it meant he thought we were sound. Wasn't too sure what the other employees thought of us though. There was Danny, a guy in his twenties with stale stubble who was always hung-over from partying the night before. Looked a bit like John Travolta in *Saturday Night Live*. No girlfriend to tie him down. Too busy loving life. Actually started out doing his work experience in GQ as well and then managed to get a job out of it. Instead of going to university after secondary school, he just went full-time at GQ. "Haven't looked back since," he told us. I still think he works there to this day, smoking and humming his favourite Bee Gees songs out in the stockroom. "Night fever, night fe-ver, we know how to do it, *oh yeah*!"

Then there was Lisa, a girl in her mid-twenties, who was also studying Arts at U.C.C, the main university in Cork. The phrase "mutton dressed as lamb" springs to mind. Dirty, bleached blond hair that looked like someone cracked eggs over her head. Lots of coats of make-up, slathered on like someone was applying cement to a wall. Push-up bra that had them up almost choking her neck. In the right light she looked good from afar. Up close, too personal. She hated the job but loved fashion, so at least there was that, she told us.

Also seemed to go on a lot of bad dates all the time, complaining to myself and Ronnie about them all. Apparently she used to be into guys who played Gaelic football but now she preferred rugby players, "just more mature, you know?" As soccer players, we didn't really but we nodded and shrugged along like we had a clue. Connor warned us on the sly not to drink her water bottles in case we caught anything from her, even though she didn't ever really complain about being sick.

"Have you seen the cold sores on her face? Guess where she got them from."

"Herpes?"

Connor's wide eyes and slow nod said it all. That explained the crusty make-up around her mouth. Delightful.

The least friendly out of the group by far was Sean, an older, overweight guy in his thirties who looked like a dairy cow standing up. Heavy breather, always snacking on mysterious food from his pants pockets. Cake Pants, we called him. Quiet too, kept mumbling to himself. First thing he said to us was "I've nothing against queer folk, just so ye all know." So that was weird.

Didn't seem to do much work. Just hung around up on the third floor with the in-house tailor, Ann. She was an older lady who used to just knit all day, waiting for a suit to be tailored or the likes. Sean would stand by the window looking out, keeping an eye on his motorbike parked across the street. Ronnie was a fan bikes as well at the time so he'd tried to spark up conversation with Sean while I looked at whatever Ann knitted that day. Nice pair of wooly socks, typically. Sean never really responded to Ronnie's small talk about bikes, only to correct him,

"No, impossible, no engine can be that big. Go back and check your facts."

To wind him up, I'd always back up Ronnie's engine size claims, just to stoke Sean's burning fire.

"I think he's right, I read it in a magazine the other day."

"SHUT UP THE TWO OF YOU, YOU'RE JUST CLUELESS KIDS, OK?!"

Sean was easy to get going. I think he was on edge so much as young knackers would always spit on his motorbike and try to push it over. Whenever he saw them go near his bike from the third floor he'd make a sprint for it, screaming,

"I'LL CATCH THOSE LITTLE FECKERS I SWEAR TO GOD!"

By the time he got downstairs his bike would already be covered in spit and lying on the ground. Sean would chase some of the knackers up the road. They'd respond by throwing eggs at Sean who would then have to turn and run back to the safety of the shop. Pack of clowns going at it. Myself and Ronnie thought it was hilarious, watching from our bird's eye view. Even Ann found it funny. Sean got us back by telling Tony we needed to clean up the egg mess off the windows and footpath. Prick. Overall it was worth it. Angry red and purple Cake Pants head and cow body up on him.

Each day we were given one big break around one in the afternoon. Myself, Ronnie, Vinnie and Leo would all meet up for lunch at the McDonalds by Virgin Records at the top of Patrick's Street. McChicken meal, please. Sample of fine American cuisine right on our doorstep. Discuss what the payment at the end of the two weeks might be. I more or less knew that mine was the pair of leprechaun shoes but I held a glimmer of hope that maybe I would get a suit out of it. We all wanted a free suit. In fact, Tony led us all to believe we were getting free suits,

"What size suit are you, kid? Let's get you measured, we'll have you looking sharp."

Turns out he was trying to sell us suits. He'd throw in a free tie at least. We all looked at him like he was an idiot. We're fifteen. How are we going to buy a suit, you dope? Even worse, at the start of the second week Connor confirmed to me that my payment was going to be the leprechaun shoes.

"What's everyone else going to get?"

"Probably a pair of jeans."

On the second last day a shipment arrived at the store. Myself and Ronnie were asked to drag the boxes out the back. Apparently Tony had bought a load of Pepe jeans on the cheap from a store that just went out of business, he was going to sell them off for £20. Brilliant. I knew this would be the payment for everyone else, ha! Pepe jeans used to be cool but not anymore. There was a big campaign with the guy Brandon from the TV show *Beverly Hills 90210* whose photo was plastered all over Cork but that was about three years ago. Pepe were *over*. Done. Dusted. Even my leprechaun shoes were cooler than that!

On our last day we were let go early as a bonus for being so great. Sure. "One last thing," Tony remarks, "As a special thank you, you guys can pick a pair of Pepe jeans. Except you Mark, you got shoes."

"No worries Tony, I love the shoes!"

The others pretended to be thankful and happy. Everyone but Tony knew the truth. Only two colours to pick from as well, black or white. Everyone went with black. Nobody even bothered trying them on. All knew how bad they were. Sean made sure to mock us while standing behind Tony, pointing at the jeans and laughing. Nice man.

We all say goodbye and head out the door. As we're standing outside debating whether to go play pool or just go home, we hear a banging noise from upstairs. Look up and see Sean standing by the window on the third floor, giving us all the finger. Ronnie waves back as he strolls over to Sean's bike,

"Up yours, ya wanker!"

Pretends to kick it. Sean's face drops. Freaks out. Starts banging on the window. Just eggs Ronnie on. Pushes the bike to the ground and gives Sean the finger back. We all rip off our ties and wave them around our head. Next minute we see an angry Sean sprinting down the stair after us.

"Sketch!"

"Screw you, Cake Pants!"

Everyone throws their Pepe jeans into the air as celebration, no more crappy work for the week. Run away laughing as we see Sean's red head come out the door. Cow body starts chasing us up the street yelling and mooing at us. His ruckus is drowned out by my leprechaun shoes clip-clopping on the footpath. Kind of makes us sound like wild horses running free. Clip-clop, clip-clop, clip-clop, all of us chanting,

"Pants off, shoes on! Pants off, shoes on! Pants off, shoes on!"

Great week of work.

For my second stint I went to work at a carpet shop called Rosie Carpets. Really scraping the barrel. None of the usual back-ups I was told about were available: Accountant, doctor, candle stick baker. Every position filled around town. My motto "I'll be grand" was not serving me well. The alternative was to spend the week at school studying. So, random carpet shop that I happened to be walking by on my way to get the bus home from town three days before work experience started it is. Told my teachers and parents it was my life ambition to work with carpets. Carpet Man Hayes!

At least I wouldn't be on my own. Ronnie blagged his way in there too, swooping in last minute like me. Zach Morris and Hey Arnold, the carpet selling dream team! The store had a showroom in the front with a warehouse out the back. Rolls and rolls of dusty looking carpets. Owner's name was Brendan and it turns out we kind of knew his son Joe. I think that's why we got the job.

Myself and Ronnie both showed up on our first day of work in a shirt and tie, ready and raring to sell carpets. Laughed at when we said this to the boss. No chance, he said. We were destined to be delivery boys with a burly, gruff man named Paddy, who looked like a brute of a caveman dressed in denim overalls. Big, callused hands with hairy knuckles that he dragged along the floor as he moved carpets from one wall to the other. Impressive mustache too, looked like a hairy leg of lamb over his crusty top lip. And so, we were to be Paddy's right hand, knuckle dragging men.

Initially this involved hanging around the drab warehouse section out the back, in with all the carpets. Seeing as we had nothing to do, Ronnie and I killed a few hours by playing a game where we would run into a stack of carpet rolls and just bounce off them onto the ground. That was the whole game. Sometimes we'd try to grab onto a carpet to use to help break our fall but more often than not we failed. Fun few hours.

After lunch we were given our first piece of work: Deliver a carpet. Hop into Paddy's old white Transit van. Empty coke bottles, crisp bags and various other bits of rubbish dumped on the floor, bench seats in the front, with an oddly pristine carpet storage area in the back. Now we're workers. Now we're on the road! Time to get to know Paddy. See what the life of a carpet man is really like. Kept trying to spark up conversation but he was having none of it,

"Do you like carpets?"

"Huh?"

"Do you hate tiles?"

"Shh."

"What do you make of wooden floors?"

"Will you shut up and pipe down. Listen to music."

Fair enough. Radio on. Ronnie was a fan of Radio Friendly, a pirate station that played dance music, whereas I was a fan of Atlantic 252, another pirate station that played pop music. Not the cheesy kind, mind you, the cool stuff. Seeing as I was in front of the radio it was my duty to pick. Atlantic 252 all the way. After a while Ronnie changed the channel to Radio Friendly which was annoying as it was right in the middle of my favourite Ace of Base song, *I Saw The Sign*. Dialled the tuner knob back to my station. Ronnie did the same. Only one way to solve this - Hands start slapping each other.

"My station!"

"No, mine!"

"I was here first!"

Tuner knob whizzes into no man's land. White noise booms out of the speakers. After a minute Paddy flips out,

"ARE YOU TWO GOING TO BE DOING THIS THE WHOLE WAY DOWN?"

Jesus, I thought, *calm down Paddy.*

"It's not me, it's him. You even said you liked the Ace of Base channel as well."

"Just give Radio Friendly a listen, Pad," chimes in Ronnie "It's way better."

Paddy turned off the radio and politely asks us both to,

"Shut the f**k up."

Myself and Ronnie looked at each other, rolling our eyes. *Just a bit of music, Paddy.* Seeing as we were only ten minutes into our journey we needed something else to entertain ourselves for the ride down. No music. Next best thing? Make our own music! Start making a popping noise with my mouth. Ronnie joins in by drumming on the dashboard. Now clicking my fingers and hands together. Ronnie adds a bass sound from his throat, kind of as if he's choking. All we need now are lyrics. Paddy? Sing!

"I swear to God if you don't be quiet I'll murder the pair of ye."

Talk about touchy. Obviously this led us to asking Paddy if he ever murdered anyone, which in turn lead to Paddy asking us if we were retarded in some way. Clearly myself and Ronnie have no real world experience. No clue how to not be annoying. How we wrecked poor Paddy's caveman head.

An hour later we arrive at our destination, a country town called Mallow that has one main street and lots of pubs. Myself and Ronnie carry the carpet inside, up to the top floor of a narrow four story house just off the main street while Paddy has a quick cup of tea with the owner of the house in the kitchen, a typical Irish housewife. Once we dump the carpet in the spare bedroom and head back downstairs sweating, we watch as she slips Paddy a tenner tip, thanks us all and we're on our way. Hop in the front of the van. Broach the obvious elephant in the room.

"So, eh, Paddy, do we all split the tip she gave you or how does it work?"

For the first time all day Paddy laughed.

While I'm trying to convince him that a three-way-split is fair, I hear the radio go on - Ronnie you snake! Quickly change the channel over to Atlantic 252. Ronnie changes it back. Just as I'm about to do the same the truck screeches to a halt.

"Lads, I'm warning ye, one more time and there'll be trouble."

Seeing as my hand was already on the radio knob, I kind of changed it by accident exactly as Paddy said the word trouble. Didn't mean to, not right at that second anyway.

"SWEET F**KING JESUS CHRIST ALMIGHTY!"

Oh Jesus. Myself and Ronnie look at each other a bit worried.

"Sorry Paddy, won't do it again."

"I need you two to go check if we have a flat tire."

"Huh?"

"I just need you both to jump out and check if there's a flat tire at the back on either side. Can you do that for me?"

"Sure thing Paddy!"

We were great workers. Out we pop, rolling our eyes at one another again. *Same old Paddy.* Stroll to the back of the truck and kick the tires, me on the left, Ronnie on the right. Paddy shouts back out the driver's window,

"Step away a second, let me test them."

"Sure thing, Paddy!"

Into the ditch on the side of the road myself and Ronnie step, off down the road Paddy drives. Watch as the white van carries on through a set of lights, and just keeps on going up the country road. Hmm, Paddy must be doing a thorough test to make sure the tires are fine. Myself and Ronnie stand on the side of the road and debate over radio stations for a few minutes, then realise Paddy's been gone a while now, hasn't he?

"Do you think he just left us?" Ronnie asks me.

"He couldn't do that to us, he'd be arrested."

"I don't think he's coming back."

"He's definitely coming back."

Paddy never came back.

Through a combination of hitchhiking, walking and buses, we eventually made our back to Cork, only twenty-two miles or so. Took a good few hours. Next morning we went to work wary, unsure who was at fault. What if Paddy made up a story? Don't want to get in trouble. Were we fired? What happened? Did Paddy leave us there by accident? Said good morning to Brendan, waited to see if we were giving our marching orders.

"I hear you were great help to Paddy yesterday."

"We were?"

"Ye can do the same again today!"

"We can?"

Paddy arrives in. Looks at us and nods his head towards the warehouse. Wants a word.

"So here's the plan: Nobody says a thing about yesterday. From now on I'll pretend I need ye to help me with deliveries. You get in the van, we drive down the road, I leave you out and when I come back here I'll say I dropped you off on the way home. Otherwise ye will drive me mental, OK? I don't want to see or hear from you again."

"Fair enough."

For the rest of the week the carpet selling dream team of myself, Zach Morris, and Ronnie, Hey Arnold, went off playing pool and arcade games in the Vic. Great work if you can get it. Can't tie us down, man! Tough week. On our last day we went back to the carpet shop after lunch to get our cards signed for school. Also wondered if we might get paid. Not obliged to but most places did pay something for work experience. While waiting around for Brendan to show up and sign our cards a married couple come into the store. Ask myself and Ronnie if there's someone that can help them.

"Emm, not sure, Ronnie you go check."

Off he goes. Time for me to shine. Pretend I'm a salesman. Show them a wide variety of my favourite carpets (the ones I ran into earlier that week). Within ten minutes I sell them their dream cream pile carpet, roll and rolls of it. Just made the shop a bomb of money. Brendan shows up in time to ring them up. Beams at me with delight.

"Happy days," I whisper to Ronnie, "We're definitely getting paid after that sale."

Once the couple leave, Brendan comes over with our report cards,

"Brilliant, *brilliant* workers! You just got the record sale so far this month, beat all our other employees! I should hire you full time."

"Not sure if you can afford my salary, Brendan. I'd do you a good deal though."

"Ha ha, very funny. Well, thanks for being here guys, all the best."

Shakes our hands goodbye. Stands there. Silence. Uncomfortable. Is he waiting for us to leave? That's it? Well this is awkward.

"Ehh, anything else before we go Brendan? Any way you might want to say thanks to us maybe?"

"Do you mean money?"

"Well no we'd never say that, I just heard our friends all got paid at their places is all."

"Oh did they now? Here's what I'll do - I'll write you both a big cheque and give it to your friend Eoin, OK?"

"Eoin?"

"He's friends with my son. He said he knows you two as well."

"OK so? Not too sure who that is but sounds fair."

There was no Eoin. There was no money. There is no carpet God. At least I got my first lesson in the business world: Always get the money upfront. Something like that. Or else steer clear of carpet folk. Maybe that was it. Did I mention Paddy had a tattoo on his lower back saying *'Carpe diem! (Or else just carpet it.)'* So actually yeah, that was the lesson. Steer clear of carpet folk.

Chapter 13
Money Money Money

Never really got into too much trouble when I was growing up. Well, not real trouble anyway. Always some small, day-to-day stuff for a bit maybe. Growing pains. At least I never got into trouble with the police. Well, except maybe this one time when I was fifteen. I blame fourth year.

Beginning to think this whole year was just a ruse to give our teachers a break. Every chance they got we were being shipped out into the real world, far away them and their sacred teachers' break room. This room was their VIP area of the school, off limits to us lowly students. Always wondered what went on in there behind the velvet rope of the elusive, always shut, weathered looking, brown wooden door. So much so I would forever be knocking on it, pretending to have a question for whatever teacher just went in. Try and suss out what the teachers on break were up to as I made up some awful gibber on the spot,

"So, eh, Mr. Clancy, just wanted to clarify from class earlier, there is no homework?"

"Hayes: Go away."

"OK, but just one more thi- Hang on. Is that Mrs. O' Rourke *smoking*? And is that a naggin of whis-"

Door shut in my face. Click my fingers. Rats. Almost got a good look that time.

Anyway, I'm convinced we were shipped out so much just to give the teachers an extra few hours break here every day. An ongoing activity we were required to do was Community Service. Give back to the community. This involved us going to volunteer at a charity organisation every Monday. Spending the day helping out. There were a load of charities in and around Cork but the key, in my opinion, was finding a charity you were comfortable with.

Mental health places threw me off purely because of the mental image they conjured. Reminded me of my old piano teacher which in turn brought up my embarrassment over the pants wetting incident. The main mental health place in Cork was called Lota. This was an old stately manor that was donated and turned into a hospital. Hidden behind big, old, rusty gates and an imposing grey-bricked wall, the place looked like a fortress. Didn't help that the zoo in Cork is called Fota, so it was kind of compared to being a zoo for mental people. Fota Lota, Lota Fota.

My little weak mind couldn't handle such a place. Nor any place like that. I always felt bad that I was so fine and they looked so frail and helpless. This left me with dwindling choices. No blind options were available, all taken. Homeless shelters didn't seem like my cup of tea either so in the end I found a place called the Cork Deaf Association, near to where I went to play pool some Wednesdays in town.

The building was closed when I spotted it but looking into the window it looked like it was just an office. Maybe this was just administration, that kind of work. I could handle that. Volunteer on. Found their number in the Golden Pages. Phoned them up the next day. Lady answered. Delighted when I asked if I could work there. Pretended I had a friend who was available as well.

"Even better!" she said.

"Great," I spoofed, "See you Monday!"

Didn't want to do the community service on my own so asked my friends if anyone was still looking for a place? One was, Seamus, my tall, gangly, glasses wearing buddy who looked and acted a bit like the character *Where's Wally?* Handy handy, cushy community service for us.

The following Monday morning we got the bus into town together from school. Happy days. Out and about. No classes for the day! Made our way from the bus station to the Cork Deaf Association office, near enough to the quay where a gang of pikeys once held me up at knifepoint over a fiver. Fond memories. Cold morning but at least it's dry. Empty streets. As we're waiting for the lights to change so we can cross over the bridge, Seamus 'Where's Wally' nudges me in the side,

"Look to your right, say nothing."

"Huh?"

Seamus nods hard over his shoulder. Look over and see an enormous man with wild ginger hair, a flustered red face and a pregnant looking belly, wearing a dirty white string vest and stained yellowy-white y-fronts. That was it. Nothing else. No pants. No shoes. No socks. Nada. Looked like he just got out of a bed of dirt, like a character out of Oliver Twist. Fidgeting hands, mumbling words and scratching his head non-stop as he paced up and down in the same spot, looking like he was bursting for the toilet. Catches me looking at him. Stares back at me with crazy goat eyes,

"What time have we?"

"Pardon?"

"What time have we I said?"

"Almost nine."

"Almost nine, that's good, that's good, almost nine - Almost nine what?"

"Almost nine o'clock."

"Oh that's good."

It was as if I gave him some magic code. Stops pacing. Stands still. Closes his eyes. Takes a deep sigh. And grunts. Long, slow, heave. Ah no way. Jesus. Is he really doing what I think he's doing? Ughing for dear life. Dumps a load. Underpants weighs down like a nappy. Face almost purple now from the big push.

On cue but moments too late, police car sirens sound up from down the street. Naked friend comes back to life. Eyes open. Crazy twinkle. Looks around. Runs off down the road, nappy underpants swaying in the wind as he does. Police car whizzes by. Chases him down the street. The green man goes green. Seamus and I cross the road. Odd start to our Community Service.

At least the people in the deaf office appreciated our story. Only three of them working in there so I think they were happy for the new conversation. We raised the bar pretty high from the word go.

First off there was Sandra who I spoke to on the phone. Small lady. Purple hair. Early forties. From the smell I gathered she was a heavy smoker. Maybe that's why she wore a lot of overbearing perfume. Gave her a sweet, sickly, flowery, ashtray kind of smell. Showed a lot of sagging, middle aged, pinkish cleavage. Said stuff like "I'd jump his bones" when talking about celebrities in the gossip magazines they had in the office.

Then there was Tom, a quiet, bald, deaf man who seemed sound. Nice green cardigan. Couldn't really communicate to him too much though over our lack of sign language knowledge. I imagine he was a bit like Walter Mitty, preferring to live out life in his head than in the real world. Or maybe he just got wet and wild when he clocked out of work, hard to tell.

Finally there was Nora, an older grey haired woman who wasn't deaf but seemed to be mute by choice. Wore purple, pink and green flowery designed dresses that covered her neck to toe. She looked a tad gruff like a goat that potentially was just about to head butt you but actually Nora was pleasant enough. Kept nodding and smiling at our jokes. In fairness, everyone in the office was very nice to us. Maybe Seamus and I added some light to the place.

The office was a dreary, old, dusty brown, dark, dank place with a flickering fluorescent light. Front office had three wooden desks, three plastic orange chairs and one grey metal filing cabinet. The back office was the break room. Just a kitchen area really with a table and some kitchen chairs, all a slightly yellowing-yellow version of the front office. At least the kitchen had two giant, green-pea beanbags. This is where Seamus and I would sit and discuss soccer topics. Not much else for us to do.

Sandra was our liaison officer and assigned us work as best she could. Put some stickers on a poster. Count how many pencils are in that box. Arrange those sheets of paper in a nice pile. Make cups of tea for everyone. Go to the shop if anyone wanted biscuits. Not too much happened at the office. They seemed to just organise events by phone, arranging for collections and donations to take place in certain shopping centres around the city. Slowly but surely we managed to whittle away our day until we were allowed home. This would be the way for the first three weeks. The fourth week, however, things took a twist.

When we arrived back from our eleven o'clock break, Sandra was excited,

"We have something for you to do! Are you ready? You won't be bored."

"Sounds great, show us the way."

On the floor of the kitchen area were two big black refuse bags filled to the brim with collection boxes, the plastic red goblet kind with the little slots on top.

"OK guys, two of ye are going to count all the money from the big collection we had over the weekend. Can ye do that? Here are some moneybags to put the different coins into, should take you a few hours but you can go home once you're done."

"Mighty."

"Any questions?"

"We can go home straight after counting them?"

"Yes. Now. Go!"

Myself and Seamus grab the bags. Empty out the collection boxes onto the ground. Box after box after box. Coins and coins and coins. Just flowing out non-stop. Big shiny silver pound coins, solid heavy fifty pence coins along with large twenty pence, ten pence, five pence, two pence pieces and lots of small copper pennies. Created this bronze and silver swimming pool on the ground that looked unreal, something you wanted to dive into, Scrooge McDuck style.

For some reason I really wanted to swim in these coins. Probably because I'd always been fascinated by my Dad's coin jar at home. Compared to my measly one my Dad had a load of coins in his, some notes too.

"Must be over £100 in there, Dad!"

Thought it was the coolest thing ever. All. That. Money. Loved handling it and letting it run through my fingers. Seeing this pool of cash pouring out of the collection boxes triggered some dormant spark in me. All the coins shining and sparkling like diamonds. The minute Sandra left the room I started throwing the money in the air like I just won the lottery. Seamus joined in as I started singing the Abba song,

"Money money money, dun dun, isn't funny, da-dung, in a rich man's world!"

After a few bars the sheen wore off. Decided we should count it quick so we could get home early. Pretty soon we copped on that we'd been stung with a stinker of a job. So many coins and each bag had to have a certain amount exactly. Fifty pennies in this bag, twenty-five two-pences in this bag and so on. After an hour we were like zombies, irritated to the max.

"Seamus! Fifty pennies, FIFTY, not forty-eight."

"That's your bag you dope, not mine."

"It's in the pile you counted so it must be yours."

This was about the fourth time Seamus had got something wrong. My patience was wearing thin. If we kept messing up we'd be there all day. Flicked a big fifty pence piece at Seamus to make him cop on. Bounced off the back of his head and fell down the collar of his shirt.

"Ha, goal!"

Did it again. Same result. Kept doing it until Seamus figured out what was going on,

"What are you doing, boy?"

"Scoring goals."

"I'm keeping those."

"What do you mean?"

Seamus grabs the coins from down his shirt. Stuffs them in his pocket. It was then I saw his other pocket bulging too.

"What are you doing?"

"I don't know."

Before I know it, my hand's reaching for a pile of coins. Fill up my pockets. Wicked cackle is heard inside my head. I had heard of students taking money from collection boxes before but never thought I'd be doing the same. Once we started we couldn't stop though. Shoving coins into every pocket we could find. Made no dent whatsoever in the four-foot wide by three-foot high pile of money. Myself and Seamus filled ourselves to the brim with coins. Stuffed down our shirts, the inner lining of our jackets, in our socks, our shoes, underpants - Everywhere! We both said, "Don't tell anyone," then went back to counting the huge pile of coins.

Half three came around and we still hadn't finished. Sandra came back in to say we could leave, our time was up. Thanked her kindly, then waited until she went back to the front office before we crept out the front door. Could barely walk with all the coins down our shoes but we tried best we could, exclaiming loudly as we left,

"There are lots of pebbles in my shoe, how did that happen?"

Slowly shuffled out the door then bolted for the hotel two doors down from the office to our left. Raced into the fancy bathrooms and locked ourselves in adjoining cubicles.

"*What did we just do?*" I hiss at Seamus.

"I don't know. Shut up and count yours."

"OK. One, two, three, four…"

Five minutes later we emerge from the cubicles. Between us we had £200 (about $350). One hundred pounds each. Jesus Christ. Some amount of money. Could we go to jail for this? Was that wrong what we did? We both swore not to say it to anyone ever, then departed company and went home. Hid the coins in every nook and cranny available in my bedroom that night. Could barely sleep a wink for a week. Prayed to God every night for forgiveness. What did I just do?

That week in school Seamus and I went through every possible scenario of how we might be caught. Paranoia kicked in big time.

Thankfully, we weren't. Showed up the following week at the deaf office. Nothing was said. We got away with it. Say nothing. Move on. Unfortunately, there was nothing for us to do again this week to keep our minds distracted. Just hang around the peapod kitchen area. Bored. Couldn't go back to this lifestyle after the high we had the week before. Needed some rush. That's when we spotted the empty collection boxes.

"What if we went collecting for them?"

"That'd be a nice thing to do, wouldn't it?"

"Yeah. Let's do it."

Both stuffed a collection box into our jackets. Seeing as it was so dead we were let go early. Great, this meant we could go collecting. Once we were out of view of the office we took out the boxes and started rattling them in people's faces as we walked through the streets of Cork.

"Support the Deaf Association, help a good cause."

"Spare a few pounds for the deaf, come on now, be nice, help us out."

In half an hour Seamus and I almost had a full box each.

"Jesus, how much do you think's in here?"

"Don't know, hundreds?"

Time to call it a day. Made our way to the bus stop on South Mall to catch a bus home. Still not even two o'clock, this was the best day ever. Just as we went to get on our bus, I decided to ask one more guy for some change. Scrawny guy in his forties with brown, balding hair, with a pencil thin mustache, a big, red, whiskey nose, and an angry scowl etched on his face. Why did I pick him?

"Sorry, any change for the deaf?"

"What did you just say?"

"Change for the deaf."

"Where's your permit?"

Permit? Why's he asking me that? Oh Jesus. Abort.

"Oh no, doesn't matter, thanks."

Swivel to go back towards Seamus who's queuing for the bus.

"I said show me your permit."

By now the angry man has me by my shirt collar, pulling my school jumper as well.

"Get off, you're hurting me."

"I don't like f**kers like you, you're going down!"

"What are you on about?? Help! Wally! Seamus! HELP!!"

Angry man slams me up against a stonewall of a building.

"YOU'RE GOING NOWHERE!"

"STOPHELPANYONE!"

All the commotion makes a crowd of people gather around. The South Mall is known as the 'richest street in Ireland' because of all the banks and businesses that are on it. Lots of well-dressed and well-to-do people have stopped to look at what's going on. An old woman exiting a bank starts shouting for someone to call the police as the angry man is now almost choking me by the neck. Even though he's a fully-grown man and way older, he's still smaller than me. Thoughts race through my head as I size him up. Should I fight him? Punch him? Head butt him? Don't think I can, choking me too hard. Start kicking him in the shins instead,

"Help. Help me!"

Only now does Seamus spot what's going on. Starts walking over to help me when the old woman tries to grab the angry man by the jacket,

"Leave that poor boy alone, the police are coming."

"I am the police, I'm an off-duty guard."

Oh no, he's a *guard*?

"This is a citizen's arrest. He's collecting without a permit."

Funk me pink. *No way!*

The affluent crowd's sympathy for me disperses, all now siding with angry man. Next moments go by in a blur. Hear the shrill of police sirens. Police car pulls up on the curb next to us. Two guards jump out, one male one female. Angry man flashes his badge at them. Explains what's going on. Try to plead my innocence. Fruitless. Handcuffed. Arms behind my back. Get put into the backseat of the police car. Tuck my head under the door. Freaked. Start shouting for help. Police go to talk to other people in the crowd. Seamus pops his head in the open police car door.

"Are you all right? Let me know what happens, I'll call you later."

Angry man sees that Seamus is holding the same collection box as me. Where's Wally has been spotted. Seamus is then shoved into the back seat of the car with me. My head flops against the backseat window like a scene from the American TV show, *Cops*. "Bad boys, bad boys, what you gonna do, what you gonna do when they come for you?" How am I going to get out of this? My parents will kill me. Seamus is looking at me mute, too freaked to talk. How did he just get caught too?

Now the car is driving. Angry man in the passenger seat, female guard driving, both of them taking us to the police station. Keep pleading our case on the way,

"Why are we being taken away? We didn't do anything."

Angry man shouts back,

"We know you beat up two other kids and stole those boxes from them, we had reports."

We didn't do that!

"That wasn't us, I swear. We work at the place."

"Sure you do. Tell it to the judge."

Judge? Court? Prison? Jail? No, no, NO! Can't be. Have to get out of this. Must get away.

Drive to the station is awful. Dread filling up our bellies. Verge of puking the whole way. Thinking of going to jail was even worse. Drive along the banks of the River Lee. If only I can escape and jump into the river I could swim away, even with my hands are tied behind my back. I'd find a way. I could do the backstroke. My thoughts are getting desperate. Rash. I'm going to do it. Something. Anything. I am *not* going down.

Pull up outside the station, a two-story, red-bricked building in the middle of the city. The woman guard in the front opens my door and helps me out. Angry man takes Seamus out his side. For a split second I realise that even though I'm handcuffed, no one is holding on to me. This is it. I'm going to escape. So I just start running. Straight ahead. Down a cobbled road. No clue where I'm going, I'm just *going*! I get about three feet when the woman guard spots me. Quick as a whip she rugby tackles me onto the hood of the car. Down in a heap I go. Bounce off the hood. Hit the ground. She picks me up and shoves me inside the front door of the police station. Now I'm in real trouble.

Get inside. Looks like a scene from a very old black and white movie. Stonewalls. Grey floor. Wooden front desk that looks like a bank teller's window. Main chief is called out, Sergeant O'Malley. Big guy with a thick head of grey hair and a face that's seen it all. Seems patient at least. Listens to angry man explain his side, then to Seamus and I.

"We didn't rob or beat anyone up, I swear."

Show him our letterhead paper and pencils from the Deaf Association. He phones them up. They verify who we are. Asks if we were meant to be collecting for them. They say no. We're still in trouble. I try one last time to say it was going to be a surprise for them but no joy. Tut. Sergeant O'Malley tells us he is booking us for the crime. But. We won't have a record. Instead he's going to phone our school and let them deal with us. Our parents would have to come collect us as well. This is the worst news ever. Not our parents.

Seamus' Dad answers the phone straight away when Sergeant O'Malley phones his house. He's in to pick up Seamus within twenty minutes. Nobody answers my home phone - both my parents are at work still - so I'm told I'll just have to wait until somebody does.

One of the guards brings me to a holding cell in the back. Led through a heavy grey door and down a stark grey corridor. Rows of cells and metal bars. New movie set: Now looks like I'm in *The Silence of the Lambs*. Jesus Christ. This is jail. I don't want to be here. Need to get away and pretend like this never happened. Ask to go to the bathroom. Pretend that I'm going to be sick. Guard brings me to a cubicle. Lock the door behind me. Everything clangs and echoes. Small bathroom but it has a window. I try my best to climb out but it's too small. No hope. I'm stuck.

Guard brings me back to a cell. Locks me in and tells me he'll be back whenever my parents answer. Being locked up is horrendous. Feel like scum. My stomach is in the bottom of my bowels. Getting dizzy and feel faint. At least my cell is empty. In the one next to me there's a grown man covered in blackened ash. Pikey. Apparently burnt down his brother's caravan after a dispute over where their mother should live. Tries to spark up a conversation with me,

"Don't mind these guys, huh, all right. You and me stick together in here, we got each other's back, alright boss?"

Help me, God.

"Hey, come 'ere to me willya, what are you in for?"

Did well not puking out of terror when he tries to shake my hand through the cell bars. Call out for the guard,

"Help! There's been a mistake, I shouldn't be here!"

My cries are futile. All I can do is sit and wait in the cell silence. Twenty minutes later the police bring another guy into the cell area. Red haired guy in a white string vest and a blanket around his waist - the guy who I saw on my first morning! This gets even better. Now there's a pikey, the naked nutter and me. How did I end up here? Where's Wally?

Half an hour of the most awkward small talk ever later, I'm brought outside. My Dad is waiting. Looks furious. Politely thanks the guard at the desk and escorts me out the door. Deafening silence as we make our way to where the car is parked. Sounds from the passing cars and passersby magnify it even more. In attempts to make things normal, I try to spark up conversation,

"Any soccer news today, Dad?"

"If I were you I wouldn't say another word until we get home."

Worst son ever.

Get home. Sent to my room. Rollicking. Brutal. Rattled. Parents are furious. Even worse is how ashamed they are of me. Disgrace to the whole family. Feel awful. Grounded for the next foreseeable future, which is a few months at least, I'm guessing. Wonder if I'll be expelled. Hang my head in shame. No dinner for me. Left to rot in my own guilt and shame in my bedroom for the long, hard night.

Go to school the next day. Shadow of my former self. Seamus and I are in knots all day wondering what will happen. Teachers don't say a thing to us though. Maybe they weren't told? Maybe we got away with it. Five minutes left to go in class, our names are called out over the intercom.

"Mark Hayes and Seamus Wally to the principal's office please, that's Mark Hayes and Seamus Wally to the principal's office."

Everyone in our class turns and stares at us. Some know. Others don't. Everyone assumes trouble is going down. My stomach assumes the position of sinking to its pit. Feel it go plop like a potato hitting a pool of brown water. This is it. It's all going to get even worse.

The walk from our classroom across the schoolyard to the principal's office feels like we're on death row. Out to meet the firing squad. Take one last look at daylight before I take a deep breath and enter the punishment room. Seamus is called into the vice-principal's room while I'm brought into the principal's room, Mr. Power. Usually he's a friendly, pleasant guy who looks like a grey-haired Mr. Bean, Beansie we called him. Not today. Walk in to our school's Oval Office. See my Mum. No way. How is Mum here? This just keeps getting worse. Can barely talk. Oh God. It's all gone wrong.

Mr. Power starts off by telling me I'm going to be expelled. Knees go weak. Stomach sinks. Bowels burp. Almost faint. Don't do it to me, please Beansie, we always got on so well. Black out for a bit when I hear the word 'expelled' again. Start imagining my life on the streets.

Ran away from home once before when I was young, about seven I think. Grounded for not cleaning my room and doing my chores. Not allowed to watch my favourite Saturday evening TV show *The Munsters*. Unfair punishment in my eyes. Packed a bag. Ran away. Well, almost. Raining outside. Hungry too. Didn't fancy it. Cleaned my room instead. Neat freak ever since. I could survive on the streets this time though. Life on the run wouldn't be too bad. Jesus, who am I kidding? Won't last a day. Except, hang on. Mr. Power is still talking,

"But then I decided we wouldn't expel you after all. Instead, you are going to be suspended."

Almost faint again from the head rush of the confusion. Except, again, there's more.

"I decided we wouldn't do that either. Instead, you're going to be…"

This went on for all the levels of punishment. As I was a good student with good grades and played sports, I was more or less left off the hook. Seamus was the same. In the end we were given two months after-school detention. We had to clean up the toilets, the football pitches outside and any litter around the school. Mr. Power and my Mum told me I would also have to make a £100 donation to the Deaf Association. This would be the real stinger as I wasn't working and didn't really have any money of my own. Now I'd have to get a job. Except. Well. Oh yeah. Ahem.

Pots.

Nooks.

Crannies.

Face went red as I remembered what we did the week before. Say nothing about the stashed money in my room, I repeat in my head. The meeting ended with my Mum asking if I had anything to say for myself?

"Emmm, would it be OK if I paid in coins?"

Mr. Power and my Mum both cocked their heads to the side and looked at me oddly. Did I say too much, too soon? To avoid their gaze I put my hands in my head and ran my fingers through my spikey-gelled hair, making sure not to mess it too much. For some reason I felt a fit of laughter coming on, the nerves and tension had broken me to hysterics. Just as I felt my throat about to warble out a chuckle Mr. Power and my Mum said in agreement,

"Yes, that would be fine."

Phew. Got away with it. I'll just say I won a load of coins at the slot machines or something. Say nothing. Lesson. Learned.

All in all, not too bad. We actually ended up be allowed off the detention after only three weeks as well. Let out on good behaviour. Paroled. Second chance at life. The system cured me. Well. I think.

Chapter 14
Sexual Debut

'Twas the night after Christmas, when all through the house, not a creature was stirring, not even a mouse. Well, no, not really. My house was pretty busy. Except for me. Just sitting in my bedroom. Waiting. Bored. Restless. Fifteen-years-old. Still grounded over the Deaf Association affair. Counting down the minutes until my relations were all due to arrive at our house for a Hayes Christmas party, one of our family Christmas traditions.

Each year after a fine feast cooked by my mighty Mum, we all go to my Nana and Grandad's house in Passage West for Christmas night. When I was young this was the greatest time ever. Down with all my cousins, showing off what we got for Christmas. Playing charades in front of the sitting room fire with my aunts and uncles. Eating my Nana's renowned trifle dessert and frosted apple-filled cupcakes. Turkey and ham sandwiches. Cups of tea. Glasses of coke mixed with fizzy orange. If we're lucky they'd have supplies of the greatest soft drink ever made and only available in Cork, Tanora, that fizzy tangerine flavoured drink. More trifle. Christmas cake. Cups of tea. Some grown-ups in the kitchen, some in the dining room, the rest in the sitting room. Cousins scattered all over. All ages. All happy. All full. Some laugh.

As you got older the sheen went off a tad. Awkward teenage years when charades were no longer as fun. Too young to drink (technically, anyway). Night dragged a bit more than you remembered in your early days. Still a laugh though. My cousins Nick and Jonathan would bring their computer, Nintendo 64 being the new hot one we all played. Set it up in one of the spare rooms upstairs and start a round-robin style *International Superstar Soccer* computer game competition with all the boys in the Hayes clan.

Instead of watching whoever played first I'd go into our Nana and Grandad's room while waiting for my go. Look at the old photos on the wall. My Dad, my aunt Jean and my uncles Harling and John when they all were young. Black and white photos everywhere. How old are these people? There's my Grandad when he played for the Irish international soccer team. Made his debut against the Ivory Coast I think, some of their players played without any boots and socks. Bare feet? Nutters.

See the photos of my Nana when she was a young dancer. Not an actual dancer, more photos of her before she went off dancing at the local club down the road from where they lived. Might have a go on the old pink exercise bike in their bedroom next. Looked like a weary old donkey. Felt it let out a sigh as I sat on and pedaled my way to nowhere. Looking around the room. Everything always so neat. Bed always made. Carpet always hoovered.

Get called for my turn in the computer competition. Time to play my younger cousin Jack who just beat my older cousin Alan. I win after extra-time, tight enough against the fiery six-year-old who looks like Stewie from the cartoon *Family Guy*. How did he get so good, so young? Sing an edited version of Queen's *"I Am The*

Champion" song in Jack's face as I progress to the next round. All good banter. Have to wait my turn to see who I'm playing in the final. Go hang out with my younger cousins on the stairs, Jack's younger sisters Kate and Jane, all playing some card games with my sister and my cousin Gillian who's my age. Gillian looks delighted.

As all the cousins play upstairs our parents watch sport and news in the sitting room below. Approaches eleven or twelve. Party's over. Homeward we go. No time to play Darren in the final of the soccer competition. Next time, we all say. Find out whose family is having the next Christmas party. Everyone on my Dad's side would host one over the coming week or so. Same thing, more or less, just a slight variation of food really. Fine family gatherings. New Year's would come along. And then we went back to school. Holidays over.

Anyway, this particular year my abode was the venue for everyone to come to on St. Stephen's night, December 26th. My Mum had been preparing food all day. My Dad had been getting the house ready. Darren and I had been playing our new Nintendo 64 computer game, *Golden Eye*. And my sister Sarah had been playing with one of her penguin teddy bears. She *loves* penguins for some reason. Around six I go to get changed. Put on good clothes seeing as we're having visitors over. Shorts and t-shirt not sufficient attire, apparently. Tut. Change on.

Throw on my new white jeans and black turtleneck jumper (finally got my own, no longer a Granvestite). Fashion, to my fifteen-year-old eyes. Comb my hair. Gel. Water. Spikes. Ready to go. Check watch. Dose. Still early. Time to kill time.

Everyone downstairs seems busy. Better not get in their way/get stung to do hoovering. I'll just hang out in my room. Listen to the new Puff Daddy album I got as a present. Put it on my CD player. Do some shoulder shrugs as I dance along in front of my mirror, singing something about the Benjamins. Never the best for understanding lyrics. My cousins on my Mum's side, Adrian and Martin, have been trying to teach me how to rave dance recently. Not sure if this is the right music for these moves. Stop dancing.

Stand and look out my window for a while. Gets dark early, already almost nighttime outside. Watch the bare skinny trees sway in the wind across the road. Look up and down as cars pass by on the quiet main road. See a bus pull up and let nobody out at the bus stop. Wonder if it's going to start raining again? Wet ground outside. Watch some raindrops from the last shower run down my bedroom window. Well, this is fun.

My mobile phone starts ringing on my bed. I was the first one of my friends to get one, a big, huge, black brick of a thing that was a present from my parents for getting good Junior Cert results. As I go to answer the phone I spot my buddy John's vintage black Mini Cooper pull up outside my house. Huh? John knows I can't come out tonight. Click answer on the phone,

"You got to come out for a minute."

"Can't, family party is on."

"Just come out, trust me. That girl Eve wants to meet you. I think she's up for it."

"Up for what?"

"Just come on, willya?!"

Hmm. Look at the clock. Six-fifteen now. Party set to start at seven. Could stay here. Hang out on my bed. Lie on my bed. Pump my bed. Or. Go out and see what John's on about? I know the girl Eve to see. I started work about a month ago in the fancy four-star hotel up the road, Rochestown Park Hotel. This was a white, three-story, grand manor type hotel that looked a bit like the White House in America. White columns at the entrance, rich red door with a gold door knock, surrounded by lots and lots of big, proud looking oak and chestnut trees.

Only just opened up. Originally it was built as a home for the Lord Mayor of Cork back in the early 1900s. Then I think it was handed over to the monks in 1947 and became a monastery. Now the corporate side has swooped in. Hotel on. One hundred rooms, two bars, a gym and a conference hall all on an eleven-acre plot. Quite fancy for a Cork hotel, one of our best. Most of the people in Rochestown were happy to see it open up I think, although it did mean we weren't allowed to climb the trees there any more (sure we won't).

I needed to make money to pay my donation to the Deaf Association, or at least give the illusion that's where I got it from, so I got a job as a glass collector in the banquet hall. Great laugh. Weddings. Concerts. Events. Place was always packed with women. All ages, all sizes, all out to get drunk and feel up younger guys.

That was my experience anyway. Must've thought I was older than fifteen. Maybe I looked dapper in my outfit. Crisp black shirt, trim black waistcoat, uncomfortably tight black pants and dark green dickie bow. No complaints about all the women feeling me up. Some hot ones so I took the good with the bad.

One concert in particular was mental, this guy Joe Dolan who's like the Irish version of Tom Jones. Showband and cover singer, famous for his advertising slogan "There's no show like a Joe Show". Old guy in his sixties, slightly overweight with a red face from either singing or drinking too much, looks like he might be wearing a grey toupee. Rumour has it he swings both ways but no one seems to say anything. Women love him.

Long tables set up in rows for his gig, banquet style, with a stage at the top. Maybe four hundred, horny, drunk women. Every time I went out to collect glasses they treated me like I was Elvis, The Beatles, Joe Dolan himself! Hysteria as I squeezed in between the tables collecting empty wine and pint glasses. I always made sure to go out for the Tom Jones cover songs in particular. Women's hands all over me. Down my pants, up my top, slipping me money, some trying to slip me tongue. Nuts. Feel on!

Anyway, this girl Eve had been at a wedding at the hotel just before Christmas. John was seeing her friend so I knew Eve to see. The longer the night went on the more and more she asked me to dance. Couldn't though, boss would've killed me. I had already got in trouble the week before after I was caught in the bathroom with a girl who was at her sister's wedding in the hotel. Her five-year-old nephew walked in as we were getting it on on the bathroom sink. Only kissing at that point but it didn't look good. Thank God my pants hadn't been down. We didn't think the nephew would tell anyone but not the case. Got back to the bar manager but I denied it when he called me into the office, he had no real proof and the kid didn't see my nametag. Dodge on.

Anyway, kept telling Eve I'd dance with her another time. Looked hot that night. Silky blond shoulder length hair, wide green eyes, slim body in a figure hugging black dress, and cleavage spilling out like two big melons she was struggling to carry. I'm sure she's older though, about eighteen. Three years is a huge gap to a fifteen-year-old. Maybe I'm reading it all wrong.

In truth I was no Don Juan growing up, more of a Donal Juan, Don's awkward Irish cousin. Wasn't too clued in about women at the time yet I still had ridiculously high standards when it came to what I liked. Watching too much *Baywatch*. American perfection. Used to hold out when others would've folded. Not going to hook up with a girl if I didn't like her. Eve wasn't unreal but she was tasty enough. I presumed it was just the drink and lack of single men at the wedding that had her all over me but now according to John, apparently not. Eve was interested. And I needed some loving. My poor bed was being worn out.

"Alright," I tell John after a ridiculously long pause, "I'm in."

Douse myself in the brand new cologne my Nana bought me for Christmas, Joop. Despite the pink bottle and it smelling like sweet cherries mixed with strawberry cough syrup, my Nana told me it was *definitely* a man's cologne. "The ladies will love it!" We shall see, Nana. We shall see!

Scuttle down my stairs. Shout out to my Mum, "Back in ten minutes!" Before she can answer I'm out the door. Not sure if she heard me. I'm still grounded but it technically doesn't start until seven every night. Drizzling again outside. Go away, rain. Run to John's car. Hop in the front. John's eating a choc-ice like I guess he thinks a gangster might be smoking a cigar. Slowly enjoying it, making me wait until he finishes up. He loved those bars of chocolate ice cream. Tubby bastard.

At least there's no one else in the Mini. Smallest car ever and my legs are getting longer and longer. Some days we'd just sit in the car, parked in a dead end, doing nothing. Pretty sure I became claustrophobic from sitting in the backseat with four or five others somehow squeezed in. No one else has a car and this was the best John could afford. Five guys. Listening to music. All the rest chain-smoking cigarettes. Me being the only non-smoker, depending if Darren was with us or not. Not the most fun really. Squashed in the backseat wondering if there was more to life. But. There wasn't. Nothing else to do. That's all we had at the time.

John gives me a nod.

"Eve wants to meet up now. I told her you would."

"I have this party and I'm still grounded. How long will we be?"

"I don't know, boy! Just don't mess it up, I think she's up for it. She won't stop going on about you."

Not sure if he means up for kissing or what? Say nothing. Pretend to be clued in as John drives us from my house to where his girlfriend Sinead lives close by. She's there with Eve, who lives a good bit away. So, either meet up now, or, probably never. Fair enough. Drive on!

Reach the house. Drizzling full on. See Eve and Sinead outside. Get out the car. Hands. Feet. Sweating. Realise John has stayed in the car. Sinead goes to meet him. I walk over to Eve. She's wearing a tight, zipped up, black jacket and white jeans. Looks good. Awkward small talk. Mumbles. Smiles. Head nods. Ask her what she's up to,

"Not much, you?"

"Not much."

"You smell good, is that Joop?"

"Yeah! My Gran got it for me."

"Right."

"Where should we go?"

"I don't know. Follow me."

Head down along the side of Sinead's house. Nerves are kicking in. Powerwalk down the narrow grassy knoll that leads to a woods. Behind the house there's a trail of a path with some bushes and the back of garden sheds. Seems like a good spot here, in between a couple of bushes. Except the path is now a wet muddy pond from all the rain. Eve stands up against a shed wall, chewing gum. Unzips her jacket a bit to reveal a tight, low, black tank top. As I'm remarking to myself in my head how we're kind of wearing very similar outfits, Eve takes out her chewing gum. This is the sign. Time to start. Eyes. Shut. Heads. Tilt. Tongues. Embrace. Giddy up!

After a couple of minutes Eve breaks the lock,
"Have you done this before?"
"Eh, yeah."
Embrace again.

When Eve asked me that, I thought she meant have I kissed girls before. Of course, can you not tell by the way my tongue flicks and twists?! What she actually meant was something else, a step up a level.

In America guys use the term first base, second base, third base and so on describing what they did with a girl. Let's just say I started off on first, and then quickly got the green light that all bases were open. I just didn't realise this, at all. So, while my hand was being directed around the various bases and so forth, I never fully copped on what was going to happen. I just thought the whole time I was getting away with doing stuff. Better keep going to see what else was on offer.

First base. Peg it to second. Although, is this second? No clue of what's what in baseball? Is second suckling? I remember thinking her breast was tender, like a nice bite of roast lamb you might enjoy with a roast potato and some gravy. My thoughts get interrupted and I think I'm being moved to third. Not sure. I'm on my knees in the pond of mud though. Wearing white jeans. Cursing the weather. Don't ruin my Christmas present. Give me a break, God.

I'm staring at pale white legs. Pull down her pink and white panties past her knees. Now I see another bush. Her chicken coop, as no one ever calls it. The golden grail. Rain is blurring my vision. Unsure what to do next, never did this before. Quick kiss? Mwah. There we go. Satisfaction guaranteed. Meh. Reminds me of the fish fingers I had for lunch earlier. Ooh arr, Captain Birdseye, my favourite brand!

Now I'm back on my feet. Wondering what time it is. We're both getting wet, from the rain. I need to be home soon for that par- Thoughts interrupted. Her hand guides my ponder pipe. Not sure why I call it that, maybe because it has a mind of its own. It's having the time of its life, if not a tad unsure of these new grounds. Feels like it's conquering the moon or something. Her hand shows it where to go. Shifts. Slots. Slips in. Oh Jesus. I think I'm doing a home run. Is that what I'm getting waved in to do, AM I DOING A HOME RUN? I'm in, I'm in, *JEEESUS* I'M IN! THE ROOSTER IS IN THE COOP, MY POTATO'S IN HER ONION PATCH! PARDON? NO CLUE! THIS FEELS UNREAL!

Well, really it feels like I'm getting soaking wet from the rain but every second thrust feels nice. She seems to have found shelter against the wall whereas I have found a slippery lake of mud to stand in. Awkwardly maneuver myself, white jeans around my ankles, struggle to keep my balance as I slosh around on uneven ground. Rain is really pelting down hard now. Big heavy drops splatter off my face. Blinding me in the eyes. I'm not sure if I'm at fourth base or inside the dugout. Which is it? Don't know. But I did it. I got a home run? That's it isn't it? We're good? We're in? Time to go the changing room? Is it the game over? Or just rain delayed? What do we do now? Maybe I should ask her,

"Should we go back or what?"

"O-K?"

Not the response I was expecting. Did I do something wrong? It was in. We were on? The rooster landed. What happened? Pull up my pants and zip myself up as we make our way back to where we started. Eve walk-runs back to Sinead's house. I sheepishly gallop back to John's car. He looks at me. I nod. Wink. Hey hup. Drive on.

"What happened?"
"I did it."
"Did what?"
"Did *it*. You know, come on John."
"Lies."
"I swear."
"You were only gone about ten or fifteen minutes?"
"I know. I did everything."
"No way."
"Seriously, ask Sinead! I got to go home, I'm late for my party."

Car stops outside my house. Hop out of the Mini with a pep in my step. Manage to run inside right as my front door is opening to my Nana and Grandad who just arrived. My Mum looks at me confused,

"Where were you?"
"I was off becoming a man."
"Pardon?"
"I said, hello Nan!"
"Is that you Darren? Or is it Sarah?" my Nana replies looking around confused.
"It is yeah, you were right about the Joop!"

Great party that night in my abode, in case you're wondering. Didn't tell anyone what happened but I strutted around my house like a stallion. Couple of my younger cousins gave me weird looks when I gave them high fives and ruffled their hair for no apparent reason. Neighed a few times as well. Couldn't help it. Donal Juan had done the deed!

I did get asked why I had mud patches on the knees of my white jeans. Claimed I must've slipped. Managed to dodge any awkwardness. No one would've even suspected the real reason. Not that I cared. Food now tasted better. Drinks were wetter. Laughs were longer. Entered a new stage of my life - I was a *real* boy. Marky Boy! Just made my sexual debut!

Technically I did, anyway. Word on the street wasn't what I had hoped. Looked forward to praise and being carried aloft through my school when the news got out amongst my friends of my great deed, like Fionn Mac Cumhaill returning from the battlefield. I am the great warrior of Ireland! Actually. Huh? Nay? No mythic style legend here. Fionn Mac Not-so-cool-at-all, it seems.

See, John did ask Sinead to verify my story, which she did. Confirmed what happened with Eve. Also confirmed that I kind of just touched each base, paused there for a few seconds (minutes, in my eyes) and then kept on running. Like I was playing the game tip the can, sprinting around like a mad man.

Eve thought that I knew why we were meeting whereas I just thought she decided on the spot she was up for it. Seeing as I didn't realise that it was all about *how long* you spent on each base, I thought I was better off to keep on running before an umpire called a foul ball. Didn't finish the deed or anything. There was no cock-a-doodle-duu, if you know what I mean. In fact that never even really popped in my mind. Just made my way around the track in record time.

Who's to blame here for my lack of knowledge of what I was meant to do? Not too sure. The whole birds and the bees' situation was only explained to me officially a couple of weeks before by my Irish teacher in school, Mr. Devlin, otherwise known as The Bull. Sound teacher but also a *very* tightly wound up man. Passionate in the ring, you might say. Looked like an angry bull with a big mop of short, curly, fire-red head of hair a flame up on him, bit like a mix between a Brillo Pad and a ginger Don King, the American boxing promoter. Forever telling us he'd wipe the smile off our faces if we didn't cop on and shut up.

Not sure why it was Mr. Devlin that gave us that chat. Happened to be supervising us for a free class and decided to spring "The Talk" on us out of nowhere. I think he got sick of us asking him stupid questions like,

"Sir, what's the Irish for gay?"

Pretty sure he was also separating from his wife at the time too so it was more anger filled instructions snorted and barked at us as we sat in class watching a video full of scientific biology diagrams about what goes where,

"You insert your, youknow, into her, whatdyamaycallit and then it gets going, alright?"

Awkward silence.

"ARE YE LISTENING?"

"Yeah."

"I said: ALRIGHT?"

"Alright," we all chimed back.

Didn't learn too much from that chat except that Mr. Devlin probably wept after he did the deed. Teary eyed and mumbling words in Irish to himself by the time the video was over. Eve was kind of lucky I wasn't yelling "IS IT IN? ARE YA LISTENING?!" at her.

A week later a weird group of Americans came to our school to give us a chat on why celibacy was a cool thing to do. I think they were Mormons or something. Or else just on drugs. Six of them, three guys and three girls, all in their early twenties with gleaming white smiles, deranged looking staring eyes and boundless energy. Odd group. Turned me off the idea of being celibate if that's how I might end up. Those girls were definitely giving glints at a few of us in the class as well. Their talk ended early though when a funny little guy in our class, Anthony, asked them,

"Is masturbation considered breaking celibacy?"

Anyway, when my parents asked if I knew about the "hey and the ho and the you know what now yourself sure", I said I did, Mr. Devlin told us all about it and so did these American people. Awkward conversation in the kitchen with my parents dodged, thank God. Close to my Mum and Dad and all but I don't really want to be having that sort of conversation with them, come on now.

None of my close friends had actually done the deed before either, so they were no help. Read articles in magazines like FHM and Maxim but they mainly stressed that you didn't want to, ehm, disperse your knowledge too soon. Which I *didn't*, as previously stated. (Just want to make that clear.)

Look, I don't know. What I do know is that the most popular song that Christmas was called *Seven Seconds Away* that had a chorus sung by Neneh Cherry. This in turn became the song everyone at school sang to me when I went back after the Christmas break. Mr. Seven Seconds. Fun nickname, for half a year or so. Even more fun trying to explain each and every time what actually happened. Deaf ears all round.

In fairness one buddy Steve did at least congratulate me away from the crowd,

"Fair play to you boy, you stuck it into a girl, more than I've ever done."

So that was nice of him to say. I found out from another friend that Eve apparently stoked the flames as much as she could as well, almost enjoying the fact that I got mocked for what happened. Nice of her.

Few years later she would try and have a second go at the champ, even publicly professing her love for me. Unfortunately I had to turn her down. Like my taste in cologne, I had moved on. No longer was I doused in that sickly, sludgy, strawberry Joop scent. Now I was a Davidoff Cool Water man - Fresh, crisp and busy conquering more beautiful lands. Fionn Mac Cumhaill had returned. We all had to start somewhere though. Sexual debut, a-duu!

CHAPTER 15
TO BE OR NOT TO BEJESUS

Looking back at it, dossing out of class was the main pastime during fourth year. After the Christmas holidays the primary objective in my fifteen-year-old life seemed to be: How can I do nothing? Hiding in the toilets for as long as possible was always a good option. You'd get in trouble if you stayed there too long though. The same went for hanging out in the library with the potted plants and wooden walls looking at old, frail books. The key was to somehow get a permission slip from another teacher that let you stay out of class as long as possible.

Volunteering to be a still-life model for the fifth and sixth year art classes was a handy but rare option. Also a bit boring. Sitting there while a group of uninterested boys drew different parts of you. Some good shoe drawings but the facial attempts were brutal. *I don't look like that, you buffoon!* I'd think to myself while pretending to be impressed by the results being paraded around the classroom afterwards. Delusional about my looks, even from an early age. No one appreciated my 'me in a toga with one of the good-looking female teachers feeding me grapes like I'm a Greek God' portrait painting suggestion either. Tut.

Pretending you needed to go pray in the chapel room was another option. Some schools had priests to take care of the religion classes. Not us though. Up until fourth year one of our P.E. (gym) teachers or else one of the French language teachers usually took the class. Cushiest forty minutes ever. These teachers had no real clue about religion besides what we all already knew, so usually we were just allowed do our homework or sleep, just as long as we didn't say that's what we did. If anyone asked, we learnt about the Lamb of God.

We all loved that class, well at least until our school decided to get a chaplain, Mr. Lyle. The day he was introduced to our class we all thought the same thing: What the funk's a chaplain? As in Charlie? Nope, this guy is tall, skinny and has white hair. Is he a priest? Kind of looks like one but he's not that old and doesn't dress like one. Dressed like a teacher. Brown wooly jumper, green shirt underneath, brown cords and beady eyes squinting out through his thick bifocal glasses. So he's a teacher? No, he doesn't teach anything except religion. *But you're not a priest?* And he has an English accent? Ehh, what religion is he?

On the downside, the mysterious Mr. Lyle now actually made us discuss religion in religion class. How dare he impose such a thing! Although I suppose it's not illegal like in America. Fair enough, Mr. Lyle.

On the upside, he introduced the chapel room to the school. *Superb* dossing option. As long as you made your case beforehand of needing a good praying session, you could go pray at the chapel (previously a storage room, now decked out with an altar, chairs and a painting of a really pale, Irish looking Jesus on the cross). Forty minutes of kneeling in silence, pretending to pray and think about God. Most of the time Mr. Lyle wasn't even there so you were free to pray away on your own. It was heaven.

That was until a group of us were caught having a sneaky game of indoor soccer in there one day. It didn't help that I was playing soccer with some of the biggest messers/troublemakers in school. Not sure how I ended in with them but once the game started it was hard to say no. The main troublemaker was Ger Leahy, a great ox of a boy with the temper of a giant Robert De Niro in *Raging Bull*, both fists covered in gold, sovereign rings just to make his punches hurt even more. Nice chap. Bit of a pikey. Pretty sure he was the reason we all got banned from praying in there. Excommunicated from this new chapel for life. Dose.

One guy who would never ban us from coming to see him was the career guidance counsellor, Mr. O' Sullivan. Sully Bags, we called him. Small, nervous and frantic, always carrying two plastic bags with food. Sully Bags was like an Irish version of Woody Allen, just without the humour or wit. Beaten down by his life choices but always tried to smile it off if ever he caught us looking at him with pity. Maybe more like Willy Loman in that sense. Depressed, yet hopeful.

Every day Sully Bags would just sit in his small, narrow office with the door wide open, waiting for someone - *anyone* - to come and have a chat with him. Looked like he could've done with some guidance himself. If only he had a career counsellor when he was growing up, then he might have known not to become a career guidance counsellor later in life.

In fairness though, Mr. O' Sullivan was sound. Almost always gave you a permission slip to come talk to him about careers paths, as long as you didn't push it. Usually it was reserved for sixth years but some fifth years were allowed to go too. A few of us clever fourth years even managed to slip in the net, pretending we were starting young with our career choices. Thing is though, you had to be careful not to actually go too far with the whole "What should I do with my life?" angle, otherwise you'd be asked to stay after school and discuss the possibilities even more, doing numerous multiple choice questionnaires that you just lied on anyway to get what you thought would be a cool outcome,

"Says here I'm going to be a millionaire. That's exactly what I want to be, thanks Mr. O'Sullivan!"

My test results were almost always business or maths related. Sometimes sport-ish. Depends on how I tailored my answers. Never once did I get a result that suggested I was destined to have a career in the arts though. Shows how crap those tests were, tut, especially as I was just about to become heavily involved in the arts world.

One day in music class our teacher Mrs. O'Shea asked who would be interested in being part of a school play. After zero enthusiastic replies, we were told we were going to all be part of a major school play, "like it or not, ye ungrateful shower of fecks". Mandatory. It would be the first of its kind in our school so we should all be proud and excited. Cue groans, wails and everyone quoting Shakespeare with an Irish twist,

"Ah to be or not to *bejesus* - Are ya serious?"

Mrs. O' Shea was deadly serious. Almost had a heart attack shouting at us to quiet down. She was an older lady who looked like a sweet old grandmother but really was more like a rusty old nail sticking out of a wall just looking to injure someone. Old-school teacher who liked to give students raps of the ruler across the shoulders if you did something to annoy her. Like sneeze. Or cough. Breathe. Made us sing a lot in class, which was unpleasant. She had huge globs of fat on her arms that swung like cow udders when she conducted us. Sometimes she showed odd glimpses of kindness by letting you out five minutes early but they were rare glimpses, like how you might spot a drunken pixie in your back garden.

The play was going to be held at The Everyman Palace, a historic 650-seat Victorian theatre built in 1897. Oldest theatre in Cork. I vaguely remember seeing a Christmas pantomime there when I was young. Everything inside was in red and gold and looked grand. Red velvet walls, red mohair velvet seats, red carpet, big red velvet curtain covering the stage, the scale of it making me feel like Jack staring up at the beanstalk, a giant feel to the whole place. Handed painted gold trimming everywhere. Arches, boxes, balconies. Intricate, handmade plasterwork dripping from the ceiling, looked like something Mick Angelo toiled over (Michelangelo's famous Irish cousin). Place had a warm, regal feel to it. Rich history too, hosting the likes of Laurel and Hardy and Charlie Chaplin in its heyday. Mighty venue. Us Corkonians in the People's Republic of Cork are very proud of it.

An assembly was held the day after the class announcement where we were introduced to the two people in charge from the theatre: Winnie and Pat. Winnie was a bubbly, jolly looking lady with funky, wine coloured hair, wearing all black and a pink shawl around her neck. Pat was a nervous, rakish hippie with long grey hair, quite suspicious looking, wearing a purple cardigan, green shirt and orange pants. Both looked to be in early forties while Winnie looked far more excited than Pat to meet us. They seemed to be breathing heavily, as if they had been prancing around on stage when no one was around.

"CONGRATULATIONS! Ye have been chosen to be part of this *in-iti-ative*!!"

What's she on about? And why is she singing words?

"This is the first of its *ki-nd* and we're so excited to be doing this with your *scho-ol*!"

Flutters her pink shawl around the stage like a butterfly on drugs.

"Now who's ready to make *the-atre* magic with us?! Hip hip –"

Go away!

Mrs. O' Shea gives us a dirty look, fake smiles at Winnie and Pat then tells us,

"OK lads, those interested in being part of this stay behind, the rest are dismissed for now."

Hmmm. Go back to class or stick around and pretend to be interested? I think I'll stick. Most of those who left were too slow to cop on to this golden opportunity while the rest who left were just plain stupid. This was dossing jackpot *gold*! Fools, how they missed out. Out of about a hundred people, thirty of us stayed behind to hear more. Winnie and Pat informed us that the play they chose for the big production was called *Laughter in Transylvania*, a comedy about Dracula.

"Sounds hilarious. I'm sure Bram Stoker would be very proud."

Winnie beams, missing my sarcastic tone, while Pat asks,

"Why would he care?"

"Well he's Irish and all."

"No he's not."

"I'm pretty sure he *definitely* is, Pat. Come on, you're meant to be the arts guy!"

Mrs. O' Shea nods an apologetic smile to confirm I'm right. Pat the Hippie's not happy. Winnie continues on. It would be a six-week production and those involved would be thrown in at the deep end, working on it non-stop, depending on your role. Six weeks you say?

"Who would be involved the most?"

"The actors - obviously."

"Obviously."

Didn't really have any interest in being an actor in a play that had that title. If it was a movie with Oscar potential, then perhaps I might have, standards and all. Surely some other people were fully involved too though.

"And what if we didn't want to be actors, anyone else involved fully for six weeks?"

"Yes, the director of course, he would run the whole show."

"Of course."

The director, you say? I think I'll have a bit of that. Turns out about ten other students had the same idea. Shane, Rob, Paul, John Mc, Andy, Consie, Barry, Seanie, Sean Óg, and myself. All gunning to be the main boy. Unsure how to choose between this random group they've just met, Winnie gives us a task: Make out a six-week work plan for what you would do if you were the director. Best one wins. This included casting, set production, rehearsals, ticket sales, make-up, costume design - The whole shebang. Jesus, sounds like work. Still though, six weeks of freedom in and out of school, class free? Well worth it. Ultimate dossing ticket.

We're told this on a Friday morning, then informed that we had to have our plan handed in to the front office of the theatre by six o'clock that evening. Sweet Jesus, how are we meant to do that?!

"Well it's to be or not to be so whoever does the best one will be the director."

Cheers, Pat, ya hippie.

Scurried home and started figuring out my plan. First things first, make out a really cool looking six-week chart on this huge poster sized sheet of paper I bought on my way home from school. Spend two hours on the design of the chart. Realise it's almost six. Oh no. I'm going to be late. I'm going to miss out! Quickly fill in each day slot for the six weeks,

"First we'll cast, then we'll rehearse, then we'll make the props, then we keep rehearsing, then we can get make-up, then costumes, then we'll recast, then we'll have a run through and then we can perform. Done!"

My Dad kindly gives me a lift into town. Friday evening. Bad traffic. Dose. I'm late. Won't make the deadline. Cursing myself on the way in. Can't believe I won't be the director, for God's sake, stupid class. Arrive at the Everyman at six thirty. Make my way inside to the front office and knock on the window. Winnie pops her head out,

"Sorry I'm late. I know there's no point now but here's my plan."

Before I even whip out my big huge poster plan, Winnie tells me I got the job.

"I did?"

"Yeah, no one else showed up."

"Oh. Right. Still, you chose me over everyone else. I'm some director already, huh!"

Went home and told everyone my plan was by far the best. I got the job. Made a mental note to inform Sully Bags that his career guidance tests were all wrong too. I knew I wasn't destined to be a P.E teacher: I'm going to be a director!

Week One: Production's off to a flying start. Casting done in a day. Main roles all brilliantly chosen by me. Andrew as Dracula (looked like a vampire). Dave as Gorum, his hunchback assistant (showed up with a pillow under his jumper to look like a hunchback, got the role on the spot). Frank as Mary, Dracula's true love (willing to play the part of a girl and wear a dress although he does look a bit more like an ogre). Tom as Count Duckula, Dracula's rival (also tall and looked like a Goth).

The minor roles - Dracula's Mum, his aunt, the slow-witted neighbours, a few leprechauns, and a talking horse - could be filled with the leftovers of which there were plenty. Set production and props to be taken care of by Andy who has the woodwork and art classes at his disposal. Winnie appointed Shane as my assistant (not my first choice but he at least liked my production plan poster). Rob was in charge of make-up seeing as his sister agreed to help him out. This directing malarkey was a doodle, almost too easy!

Week Two: Mutiny. Dave wants Frank's role and Frank wants to be Count Duckula instead of Tom. After rigorous negotiations, Frank compromised and swapped roles with Dave. So Dave is now Mary which is good as he kind of looks a bit more feminine, Frank is now the hunchback which is good with his squinty eye and the ogre look he has going on, and Tom is still Count Duckula. Side note: Our horse outfit has gone missing.

Week Three: Rehearsals are going well. Except, Andy informed me they were behind on set production. They got distracted (by what, he never told me) and were yet to start. I assigned Pat the Hippie the job of monitoring them. Pat the Hippie was not happy that I'm now giving him orders. I'm enjoying being a director.

Week Four: Rob quit as people were calling him gay for being in the make-up department. He was replaced with Karl, a tall, skinny, flamboyant lad who looks like he wears lipstick, should really have been involved in the production earlier. Pat the Hippie somehow lost control and respect of the woodwork class. He too has quit the whole production.

Week Five: Shane quit as assistant director because his useless suggestion of including a spaceship in the final scene was ignored. I have found him to be unhelpful, snarky, and, quite frankly, annoying so I don't mind too much. Also, our school principal threatened to have the whole thing shut down if the actors didn't stop acting like they were Thespians who were above the law of the teachers and could hang out in the teacher's break room. Ger Leahy and a few other troublemakers in our year have asked if they can join the production now that they see what they missed out on, dossing wise. I let Winnie break the bad news to them.

Week Six: Our main actor Andrew quit because he couldn't take the pressure of being the lead. Despite looking the part, Andrew really lacked the depth, charisma and stage presence needed for the role so it isn't the worst thing ever. Still, this leaves me with no Dracula in a play about Dracula. Some are calling for me to play the role but I told them I cannot possibly do the role of director and lead actor at the same time. I want to be out of sight if this thing sinks, not front and centre. Unless of course it's a huge success.

Shane returned to be my assistant director, bringing with him the missing horse outfit. Tom was chosen to be the new lead and the guy who played the rear of the horse, Keith, is now Count Duckula.

Week Seven: Time to perform!

Despite the shambolic weeks leading up to the big performance, I had an odd calmness the night of the big show. Perhaps it had something to do with the naggin of vodka I drank part of earlier in the evening. Everyone in the production did the same. We all needed to calm our fifteen-year-old nerves, particularly as ticket sellers had managed to fill the room. Sold-out. Packed house! Almost seven hundred people (the fact that this was over capacity was ignored by everyone). This was pretty huge. All our family, friends and girls from local schools. Even the local newspapers were here to cover it. Snapped my photo with the cast in the changing room beforehand, one big happy family. Nervous fake laughs and smiles,

"Nothing we can do now lads, go out and break a leg!"

They all highly appreciated my great pre-show speech. Noticed there seemed to be an awful lot of girls back stage too somehow. Seemed a bit wild, as if everyone was drunk. Dave had his arms around two girls who appeared to be groupies, Andrew had reappeared and started to act like he was still in the play (I made sure to tell him he was not) while Tom was in the corner doing something suspicious. Praying? Drinking? Tommy Tanking? Not sure. Not to worry, just part of show business, I told myself. Peeked my head out through the curtain and saw the huge crowd. Rows and rows of people, packed in all the way up to the balcony. Seemed to be a lot of rowdy guys from my year at the back of the hall. I'm sure they'll be grand. Check my watch. On with the show!

Head off to stage right to watch from a balcony with Shane, Winnie and Pat the Hippie who still isn't a fan of me. Bit nervous as seven o'clock approaches. Shake hands with all three of them and thank them for being part of my production. Ruffle Pat the Hippie's hair and say,

"I hope we can be friends after this."

Lights go down. Crowd start to whistle and cheer. Time to rock and roll. Nothing more that I can do now. Lights come up. Crowd goes silent. Curtains are drawn, revealing Count Duckula and

Dracula having a heated argument about who is the bigger sucker. I turn to Shane and whisper,

"This is it. To be or not to be*JESUSCHRISTWHATHAPPENED?*"

Lights out. Pitch black. Some hammering noise can be heard and boys are screaming,

"Stupid f**king play, pack of queers!"

Sounds like Ger Leahy and his gang of troublemakers. Herd of oxen and raging bulls stampeding around. Shane runs off to suss out what happened. The crowd is sitting in pitch-black darkness, thinking this is part of the show. On stage I can hear Count Duckula saying,

"Can somebody turn on the lights? What's my line too?"

Shane returns breathless, wheezing as he tells me somebody has taken out the light fuse box. Smashed to pieces. Winnie almost faints while Pat the Hippie sprints off backstage. Shane and Winnie both ask me frantically,

"What's the plan, WHATSTHEPLAN?!"

"The plan? How would I know?"

It's not like I had this on the poster.

Pat returns.

"The fuse box has been smashed in. We can't open it."

"Oh Jesus. So no lights?"

"No s**t, Sherlock."

"What's that meant to mean, Pat??"

Shane grabs me,

"Get a grip! Make an announcement, do something!"

True. Crowd is getting restless. Pat hands me a torch. Turn it on and shine it on myself as I make an announcement from the balcony,

"Hi, just having a bit of trouble with the lights, back in a minute."

"Who's that?" I hear someone shout from the crowd.

"Queer" someone else yells.

Before I can answer either of them, (was that you Mum?) I hear people rapping and beat boxing on stage,

"No trouble with the lights, it will all be all right, hip hop to the night, time to give you a *friiight*."

Shine my torch over. It's Adam and Keith, the talking horse. That's not their line? Next to them someone else appears. Pat turns on more touches. Shines them on the stage along with mine. It's Philip, Dracula's aunt, calling out in a voice that sounds like Hyacinth Bucket from the English TV show *Keeping Up Appearances*,

"Did somebody call for me? Oh dear, I appear to have turned off the lights by mistake."

"PHILIP? WHAT ARE YOU DOING?" I hiss in a whisper.

Philip doesn't hear me. I'm drowned out by a confused crowd laughing along. Is this part of the show?

"KEEP GOING PHILIP!"

The next ten minutes involve Philip, Adam and Keith all ad-libbing and rapping on stage in the dark with the only light coming from three torches held up by Pat, Shane and myself. The emergency back-up lights briefly came on after that and the play tried to start again. Those lights frizzled out after five minutes though, plunging the whole theatre back into darkness. Old building and all. Fire brigade showed up and managed to get the emergency generator going again so we got ten more minutes of the play. Dracula waking up. Trying to make himself breakfast. Neighbours calling over. Interrupting his day. That was it. The play was a slow burner. All the action was towards the end.

Just as the police showed up to arrest those who did the damage, the lights went out once again so the Fire Marshal said we had to shut the play down, the theatre had become a potential fire hazard. What was meant to be a one-hour comedy turned into a twenty-minute tragedy. Those groupie girls started puking backstage, now wearing even less clothes than before. Parents were confused and disgusted in the audience. Actors drowned their sorrows/celebrated on stage that the play experience was finally over. And finally, that ox Ger Leahy was arrested on two accounts of being drunk and disorderly, and damaging property. At least that's how the newspapers reported it anyway.

All in all, safe to say my directorial debut was an absolute tremendous success. So much so, they never did anything like it again.

CHAPTER 16
SUPER FANTASTISCH

So it's still fourth year, I'm fifteen and I've just arrived in Cologne in Germany, or Köln as the Germans like to call it. Two-week student-exchange, one of the perks of studying German. Plan is to stay with a German student in their family home. Go on work experience. Have fun. Then they do the same back in Ireland a few months later. Bring. It. On!

In fourth year we had to choose between doing either German or French. Could no longer do both for some reason. Must cull one. Preferred German purely as I could understand and speak it better. I was actually really good at it, one of my better subjects up there with Maths and Biology. Conversing away with the German teachers. Catching their mistakes at times. Having a right old laugh. I thought I was brilliant. I thought *they* thought I was brilliant. Debatable.

Our school was paired up with Scoil Mhuire to do the exchange seeing as German schools have boys and girls under the same roof. No sexual segregation over in the Vaterland. There were six of us from my school and six girls from Scoil Mhuire doing the exchange. All the girls came to our school one day to meet and greet before we left. I *jokingly* asked if anyone of them were part of the Mile High Club and if not perhaps the flight over would be a good time to join. Joke did not go down well. Pretty sure it was the first time I made an entire group of girls instantly dislike me. Collective gasp of disgust followed by me getting kicked out of class. Never could keep my mouth shut. Well done me.

In my defence when the girls arrived for the meet and greet it was fair to say we were a little bit underwhelmed. Most were more homely than I had expected. The rest were kind of pasty, puffy and pale looking, as if they'd seen a ghost and needed a good night's sleep. Scoil Mhuire girls were meant to be the hottest girls in Cork?! Maybe they weren't too happy they had to take the bus to our school. Gasp! Public transport. Or maybe make-up had been banned at the school that day, I don't know.

They all seemed a bit stuck-up too. I sensed a few thought we were beneath them. A lot of them might as well have had eyeballs in their turned up, button-nosed nostrils they looked down it so much. Maybe it was all in my head. Either way, it made me want to be cheeky and so the mile high query popped out of my mouth.

That exchange almost got me a report card. Thankfully I managed to talk it down to just a note home in my journal. Also almost got me banned from going on the trip. Luckily I had already paid my deposit. I wrote a letter of apology dripping with remorse, which was dubiously accepted. We moved passed it. So. Eh. Trip on.

And now I'm here in the Germany.

Stroll out the sleek, smooth metallic airport doors with our luggage. Notice differences straightaway. The airport doors back in Cork wheezed open and closed sounding like an old man with bad lungs. Here the doors seem youthful and healthy, efficient. I can feel the springtime in the air. There's pep in my step. Weather is nice. Not as cold as I imagined. Everything looks sharp and cool. Buildings. Cars. People. I like it already.

Look around for people holding signs with our names. Through a haze I see a Hayes. That must be the Dad of my exchange family holding the sign. Tall and trim, looks a bit like Pierce Brosnan, just with a thick black mustache that looks like a shoeshine brush. The Mum looks like Claudia Schiffer's older sister, just with a shorter, Mum like, bob haircut. Oh ja. The daughter looks like Claudia Schiffer's younger sister. Tall. Tanned. Long, flowing blond hair. Mighty! Hello to you too. And this small guy wearing a pink Ralph Lauren jumper draped over his shoulders with the blond quiff, fake tan and scowl on his face must be,

"Hallo. Ich heisse Dirk."

"Hello Dirk, how are you?"

"Kannst du Deutsch sprechen?"

"Can I speak German? Oh yeah, I'm super-fantastisch. I just didn't think I'd have to straight away."

"Ja, du musst Deutsch sprechen. Sofort. Jetzt."

"You want me to start right now? Is that what you said? OK. Hallo Dirk."

"Hallo Mark. Das sind meine Mutter, mein Vater und meine Schwester."

"Mother, father, sister, yeah I got that. Hallo. Heil. Ich heisse Mark. Ich bin sechzehn Jahre alt."

Once I informed them of my name and fake age (pretending to be sixteen instead of fifteen on the off-chance they would try to stop me going to the pub) I realised I was now out of my comfort zone. Thought I was good at German, but up to this point I only ever spoken it in a controlled classroom situation. Anything outside of that was usually me trying to flirt with my German teacher, Ms. O'Golden. I exhausted her patience and goodwill but in fairness whenever I made a funny joke she at least cracked a smile before giving out to me. She reminded me a bit of Jennifer Aniston. They both had light brown hair in the same hairstyle, similar shaped faces and slim bodies. That was good for me. And so German was my favourite subject.

Anyway, as Dirk and his family all talk at me, snapping and contorting their tongues harshly, I listen for noises I might recognise. Think the Dad's name is Jurgen. Mother is Claudia. Must be a popular name. Daughter is Ann. Or. Anna? Can't quite get it.

"Anna?"

"Nein. Anne."

"Annie?"

"Nein! AnnEH."

"Oh right, like a cough at the end. AnnEHH."

While I'm busy coughing out her name, I miss how old she said she was. Fourteen? I think. Something before the age. Might have been nearly. Nearly fourteen? Which is thirteen. Dose. Fifteen to thirteen. Two years difference. They're like dog years when you're my age, in my mind at least. Too big a gap despite how hot she looks. I'd be some sort of pervert. Shut that flirting down right away.

Instead, stare out of their brand new black BMW car window as they keep talking at me in German. Driving through a tunnel so not much to see. Feels cool at least, like I'm in some sort of Bond movie with the entire Bond family. Wonder how long I can get away with not talking? No clue what they're saying so I just smile back and nod,

"Oh ja, fantastisch."

Fantastich is my second favourite German word, superfantastisch being my first. In English I can never say fantastic without sounding sarcastic for some reason (years of saying it sarcastically hasn't helped).

"How was the meal?"

"*Fantastic*, big fan of capers."

"Have a good time?"

"Oh *fantastic*, I love sitting in wet mud."

"We lost your luggage."

"*Fantastic* news!"

At least in German people believe me when I say the word. Maybe they don't have sarcasm. Either way, for the rest of the car trip I just repeat these two adjectives, fully unaware of what they're asking me.

"You like genocide?"

"Oh yeah, fantastich!"

"Are you hungry, could you eat a stick of wood?"

"Oh yeah, super-fantastich!"

From the drive to their abode it seems they live in the suburbs. Looks like a nice place. Quaint yet expensive looking red-bricked houses with thatched roofs everywhere, chimneys tooting out rings of smoke. Not too many high-rise apartment buildings or anything like that. Everything has an opulent yet cottage feel. Cobbled roads in parts, modern cobble. Trees. Shrubs. Greenery. All very plush and well manicured. Reminds me of where I'm from, just slightly nicer.

As Jurgen parks the car on one of the quaint cobbled roads, I'm told we're going for a family dinner at a restaurant. In my honour? I think, don't fully understand what they said. Sounds good. Nod along. In we go.

Restaurant looks like a large cottage on the outside. Inside is packed. Loud. Warm. Bustling. Big boisterous Germans with big, red, smiling faces everywhere. Glasses clinking. Laughing.

Drinking. Chatting away. Looks like a meticulously well-kept grandmother's house. Welcoming. Fire roaring. Ornate ceiling that looks like a design you'd find on fine china. Paintings of the countryside and horses on the walls. Main dining table is in the centre of the room. By the looks of it all of Dirk's family are here. Grandparents, uncles, aunts, cousins, the lot. They all look like they're either from *The Sound of Music* or the cartoon *Asterix and Obelix*.

From the grunts and mutters I gather dinner isn't for me after all but I'm still seated at the top of the table. Unfold my napkin and realise they're all staring at me with bewilderment/wonder/smiles. I give a bewildered smile full of wonder back. Waiter hands me a huge map of a menu. Bury my head in it straight away. Examine the words in depth. Anything to break the silent stares everyone's giving me. Peer up. Did it work? Nope.

Our waiter looks like Basil Fawlty from *Fawlty Towers*. Going purely by his body language (still no clue of what he's actually saying) it looks like he's asking people if they're ready to order. They are, it seems. And I think they want me to go first. Yeah, they are all giving me 'shoo-shoo' or 'come here' hand motions while saying German at me. I smile back and mutter fantastisch to myself. Menu looks like calligraphy to me. No sign of the word 'Huhn' which is chicken. Dose. Just play it cool. Pick the thing top of the menu. That'll work. Point to the weird first name on the list. Basil nods. Good choice. The whole table applauds. I've done well.

To my left is Dirk's grandmother. She looks like a shriveled up prune in her old age, weathered face that looks asleep, with beady-eyes and a nose like an eagle, shawl wrapped around her head with curls of white hair peeking out from underneath. At a guess I'd say she's a hundred years old and seen a lot of trauma in her days. Not sure which side she would've been on in the world wars. To my right is Anne, looking very nice, blue eyes twinkling at me. Now I realise that maybe I'm at the bottom of the table. Hmmm. Not sure if the grandmother likes the look of me either. Just sits there staring suspiciously at me when I ask her name.

"I'll just call you Oma so, that's the German for Granny, right?"

No reply. Spot a cool looking cuckoo clock on the wall. I'll just talk to this so instead. What splendid craftsmanship. Carved right out of a block of wood. Bird pops out and I clap like a monkey. *Amazing*! Germany is brilliant. Seven more cuckoos later, I realise it's eight o'clock. Balls. That's the time we're all meant to meet at a pub called Das Glockenspiel. The boys from our school who were on exchange the year before told us it was their favourite pub to go to, ergo, now our new local. I think the name means The Xylophone. Some sort of instrument like that. Turn to Anne,

"Wo ist the pub, eh, Das Glockenspiel?"

"Ja, naturlich. Da."

While I'm busy nodding satisfaction at the word naturlich (meaning naturally, another favourite of mine) Anne is pointing out the window straight across the road.

"No way. That's it?"

Out the window I can see the sign for the pub. Also looks like a cottage, just with bigger windows showing off the whole bar. Right across the road from me, mighty! All I have to do is get out of here. Is that- I think I just saw Vinnie (Lego Head) and Leo (albino with a bright white head) walk in together. Ah balls. My two main buddies on the trip. Lads, wait for me, we're meant to have the first pint together! Time to devour my food and then slip over.

On cue, Basil arrives back with my meal. All eyes back on me. Looks like I've ordered a big, steaming hot bowl of... Soup? Yeah. Must be soup. And a plate of vegetables too I think. Or they might be Oma's. I look at her for a clue, gives me nothing. Better not touch the veg. Just enjoy the soup. All eyes still staring me down. Are they smiling or sussing? Family members telling me "Esse, esse - Eat, eat." OK, OK, if you insist.

Pick up a sterling silver antique spoon - I wonder if that's from the war? No time to think about that now. Just eat and go. Scoop up a big spoon of soup, give Oma a smile and a wink then shovel the spoon into my mouth. Balls. Funk. Dope. Straightaway I realise I've done something stupid. Argh. Can't move. Stuck rigid. Mouth full. Mouth burning. Sweet Jesus. God no. What have I done?!

All the German classes where we discussed meals come flooding back to me. Now I remember - This isn't *soup*, this is bloody boiling water! Burning the inside of my mouth like a scalding hot fire. The plate of vegetables is for *me*. I'm meant to put them into the bowl and let it all soak up together. Those Germans and their different ways, tut. Oma, *why didn't you warn me?!*

After far too many seconds of having boiling water in my mouth, I give up. Couldn't hold it any more - my poor tongue - and I couldn't swallow - my poor throat. Spit-spray the majority of the boiling water out into the air and over the table, then dribble the reminder all over myself, the bowl, and the floor. Close to choking. Gasping. Face bright purple-red. Grab a glass of water and chug. Grab Oma's and do the same. Take deep breaths to regain my brain. Fan my burnt tongue for dear life, scooping ice onto it. Wet my napkin and wipe my brow. Funk me Jesus. Is it hot in here or *what*?

Look up and see a table of shocked Germans staring back at me. Well, that's a fine first impression they have of me. Oma starts tutting loudly next to me then says something that makes the table break out in laughter. Definitely at me, so that's nice. Not sure which burnt me more - The soup or Oma. Look over at her like I know what she said. Give her a beady-eyed stare in return. Start laughing along. I'll get you back, old woman, don't you worry.

At least Claudia asks if I'm OK. Tell her I am, thanks. Might go get some air though. Would she mind if I went across the street to see my friends, we were meant to meet there? By now I'm only speaking English, gave up on German already.

"Naturlich!"

"Thanks."

"Dirk, du auch?"

Forgot I might have to invite that little weasel. Not a fan of Dirk Diggler. Laughed the loudest at me. Didn't really like him and his snobby ways already, even less so after that.

"Nein."

Mighty. To be polite I give the obligatory,

"Are you sure Dirk?"

"Hmm-"

"No? OK. *Super-fantastisch*. I'm off for a pint!"

Nod goodbye, pat shoulders, thumbs up to Basil and bolt out the door. Hang my tongue out of my mouth like a dog and let the wind cool it down. Need to compose myself before I head into the pub, the main reason we're all so pumped for this trip.

The drinking age in Germany is sixteen. Sixteen? *Sixteen*! In Ireland it's eighteen. You'd still go to the pub at sixteen with your fake ID but the whole process was usually head wrecking, the opposite of having a laugh. This trip meant we could all go to pubs and actually enjoy ourselves without worrying about being kicked out or arrested for forging made-up Irish technical college IDs.

"Yeah, my name is Martin, I go to Kerry Tech, studying Mechanical Drawing and Fish Farming. I'm eighteen, I swear!"

Made myself my first fake ID on my home computer. Got it laminated at a business supplies office in town. Pink, cheap and flimsy, I was convinced it wouldn't work. Apparently it was good enough though, according to Darren. I hadn't used it yet but it was handy to have as backup just in case. Technically I was still only fifteen but I would be sixteen soon enough. The main thing was that I looked sixteen. Good old height, always added on a few months. Now then, time for pints!

Das Glockenspiel was a typical pub really, maybe not as dark and depressing as some you'd find in Ireland. Wooden bar. Wooden tables. Stools. Pool table. Hardcore German rock music pumping out, Rammstein I think the band are called. Everything one would need.

My fake Kerry ID works a treat. Tell Vinnie and Leo what happened at the meal over a pint. We all have a good old chuckle. The booze helps to cool my tongue too. Also improved my ability to speak German. Funny how that happens. Good old booze, letting me loose.

Everyone else seemed happy enough with who they were paired up with. Vinnie and his Lego head got a guy named Dieter, a tall boy as skinny as a rake who was also a big soccer fan and looked a bit like Mozart. Leo and his small, white Albino head got a big, jolly, red-faced boy named Wolfgang who looked like a walrus. Seems I got stung with Dirk.

Few of the Scoil Mhuire girls were in the pub as well. Couple of the better-looking girls were sound-ish, the rest seemed a tad disgusted by the sight of me. At least their friendlier German counterparts were sound. Three girls in particular were delighted to hang out with us: Annett, a tall, too skinny blonde who was slightly balding in the front, Sandra, a bubbly, purple haired girl with tattoos and big breasts, and Barbara, a stocky, bodybuilding looking brunette in glasses who kind of looked like a walrus herself. They all laughed at everything we said. Kept buying us booze, introducing us to everyone, just being ever so friendly. At one drunken point Vinnie and I remarked how nice they were even though none of us fancied any of them, although Leo did wonder,

"Think they're being this nice to try and get with us?"

"No no, they're just being nice," I told him, "That's how they are in Germany."

Vinnie nodded along,

"Yeah Leo, girls can be nice for no reason, you know."

"Calm down lads, I was just wondering."

"Ahh, Vinnie, Leo's drunk I'd say!"

"Leo, are you drunk? You are!"

"I'm not, I swear, shut up you two."

Of course Leo was dead right about the girls. Within five minutes of our pep talk they were asking us if we had girlfriends and which of them we liked. Balls. Being the sound friends we are, Vinnie and I left Leo with the girls as we headed off to the pool table at the far side of the pub. Irish boys in general aren't the best at conveying emotions to girls, so walking away quickly was usually a tactic used, definitely in my case anyway. *I'm going to go over here but I'll be back in a minute*, kind of thing.

Myself and Vinnie challenged another duo playing pool for the rights to the table. These guys were older German dudes, two balding, heavy metal fans. Looked at us and laughed. "Sure, ja. Easy money." Indeed. We had them beaten in ten minutes.

Spent the rest of the night defending our honour as champions. Three hours of shots, beers and wins later, we were done, drunk on booze and adulation, with Leo in the corner cheering us on along with big old Barbara perched up on his small lap. Apparently she had a fetish for Albinos. Lucky Leo.

We didn't want to stop playing pool but we all had to be back to where we were staying by midnight. First, we had to play one more game. Challenged by the bar's local hero. This guy was going to teach us a lesson, the barman told us.

"Who?" I asked.

On cue someone starts playing Ace of Spades from the jukebox. Out of the crowd steps an aging rocker dressed in a faded black sleeveless t-shirt and tight leather pants, with arms skinny as a toothpick, a belly pregnant from years of beer and a bald head on top with a greasy slicked down greying ponytail. Looked like the wrestler Jake the Snake. Even had his own custom made, black marble pool cue with him.

Laid the case on the table like some sort of automatic weapon you'd see in the American movies. The snake slithered out his cue and raised it a loft above his head like it was some sort of sword. Felt like I was in the presence of an American gangster with his tommy gun, surrounded by the Mafioso. The pub packed with "the family" went wild for him, all doing air guitar tommy gun motions and shouting along in accented English "ACE OF SPADES, IT IS THE ACE OF SPADES, JA!"

Seeing as Vinnie and I were the reigning champions it was our break. Asked Vinnie if he wanted to start, he waved me to go first. Jake stood next to me as I broke, attempting to throw me off by gyrating his leather pants crotch in my face. Who is the fifty-year old chump?

Took the opening shot. Potted three balls off the break, then cleared the entire table in one go. It was fantastisch- Nay, *super-fantastisch*! Silenced the crowd entirely. Just the black ball left. Pot this and we win. High on cockiness, I line up the black to the bottom right corner pocket, pull the cue slowly back, look up at Jake the Loser Snake and then slam the cue forward. Hear the glorious sound of the black ball nestling safely in the pocket as I stay looking up at Jake, finishing him off with a smile and a wink. Who's the ace of spades now, boss?!

"Hey, what didn't you give me a go, you prick?"

Vinnie returns from getting us a round at the bar.

"My bad. Time to go, this crowd doesn't look too happy."

All the old German rockers are disgusted. Staring us down, muttering to themselves. The villagers in their quaint town are not happy. Village of the damned. Tightly gripping cues. Seemed to think we were cheating somehow. Little did they know we just spent our wasted youth in pool halls. Down our pints and bid goodnight to the German girls. Skip out the door just as Jake the Snake smashes a shot glass on the ground. Great loser.

At least we got managed to get away unharmed. Well, except for poor little Leo. Barbara devoured him like a walrus sucking down a fish. Nicht so fantastisch.

Chapter 17
Bob The Banker

Wake up. Early. Where am I? Drunk? Happy? Lay there. Look at the ceiling. Scan the room. Realise I'm not at home. I'm in a foreign bedroom. Nice. Quaint. Cosy. Bed. Drawer. Closet. Lime green walls, egg white curtains, butter scotch carpet. Different to my room at home. Blue walls, blue carpet, dark navy curtains. Unreal at keeping the light out. Allowed me to sleep for days.

Usually my Dad came in to wake me for school but not today. Tut. I wonder what he's up to? Eating breakfast? Knocking on my door? Probably driving to work mourning the fact I'm not in the car with him. Poor Dad. Poor Mum. They must miss me. I'm only gone a day. Feel bad for them. Not getting to have me around all the time now I'm here in Germany. Dose.

Deluded daydreams interrupted by a rap on the door.

"Mark! Guten morgen!"

"Hi Claudia, good morning to you too."

"Bist du bereit?"

Ehm, what does that mean again? Oh yeah. Am I up?

"Ja! Ich bin… up."

"Fruhstuck ist fertig!"

Breakfast? Mighty.

"Ja! OK. I komme now."

Out of bed I pop. What should I wear, what I should I wear? First day of work experience. Myself and Dirk were going to be working at the bank where his Dad worked. One of the main men in there, apparently. What does a bank executive wear? This t-shirt or that t-shirt? This turtleneck jumper or that turtleneck jumper? Ah, I know: Black turtleneck and denim jacket, the old reliable. Just pop my collar on the denim jacket. Good. To. Go. Stylish boy. Time to get my banker on.

First, must brush my teeth. Peek my head out the bedroom door. Try and remember where the bathroom was again. Big house. Lots of doors. Claudia gave me a tour last night when I got back from the pub. Also made me a ham sandwich and gave me a glass of milk. Not exactly like a ham sandwich back in Ireland - two slices of doughy bread, lots of butter and ham in between - this was more German style. Plate of cured ham, salty salami and slices of rye brown bread that tasted a bit like a leather belt. When Claudia asked if I need cutlery, I panicked and said yes please, because that's how we eat sandwiches in Ireland. Very sophisticated/confused. At least the milk tasted similar to the Irish kind. Go on the cows.

Good news was Claudia wasn't upset at all that I went for pints. Only Dirk and Oma gave out about that. Nice of them. After my midnight snack and the retelling of beating Jake the Loser Snake, Claudia showed me the house but it was dark, late and the booze made it a tad blurry. Remember it looked nice in the moonlight. Reminded me of a house from Hansel and Gretel, just a mansion version. These folk were rich.

Cool, old-fashioned looking kitchen that you might find in a hobbit's home, decked out with all the finest modern appliances, obviously. Three plush living rooms: One that looked like an antique library, walls filled with shelves and shelves of books and a cuckoo clock; a modern one with a huge flat screen TV, surround sound and black leather couches, and; the obligatory pristine, fancy one that you saw as you walked up their driveway, with the untouched cream couches that are only used for guests. Don't think I'll be considered a guest, part of the family now!

Also had a dining room dripping in mahogany and dark, rich wood, a similar style office for Jurgen and a snooker room that they would prefer I didn't use. Afraid I didn't know how to play and might rip the felt. Cheers. Not sure what else was on the ground floor. Garden in the back I think, out past the kitchen. Followed Claudia on the midnight tour, up the wooden stairs that changed directions three times on our way to the second floor. Enjoyed the staircase a lot. Each wall was covered in various artistic photos. The ones that caught my eye in particular were black and white photos of a beautiful naked blond haired lady with a ridiculously hot body, glorious curves all out for the world to see as she lay on a tropical beach somewhere. Go on the art!

Four bedrooms on the second floor: Dirk's one, Anne's and two guest bedrooms. I think I got the smaller guest room but not sure. I'll bring that up later. Third floor was Claudia and Jurgen's wing. Didn't get to see up there. Not yet. Maybe Claudia will give me a tour later in my visit. Ahem.

Anyway, that was last night. Now in the light of day I can't fully remember where the bathroom is on the second floor. Softly start knocking on the heavy wooden doors,

"Excuse me, sorry, bathroom, free?"

No answer. Door locked. Try the next, same again. Spot a small ornament of a quaint toilet hanging on the next door. Oh yeah. I remember now, this is the bathroom. Door slightly ajar. Better knock to be safe.

"Hello, is it free?"

Anne lets out a happy cry,

"Ja! Come in, almost done."

For some reason the 'come in' part of that sentence overrides the 'almost done'. Why not wait until she's done? I don't know. I just followed the come in. Wash bag in hand. Push the door. In I go. See the glorious looking Anne sitting pretty on the toilet, peeing and brushing her teeth. Smiles and waves at me.

"Komm komm."

"Ehhh."

Not only is that weird but Dirk is also in here, standing at the sink, brushing his teeth, with just a towel around his tubby waist, water dripping off him. Was he showering while she was peeing? Well this is odd. Or is it just German?

Dirk forces himself to give a nod hello, his beady eyes squinting his true feelings at me. I nod a 'thanks for complaining about me going for pints, buddy' smile back. Not sure why he doesn't like seem to like me, or anything really. He's chubbier than I thought. Flabby feck. Maybe that's why he seems so angry. Brushing his teeth like a psychotic, serial killer robot. You know the kind, a young Patrick Bateman. At this point I'm stuck, unsure what to do. Anne insists,

"Brush brush, there's room for all."

In fairness, there is lots of room. The bathroom is massive and the sink is long. Nod a hello back and put my wash bag on the counter. Wash my face and go fishing for my toothbrush. Try my best not to look in the mirror at the two weirdos. Start spiking up my hair with exact precision. Must get each spike perfect. Not too spikey, but overall more spikey than flat. Quite an art really.

All I hear is Dirk giving out to Anne about something in a whiny bitchy way. Anne just sits there brushing to the sound of her own music. Brush brush brush. Wee wee wee. Finish the spiking and dry my face. Giddy up out of there just as Dirk goes to dry himself off with the towel and Anne is standing up after finishing her business. Strange? Or just a close German family? Again, can't tell. In Ireland no one ever sees anyone else in the bathroom, much less naked. Never ever. Never. Ever.

Make my way down the stairs to breakfast it up. Looks like plates of ham and leather bread are on the menu again, some hard-boiled eggs and pickles to boot as well. Freshly squeezed orange juice tastes nice. Claudia seems chirpy and cheerful. Jurgen is reading the paper and drinking coffee. Gives me a hearty good morning. This family is sound. Where did Dirk go so wrong?

Few pickles later, Dirk comes down and we're out the door. Off to work. The drive into the city is mighty. Love seeing other countries out of moving windows. Grey morning. Light drizzle. Nip in the air. Germany looks cool. Sharp. Old fashioned. Modern. Full of BMWs.

Closer we get to the city centre the more and more skyscrapers start popping up. We don't have them in Ireland. Tallest building is about fifteen stories high. We have about three of those in total. Here in Cologne they're everywhere. Feels like a big city. New York – London – Tokyo! I'm a big city boy now, off to go work in a big old fancy looking skyscraper. Jurgen reminds me he works for Deutsche Bank, the biggest commercial bank in Germany. Oh yeaaah. Looks like I'm going in at the top. Today the bank, tomorrow - The world!

Car pulls up outside a building. Jurgen turns to me in the back seat,

"Ziemlich cool, huh?"

"Yeah, really cool! Can't wait to see inside. Ich freue mich."

I am excited, even if my German speaking level appears to be at robot mode. Either way, I'm pumped. Not sure what happens now though. Is Jurgen going to park right outside it? Or is there a valet? What's going on? Next minute Dirk nods goodbye at Jurgen who in turns waves goodbye at me. Huh? Why are we getting out here? I see Dirk go sit at a bus stop outside. Jurgen senses my confusion,

"You must go with Dirk, OK ja. I wanted to show you the building where I work but you are going somewhere else. You can take the bus."

You're just teasing me, Jurgen? You brought us all the way in to see a building? Not even that great to be honest. What was the point of all this, Jurgen? After a few seconds in silence seeing if he can or can't read my mind, I exit the car like a deflated balloon.

Starts raining full on as we stand under the bus shelter. Great. Dirk informs me we're going back to work at a bank close to his home. At least we can walk there and back from the house, he adds. Yeah, Dirk, that's fantastic.

Only now do I see what exactly he's wearing: Brown boat shoes, blue Ralph Lauren socks, cream Ralph Lauren slacks, a pink Ralph Lauren shirt with a baby blue Ralph Lauren jumper wrapped around his shoulders, tied in a bow in the front. This guy is like the opposite of me. Mirk and Dirk. Some show. He could really do with a stylish turtleneck and denim jacket combo. Some guys have no clue.

Bus pulls up and saves our awkward silence. Small talk is kept to a minimum for the trip too. Try to ask Dirk if he likes soccer. He lies and says he doesn't. Claudia already told me he loves it. I get the feeling Dirk thinks he's better than me, better than everyone. Angry little spoilt boy. The ironic thing is I now think

I'm above him. Trying to be friendly and all. Maybe we're just too similar to get on. Poor Mirk and Dirk, doomed from the get-go.

After some far more pleasant small talk with the bus driver, we arrive at our destination. Bid Ulrich goodbye and wish him all the best with the bus life. Hop off and see our new home - A crummy, run-down, weary looking bank on the outskirts of a suburb town. This is like something I'd find at home. Bright lights, big city, this is not. Well, bar the lights part.

Dirk takes the lead and knocks on the closed front door. Converses through a letterbox with a guy who looks, oddly enough, also looks like John Cleese. Turns out this is Rudi, the branch manager.

"Hallo, guten morgen, willkommen, willkommen!"

"Hallo. Ich bin Mark."

Rudi ushers us in to what looks like a building site. There's no ceiling, just harsh, bright, fluorescent lights swinging from the rafters along with tubes, pipes and scaffolding. All the walls are gutted, covered in masking tape and black bin bags. Ladders scattered everywhere. Are we here to build? Rudi starts speaking English for my sake.

"We are under construction, ja, you understand? Only temporary, you understand. You must wear these though, OK, ja?"

Hands me a bright luminous yellow builders jacket and a hard hat. Ah for funk sake, we must wear these? What about the stylish clothes I picked out? And my hair? You want me to just ruin it with this builder's hat? Took me all morning to get just right! I'm no Bob the Builder, I'm meant to be Bob the Banker!

The hat definitely annoyed me more than the jacket. I was very particular about my hair. Always have been. Appears I always will. At the time in Ireland the normal haircut for a boy my age was to have the back and sides shaved to some degree, short and flat on top and a little fringe sticking up in front. The shortness of the back and sides was determined by how tight the blade used would be. A five wouldn't be too short whereas a blaze zero was basically a wet shave. Hardcore. The older I got the shorter my Mum would let me go with the blade number, to a point of course. One time I went got a one and a half. Hated it. Looked like a thug. Not saying that all boys who got those haircuts were thugs, just that more often than not these guys would enjoy a good fight. The tighter and balder the more you looked like a convict. I can see now why my Mum was against me getting it. It'd be interesting to do a study to see how well the zero blade boys have done since back then, how many exactly flourished. As always, Mum knows best.

Anyway, I think I was at a blade three or four at this stage, not too short. On top were all spikes. Stylish, went really well with my turtleneck look. Alas this hat was going to annoy me on a daily basis. And it did.

At least the person I was paired up to work shadow was really nice. I got a lady named Elena while Dirk was handed over to a man named Bernd, who also kind of looked like a creepy serial killer. Balding with a pencil thin mustache and dodgy beady eyes. Perspired a lot and his green cardigan vest looked too big for him. Good match for Dirk really.

Elena was in her mid to late twenties I think, originally from Turkey. Never realised there were so many Turkish people in Germany until I got here. Long, brown hair, tanned skin, big breasts that weren't hidden by any means and plump lips that almost dripped off her mouth. She smelt nice too, like how an older girl who's out clubbing would smell.

Elena seemed to like me straight away for a number of reasons: One, she could improve her English by talking to me. And two, I was good at maths. Helped with her job. I too liked Elena straight away: One, see above in relation to looks. Two, she told me I didn't have to wear the jacket all the time. And three, she spoke to me like I was her age. An adult. Which I clearly was, of course.

As was the way, Elena started off by giving me a tour of the bank.

"Here we have the bank teller's desk as you can see."

"Looks like just a table."

"The usual one is under construction."

"Oh right."

"Here we have the loan department."

Again, a desk.

"Rudi's office."

Just a desk.

"And this is where we deal with our biggest clients."

Another desk. This bank was basic, a building site scattered with cheap wooden desks and uncomfortable, orange, plastic chairs, lit up by horrible fluorescent lights that gave everyone a zombie looking glow.

We continued our tour to the building next door, a bakery where they apparently served the greatest cakes ever. The Germans do love their desserts. All sorts of torts. Strawberry, chocolate, fruit, apple, strudel, the works. Most of my German classes in school were about the different cakes on offer. Hours were spent learning how to order one. I would have to go sample the goods next door at lunchtime, a carrot cake on a stick to look forward to at least. First, Elena told me, time for work.

The job was pretty simple. Here is a sheet with numbers. Input the numbers into this computer. That's about it. At times she might meet with customers about their loans. That was really all of it. Show up about nine every morning, leave at three. Rocket science. I was going to take over the world from here all right.

Not sure if this was the case with all office jobs but after a few days working, every day felt like the day before. Arrive. Small talk. Input. Chat. Listen to Elena tell me about her regrets about getting married at such a young age. Give her some wise marital advice from fifteen-year-old me. Try and sneak a glance at her boobs. Develop a crush. Break for lunch. Go next door and order two cakes for myself. Eat. Sleep. Repeat.

I became addicted to the sugar glazed, fruit covered pastry cakes, all filled with custard and delight. The women that worked in the bank would all sit around and watch me eat them, one after another. They were all on diets but lived vicariously through me, sitting there in my builder's hat, savouring every bite. Dirk was jealous that I got all the attention but Bernd kept him busy with running errands for him. At times I'd look over and Dirk would be up a ladder, fiddling with faulty wires. Never looked too happy.

Some days I would go back and get another two cakes for myself if I felt I deserved it. Now and again I'd get self-conscious and wonder if I was eating too many cakes but the women would tell me not to be silly, still a growing boy. Unlike them, who were all trying to shrink down by fifteen pounds. They all wanted to hear which kind of cake was my favourite and why. So I'd tell them.

"Strawberry. Just goes better with the custard filling, I think. Pastry is so soft and the strawberry is so juicy too, makes for a great combination. Tomorrow I'll try the strudel, just for you Gretchen."

Gretchen, one of the older, women that worked at the loan desk, would then giggle with glee, her friendly, meaty, red-cheeked face gyrating in delight. I made them all write down what cakes to try on their behalf and they even bought them for me. Cha-ching, said the cake king!

After lunch I would sit in as Elena discussed a loan problem with a worried customer. Then she would ask me questions in English asking me to point out where she might be saying something wrong. She'd enquire if I'd like to do the same in German. My answer was always the same: Naah.

From two to three I'd watch the newly installed clock on the wall tick away. Finally at five to three I'd ask Rudi if I could head off. He would say of course. Dirk would do the same but Bernd usually needed him for some sort of odd job so he had to stay on until four (trying to realign the dangling fluorescent light above his desk in most cases). Unlucky, buddy, that's what you getting for moaning with Oma about me going for pints!

Tip my hat goodbye to everyone, then off home I would stroll on my own, pumped that in a few hours I could go meet my buddies at the pub for pints, pool and fun. Must say, I was enjoying living the life of a workingman. Bob the Banker, taking over the world!

Chapter 18
The Mirk & Dirk Show

Over the next few days it became clear that Dirk and I were not going to be friends. I thought I was bad at small talk but Dirk was excruciating. *The Mirk and Dirk Show* this was not.

Ask Dirk about soccer, nothing. Girls, nichts. School, nada. Mumbles. Wince of the face. Look the other way as he became engrossed with picking dust and chalkboard off of his pink cashmere sweater. I knew he liked soccer, saw the posters in his room. Girls, I think so. Maybe not, might've been confused which might explain his odd anger. Not sure. Small talk about school was just me going through my rolodex of small talk options. After that I had little. Unless. Did he like boozing?

"Nein."

We had nothing. At least his Mum was mighty. Claudia would always have a feast waiting for us after work. The staples were always available - cured meat and rye bread - but each day would be a bit different. Chicken. Wurst. Some bitter green meat I never in my life saw before and will never touch again. Tasted like a gone off boot or something. Mank. Still not sure what it might've been.

Leprechaun perhaps. At least Dirk smiled when he saw me almost puke it back up.

After our afternoon munch, he'd disappear into the pantry or whatever was at the far side of the kitchen. Whenever I asked what he did back there, I'd get a mumbled reply and be told I wasn't allowed in there. Fair enough. I'll hang out with Claudia as she bakes more rye bread that tastes like a leather belt. She was always baking some sort of delight, reminded me of my Mum at the weekends (although my Mum's desserts cannot be topped, people travel from around the globe to sample her pavlova).

After sampling a few cakes, Claudia would suggest I go hang out with Dirk but I'd joke that I wasn't allowed. I'll go lie down and listen to music instead. Like most working men, I experienced a significant dip from the hours of four to six in the afternoon, hard day's night and all that. Everybody else on the exchange worked from nine to five, so I was the only one off. Lego Head Vinnie was in some computer shop while Albino Boy Leo was in a butcher's shop. Living the dream. They didn't get home until six and weren't ready for the pub until about seven or eight. Time to kill every afternoon.

I brought my portable CD player with me along with a case of ten CDs. Pretty sure on my first night I tried to listen to music in bed after coming home from the pub and somehow managed to scratch almost all of the CDs. No longer playable. Oasis. Blur. Carl Cox. Michael Jackson. Now 20-something. Outkast. All gone. All I had left was *I've Been Expecting You* and *Sing When You're Winning* by Robbie Williams. So every afternoon for two weeks I would just listen to those two CDs on repeat. Nap. Daydream. Bed pumping. The usual. Calm before the storm, as they say.

Once six o'clock came, Claudia would call me for dinner. Buletten (meat balls), Sauerbraten (beef, I think, slight chance it was horse but say neighthing), Frikadelle (burgers), Blutwurst (black and white pudding), and so on. Whatever it was most of the time I enjoyed it immensely, especially as I also got a glass of beer to wash it down. *I'm a real man boy now!* I would think as I smacked my lips after a cold mouthful of wheat beer, giving Anne our customary cheers. She'd always try and come to the pub with me but her Mum and Dad always shot her down. Well, her Dad anyway. Claudia would try and poke him into letting Anne come but never worked.

At least Dirk always turned down the offer to join me. Except for this one night. No clue why but he decided to come along to the Glockenspiel but it meant that Jurgen would drop us there instead of me walking and getting the bus, so that was handy at least. Only good part of the night though.

After one glass of beer Dirk was drunk. Two and he was shouting at people in the bar for no reason,

"NEIN, ICH SAGTE NEIN."

"No. You said no? Doesn't even make sense."

How did I get lumped with this beaut? The other Irish folk thought it was funny but the Germans didn't see the humour, kind of more embarrassed. Apparently Dirk wasn't liked at school, one of the German girls told me.

"Why so?"

"Because he is, oh how do you say - A dickhead."

"Ohhh. I see."

I like seeing and hearing German girls curse in English. Hot with the accent. Wrapping their lips around the curse words. Dirk, on the other hand, was now busy shouting at a table of random people,

"Halt die Klappe! Halt die Klappe!"

"Dirk, why are you shouting shut up at them? Let's go play pool."

Follows me over to the pool table. Starts smacking a cue off the floor while I rack up the balls.

"Halt die Klappe! Halt die Klappe!"

"Oh Jesus, Dirk, calm down. Have a water."

"Ich gehe zu Haus. Ich gehe zu Haus!"

"You're going home already?"

"Ja."

With that Dirk was gone. Great laugh really. When I got back to the house about three hours later he was up watching TV in the fancy living room. All the lights off. Everyone else in bed. I was pretty drunk. Dirk saw me sit on the couch across from his and started making a weird "Neeeaaaaaaaaaaahh" noise. Surely he's not still drunk?

"Have a good night Dirk?"

"Neeeeeeeaaaaaahhhhh."

Starts swirling his hand around like he was flying a paper airplane.

"I thought this room was just for guests?"

"Neneneeneneeee."

"That's nice. I see you're watching soccer."

"Nanananaanananananananaaaaaaaaaaa. NAH!"

"Are you Batman?"

"NEIN!"

"I thought you didn't like soccer?"

"I don't like *you*."

"Ha! Why's that?"

"I don't like you."

"Fair enough, I don't really like you either, *Dirk*!"

Starts laughing uncontrollably when I say this. Makes me think he's a bit of a nutter. Even worse, a drunk nutter.

"Neeeeaaaaaaaaaaaaaaaaaah."

"I actually think you're a gimp."

"Hahahananahahaha."

"And a dope."

"Hahaha."

"Oh Dirk, feels good to let it out."

"Ha ha, I do like fussball, I just say it to you that I don't."

"That's because you're an ape."

"You are very funny, ha ah ahahah naaaaaaah."

"Thanks."

"I must sleep now."

With that he pops up, runs upstairs to bed and slams his door shut. Judging by his heavy head and lack of extra awkwardness the next day, I don't think he remembered a word of it. Asked if we had stayed in the pub for long. "No, went home early. Do you remember?" Mumbles. Wince. Claims ignorance. And that was the end of Dirk coming down the pub.

As it happened, our days at the Glockenspiel were numbered anyway. Bar manager gave us grief for reports he got that one of us had been abusing customers the night. Tried to tell him Dirk wasn't Irish but he didn't care. Said it was our last chance or else barred. Strict rules. All swore to be on our best behaviour. Not everyone got the message.

While the rest of us played pool a chap in our group, let's call him Frank, stayed at the bar doing shots of sambuca on his own. Frank was a small guy, height of a leprechaun and built like one too, just with a face that looked like a pot o' mold, as opposed to gold. Couldn't handle much booze. No clue why he was doing so many sambucas, trying to impress girls I think. Didn't work.

Started puking all over the bar, abusing punters and crying out for a girl to love him back. This led to anyone with an Irish ID being fully banned. Tut. Can't take us anywhere.

At least this meant we would have to do other things at night. Managed to get tickets to a soccer game the next night, the Köln derby. FC against Fortuna. Fierce local rivalry. Biggest game of the season, apparently. Should be a cracker. Barbara's friend Marcus got us cheap tickets. Happy days. Until we saw where we were sitting - Right in the middle of the hardcore home fans behind one of the goals. There would be no sitting. More like non-stop standing, bouncing, chanting, singing and fearing for our lives.

Just as we got to our row, Marcus warns us not to let anyone know that we're not German. Pretend we're home fans like the rest of them if anyone asked. And also, Marcus was actually a fan of the other team.

"Eh, what? We'll be lynched!"

"Nein. Just sing, don't answer too many questions."

"OK, hide your scarf too."

Within ten minutes we had a guy throwing a plastic glass of beer at us. At least we thought it was at us, might have just been throwing it in general and ended up in our direction. Myself, Leo and Vinnie just drank up and sang harder.

Leo almost gave us away by wearing an English team's soccer jersey underneath his jumper but he quickly whipped it off and threw it away. Pretty soon we all had our tops off, shirtless and sloshed like the rest of the fans, swinging our t-shirts around our heads chanting along sounds to whatever words the rest of the fans were singing. Three half-naked Irish boys pretending to be Germans, giving it socks with the local ultra-hardcore nutters. Our team won three zero so at least there was no angry riot at the end of the game. Fun night. Fortuna on!

Saturday night was meant to be the big one for us. Our German counterparts had arranged for us to go to a nightclub. We were pumped until we found out it wasn't exactly a nightclub, more a church hall with a disco ball and some German pop music being played over speakers. Still, we'd make the most of it. Even the Scoil Mhuire girls were coming along.

We all met in the town square at nine. People had been pre-drinking in various spots beforehand. Myself, Vinnie, Leo and another buddy Andrew (who kind of looked like a blond haired teddy bear) decided to buy some beverages at the local liquor store to keep us ticking over at the disco (it was a bring your own drinks affair). Told the group we would meet them there. Drew a surprising reaction from some of the Scoil Mhuire girls,

"Why are you leaving?"

"Just getting some drink before the disco, we'll get enough for everyone."

"You are definitely coming to the disco though, you're not trying to sneak away and do something else are you?"

"No, never even thought of it until you just mentioned it. Maybe if the disco isn't good?"

"Promise you'll be there so, meet us there."

"OK."

Look down and see that this eager Irish girl, let's call her Lucy, is trying to hold my hand. Hugs me goodbye. That's weird. Is she drunk?

I knew Lucy to see from taking the bus home from school. Never spoke to each other, just saw her. She was the really hot one out of the Scoil Mhuire group. Long, dark brown hair, clear chestnut eyes and tanned skin for an Irish girl, looked a bit like Pocahontas. Seemed I had a thing for brunettes when I was young. Nothing to do with that Freud theory of fancying girls who share the same traits as your Mum. That'd just be weird. Mine was probably more a case of I like girls who kind of looked like me. Far more normal.

Anyway, Lucy also had a snooty look about her, button nose constantly turned up. Barely spoke to each other on this trip so far. Our conversations had been minimal at best,

"I've seen you on the bus, you live in Rochestown too, don't you?"

"Sorry, I don't think I've ever seen you before in my life."

That kind of friendly thing. Yet here she was getting very weird towards me. Asked the lads if they saw it too,

"Did ye see that? Why does Lucy want us there so bad?"

"Just drunk I'd say. Come on we get more drink!"

Good call. Into the liquor store we go. Clueless about what to get. Spot a display full of drink on sale. All spirits. None that we recognise. Leo grabs a bottle of clear stuff, Korn.

"What's this?" we ask the guy behind the counter.

"Das ist gut."

"Fair enough. One of these each, please. And this one?"

"Schnapps."

"Should be good for the girls. Four of those please. And this one?"

"Stroh 80, very good. Very strong."

"One of those so too please."

Laden with booze, we head back out into the cold night, steam puffing from our mouths. Time to warm ourselves up. Let's sample some Korn. Can't figure out if it's strong or not. Leo pops it open. Takes a whiff.

"Yeeeahhhoow!"

Start making cat howls from the smell. Must be good stuff. Takes a slug. Passes it on. We all do the same. Warms us up in one swoop. Another slug each. Now we're jolly, now we're drunk. Andrew and Leo start discussing soccer while Vinnie and I are gibbering on about the girls.

"Who are you going to go for?"

"I don't know, think Lucy is up for it? Seemed to be trying to hold my hand in the pub."

"No way boy, she'd be afraid to kiss anyone, especially you. Good looking but very stuck up."

"True true. How about the German girls?"

"Yeah I don't know, I think Annett likes me but she's not hot."

"Yeah you're goosed, she's definitely trying you tonight."

Without realising it Vinnie and I had gone a different way to Andrew and Leo. Lost them. They have the Korn. We have the Schnapps and Stroh. Tuck into a bottle of Schnapps. Why not, we both say. We're drunk now and think we're great, well traveled men around town. Clink bottles and cheers to each other.

As we turn a corner we bump into Lucy and another Irish girl, Sinead who kind of looks like Lucy's dumpier sister. Sound but has a very distracting black mustache over her upper lip that no one seems to have told her about. Mustache or no mustache, both are delighted to see us. They must be drunk too. Seems like Vinnie and I were going the complete opposite direction to the church. Both girls link us in the arms and away we go, back the way we came.

The gibber and charm is flowing out of Vinnie and myself. Sinead lights up a cigarette, offers it around. Before I know it I'm taking a drag, trying to be the big man. Spit out the smoke. Manky. Never doing that again. Just hold it in my hand instead, try to look cool. Lucy is now holding my other hand as we make our way through the quaint, cobbled streets. Schnapps is flowing, I've got a big map out, we're in a foreign country and I have no clue what's going on. Lucy seems to be leading the way. She knows where it is, follow her.

"OK but I think you're wrong. Look at the map, we're meant to be-"

"Who cares about that?"

Grabs my well folded map and throws it into a bin. Well that's not very nice now is it?

"What are you doing?"

"Just shut up."

"You sound like Dir-"

Before I knew it she pushes me in a bush. Pounces on me. Lips, hands and tongue flying everywhere. Branches and leaves are sticking into my head, back and ass but I reciprocate. After a few minutes of bush action, she pulls back,

"Don't tell anyone."

"Yeah, cool. Should we have some more schnapps?"

Appears not. Lucy goes for round two on me. Hey hup ye pup! Emerge from the bush a new man boy. I knew she was up for it. Not just the schnapps talking. She grabs the bottle and takes a swig.

"Where did you put the map?"

"Me? You threw it in the bin over there."

She roots it back out and starts going back the other way. I knew she was taking me down the wrong road. Follow along after her. Find the church hall. Sinead asks me if anything happened.

"Schnapps," I respond.

Can't remember much more of the disco. Apparently Stroh 80 is the equivalent of poitín. We all did one shot and almost puked our hearts out. Once the watery mouths subsided the rest of the night was a great laugh, I think.

I do know that Lucy didn't talk to me for the rest of the night. Told me she couldn't say anything as the rest of the girls would give her grief. I was still blacklisted for my mile high comment. In fact, now that I think of it, I don't think she spoke to me again for the rest of the trip. So that was nice. And I never did tell a soul. Ahem. Sound of me. At least that wasn't the end of my holiday flings.

Things started to get interesting during my last week at work. For some reason (dementia?) I think Elena started to have a crush on me. Kept saying stuff like how she wished I was older than just eighteen (ahem), if only her husband was as nice as I was, did I want to come to her barbeque that weekend?

In attempts to convince her I was indeed a man and not actually a fifteen-pretending-to-be-eighteen year old boy, I'd try to casually reply a deep, manly "Ja, naturlich," but instead my voice broke as I spoke so I just squeaked out "Ja!" Didn't matter how I said it, I was going home the day before so either way I couldn't make her barbeque. Elena would just have to live out that fantasy in her head. (I'm assuming she had Mrs. Robinson dementia too.)

On top of this attention, I was still quite the little fruit tart at the bank. Up to four fruitcakes a day, each bought by a different woman worker, all giddy with excitement at the thought of me devouring them. I had become a food-porn star. Began rating each cake on a scale of one to ten which led to them starting a betting pot, gambling on whether they could find me a new cake that I might prefer over the strawberry custard tart that held the top spot. Needless to say, I was enjoying being a star. Why did all these grown up people always complain about their jobs? This life was mighty!

Dirk, on the other hand, was not. Scowl got worse and worse every day. Angry all the time at *everything*. The bus. Bus driver.

Pedestrians. Customers at the bank. Weather, be it hot, sunny, cold or raining. Soccer results, even if his team won. His parents. Dinners his Mum made us. TV shows. New clothes he had, all those bright pink and baby blue outfits. The couch he was sitting on. Problems everywhere he looked. Some laugh to be around.

I remember looking at him one night while he was doing one of his psychotic low-pitched screams at the TV. *What the funk is wrong with you,* I kept thinking, *do your parents not give you enough love? Too much love?* Not sure. His parents looked and acted as perfect as mine. My own parents are mighty so I always find it hard to relate when other people don't have that. Must work on my empathy muscle really. With Dirk though, he looked like it had it all. Still wasn't good enough.

Now that the pub trips were over, I spent my remaining nights in with my exchange family watching TV. All the rest of them seemed happy as Larry. Main difference I noticed was that their humour was a bit different to mine when we watched sitcoms. Always seemed to laugh just as the punch line was delivered so they'd never actually fully hear the joke. Made the timing of their laughs always slightly off. I still joined in with their oddly timed laughs though, part of the German family now!

Dirk would usually disappear out past the kitchen when the rest of us started watching TV. His Mum or Dad would ask if he'd like me to go with him to hang out but he'd always make it clear he had no interest. Despite thinking I might ask to go do whatever he was doing just to annoy him, I'd stay and watch TV instead. Jurgen and Claudia would roll their eyes at me and smile apologetically.

"No worries, what are we watchahaha!"

One night I was up on my own watching the end of the movie *Die Hard.* Everyone else always went to bed really early so it was only about ten o'clock. Heard a noise from the kitchen. Looked over the side of the couch and saw Dirk coming from the door through the pantry, wearing just a towel around his waist, hair all slicked back wet. He's always in a towel. Not blocky either so not sure what he's showing off, big flabby body on him. Looks like a Teletubby. Reminds me of a bigger version of myself back in my cereal hog days. Where's he coming from? Was he showering out there? Hmm. I'll just ask him.

"Where are you coming from Dirk? Is there a shower back there?"

Don't think he saw me on the couch. Stopped in his tracks as he made his way up the stairs. Looked like I just caught him at something.

"Oh, hey, I didn't see you over there, Mark. Why are you still up, late, ja? Ha ha, no shower out there, I just needed the drink of water."

Sure you did, spoof.

"Oh right, cool."

"Don't go out there, OK."

"Out where? Pardon?"

"Nothing. Gute Nacht, friend."

Well I'll definitely be going out the back to see what's there once you've gone to bed, Dirk.

"And a very good night to you too!"

Waited about half an hour to make sure Dirk wasn't coming back down from upstairs. Gave out a few light calls from the bottom of the stairs,

"Dirk. Dirk? *Dirk?*"

Nothing. Time to go sussing. For some reason I never went exploring in the house. Too busy exploring outside elsewhere. Also didn't want to be rude/kind of slipped my mind. I knew the house was big but I had just been in a few rooms. I could see a big huge garden out the back but there was no clear way to get out there from the house. I'd have to get a key, go out the front, around the side, through the garage and out the locked gate. Not worth the hassle really, unless there was an easier way through this pantry door.

Tiptoed my way through the kitchen, threading along the cold tile floor. Felt like a cat burglar, the Pink Panther music going through my head. Dung, da dun, da-dun da-dun da-dun da-dun daduunnnn, dadadadun. Pantry door was locked. Key on the wall next to it. Schoolboy, Dirk, too easy. Key in. Door unlocked. Down the steps I go. Small passage leading to another door. Now I feel like I'm in an Agatha Christie novel, just about to solve a mystery. Turn the key in the lock. Heavy click. Swing open the big wooden door and - What. The. JESUS!

In front of me is a huge, indoor swimming pool, steam rising up from it. Looks as big and as fancy as the one in the Rochestown Park Hotel, that four-star hotel back in Cork. This one was all white and marble and expensive looking with little Greek statutes in each corner. Feels like I'm Julius Caesar, back in the year 48 B.C. Standing in my villa in Rome after conquering another land. Seriously. The pool is that good.

On my right hand side are massive French windows looking out over the back garden that looks like something you'd see in a gardening magazine. Lit up with spotlights, showing off all the manicured lush green shrubs, proud chestnut trees, and red, yellow and purple flowerbeds. My garden slaves must tend to it well. Spot a swing hanging off a tree and a water fountain as well right in the middle. That's what Claudia must do every day when she's not in the kitchen. What else is here?!

To my left are two glass doors: Sauna and steam room. *I love saunas and stream rooms!* Run up the steps behind the pool - Jacuzzi. *My favourite!* Behind that another glass door: Gym. Sweet Lord. Next to that a big huge climbing wall. I never tried one of them, ICANTWAITTOTRY! This is like the Bat Cave, a Caesar style Ali Baba cave. Something. THIS. IS. UNREAL!

Before I know it I'm darting silently back through the pantry, into the kitchen, up the stairs and into my bedroom. Rip off my clothes and put on swimming shorts that are in one of the drawers. Thirty silent seconds later I'm in the pool, floating on my back and spraying water into the air like a fountain. Time to make this even better. Jacuzzi on!

Worried it was loud but I had a feeling the walls were soundproof. Relaxed in the warm bubbles for a while. This is the life. Got myself a towel and dried off before attempting a go on the climbing wall. Didn't get very far, maybe I need the right shoes. Not to worry, I'll bring my runners next time. I'll be back here again. Took a shower to rinse off, way better water pressure than the one upstairs I've been using all along. Tut. No wonder Dirk wanted to keep me out of here, this place is *mighty*.

Next four nights followed a similar routine: Dirk would give me a suspicious look before going to bed, asking why I was staying up to watch the *Die Hard* movie again.

"Just one of my favourite movies, the good guy beats the bad German guy."

"OK, ja. Don't make noise, you are too loud my Vater said."

"Es tut mir leid, so sorry. I'll keep it down. In the pool."

"*Vhat?* Vhat did you say?"

"I said I'll keep it down, keep it cool."

Sucker. Your pool is now mine, Pool Nazi.

"Night-night, Dirk."

Baden-Baden time! Pool. Jacuzzi. Gym. Climbing wall. Shower. How bad. Welcome change from the nightly Glockenspiel routine too, it was getting slightly stale.

I did venture out for a goodbye party on my last night but my mind was already back in the pool, looking forward to one last swim. Snuck down from my room at one in the morning. Noticed that the pantry door was open. Always locked and closed before. Heard splashing from the pool. Balls. Surely not Dirk. Maybe I'll just go in anyway, pretend like I just discovered the cave now and happen to be wearing swim shorts. Funk it. Pop my head in the door – Anne! Ducking in and out of the water. Emerges out of deep end,

"Mark!"

"AnnEH! Shh."

"I'm drunk. Shhhahaha."

"Me too."

"Come swim!"

"Fair enough."

Swam for a bit. Anne was looking like a Bond girl in her white bikini. Took after her Mum, body wise. Asked her why she was boozing,

"It is my birthday tomorrow."

"Oh really? How old again?"

"Fourteen."

"Oh yeah, one year younger than me. Interesting."

"Ja, you will be gone for the party."

"That's a pity."

"Ja."

"Well technically it is Saturday already so happy birthday!"

Decided to celebrate by toasting some of the beer Anne had taken from the pantry. Horrible tasting dark stuff but I pretended to enjoy it as we sat in the Jacuzzi. She didn't think it was odd I had come for a swim so I got the feeling the rest of the family assumed I had known about this the whole time. Played it cool. Said nothing. Dirk had been holding out on me. Dickhead.

Anne and I soaked for a good while in the Jacuzzi, sampling another dark ale. Not much else happened in the Jacuzzi after that. Well, maybe some stuff that would've at least given Dirk a real reason to hate me if he ever found out. Ahem. What happens in the Bat Cave stays in the Bat Cave. Let's just say that despite it being her birthday, she blew out my candle. And it was lovely. Thankfully she didn't drown doing it either.

Got up early next morning to pack my bags. Trip was over. Sad day but looking forward to getting home as well. Hauled my bags downstairs. Forgot my CD player. Run back up to get it. Claudia is already bringing it down for me. Decide to take one more look at the artsy photos on the stairs. One last mental image before I leave. Pretend to be looking at them all, not just the naked lady on the beach ones,

"Do you like?"

"Yes. Who is this girl?"

"That's me."

"Wait: The naked woman is *you*?"

"Yes, when I was younger."

Oh Jesus.

"You like the photos?"

"They look very nice."

"You like the beach?"

"Oh yeah, the beach looks good too."

Give Claudia a wink and a smile. Hey hup. Takes her a minute,

"Ha ha, I get it, you are funny. I will miss you."

"I'll miss your two, too!"

Joke gets lost. Kisses me on the cheek and hugs me goodbye. Same again with Anne who's waiting at the bottom of the stairs. Look up and see Dirk at the top of the stairs giving me dirty looks while I hug and kiss all the women in his life. Thumbs up to him. Scowl and a beady eyed stare in return. Hear a beep from outside. Jurgen's waiting for me.

"Nice meeting you Dirk. Thanks for the loan of your swim shorts."

"Huh, was? *Nein*, you said you were vatching Die Hard!"

"Did I? Well, yippee ki-wahey muttervater."

"I will see you in Ireland."

Balls. Forgot about that. The Mirk and Dirk Show wasn't over yet. Dose.

Chapter 19
Hairdresser Hayes

All summer I was dreading the start of fifth year, purely down to Dirk coming to stay with me. The German students were coming at the start of October for their portion of student exchange. At least we got two weeks off class to go do more work experience. Despite the fact I was now sixteen, meant to be more mature and entering an important year of school, dossing off class was always a highly attractive incentive. Still, the thought of hanging around with Dirk and having him in my house was depressing. If only I had a secret indoor pool and gym area to keep hidden from him. Alas, I didn't. However, the gods did smile down on me.

Two weeks before they were due to arrive our German teacher Ms. O'Golden informed me that Dirk had failed his summer exams and his repeats. This would mean Dirk had to repeat the entire year. Meaning he wouldn't be able to come stay with me in Ireland.

"What? Seriously? No way!"

Did a victory lap of the classroom in celebration. Couldn't believe my luck. *The Mirk and Dirk Show* had been canceled!

Ms. O'Golden waited until I calmed down before telling me another boy had asked to take his place, Marcus.

"Oh yeah, I remember him. He got us tickets to the soccer game."

Marcus reminded me a bit of Barney, the purple dinosaur children's character. Tall and goofy, with a big fluffy head of light brown hair that just bobbed around as he spoke with a smile. Good laugh when I met him that time at the soccer game before. Still though, do I want him staying with me?

"So would you mind if he stayed with you instead? It's up to you entirely, you're not obliged."

"In that case I would mind. I prefer to have no one stay with me."

Very particular, at the time. Liked to work on my own schedule, free to come and go as I pleased. Not have to worry about being a host. Getting out of the whole affair suited me just fine. My snakey friends Leo and Vinnie had other ideas though. Insisted to Ms. O'Golden that Marcus should be allowed stay with me instead. Claimed they really wanted to see him but that was spoof. Just wanted me to suffer if they had to as well. I'd do the same really. Wore Ms. O'Golden down so eventually I was told I actually hadn't a choice in the matter. Marcus was going to stay with me. At least it wasn't Dirk. Wuu. But still. Dose.

Another reason I didn't fully mind Marcus coming to stay with me was that it meant a break from being grounded. A few weeks earlier I took my Mum's car out without permission. Ended up crashing it into a packed bus full of people while trying to do a U-turn in the middle of the main street in Cork City. Everyone on the bus looked on in amazement but I fled the scene anyway, the damage was minimal. I hoped. I had friends in the backseats wearing wigs and shouting at passersby in Scouse accents out the windows (don't ask) so that threw me off and didn't make it entirely my fault, in my own mind at least. Helped justify fleeing the scene. Also didn't want to be arrested again.

After I dropped my friends off and drove the car home to survey the damage I tried to do another U-turn at the top of my street in my park. Flustered. Dark. Freaked. Not good. Managed to drive the car into a light pole. Neighbours out for a walk saw me and asked if I was OK. Sitting there stunned, I panicked, laughed, gave them a thumbs up and drove off again. Flee the scene seemed to be my motto.

Next day I pretended I to have caused the huge light pole dent in the bumper and the smashed indicator damage by kicking a soccer ball off them really hard. My parents knew something was up. We just settled on me being grounded at weekends for a month. It was a fun time. At least now I could see some nightlife again though.

Seeing as I thought I was free and then told a week later I wasn't, I had little time finding somewhere for Marcus and I to go on work experience. As a result, he ended up working an Indian restaurant and I became a hairdresser. This came about while I was waiting for Darren to get his haircut in De Barbers one day. Busy eating an ice cream and minding my own business as I kicked an empty coke can off a wall, I spotted a girl walk out of some new shop that just opened up around the corner from Xtravision. Sweet Lord - She looks *unreal*.

Long, flowing black hair with wine and purple streaks, tanned skin, big lips, heavy eye make-up, slim figure but curvy in the right places. Older than me, in her mid-twenties maybe. Dressed in all black, tight black leather pants and tight black low cut tank top, highlighting her bouncing beauties, strutting along in her big black high heels. Where did she come from? She's definitely not from around here. Looks like Princess Jasmine. Well, I'll be Aladdin.

While trying to be cool and pass her the coke can like a soccer ball my ice cream falls out of the cone. Flops on the floor. She laughs, I laugh, we all laugh. Who is this beauty? Try to squeak out a hello. No joy. Sounds like a bird just chirped no. Not the smoothest boy in the box.

Instead I just watch her like a creep as she crosses the road and goes into the bank. I wait. Lick my cone. Kick the empty can. Here she comes. Exits the bank, walks past me again and goes back inside this new shop. She must work there. Mosey my way past to check out the sign - Douglas Hair Salon. She's a hairdresser? No way. She might be the one (to give me a good haircut!).

In a moment of rare genius I devise a cunning plan. Next door to the hair salon a new Indian restaurant had just opened up too, The Taj Mahal. In I go and ask if Marcus could do work experience there. Place is dead. Looks like a purple cave. Bean bags. Candles. Elephant ornaments. High pitched Indian music blaring out of their speakers. Marcus will love this place. Twenty minutes of charm later and the restaurant manager (who surprisingly enough was actually Indian, Ireland was getting more diverse) agrees to take on this random German boy he's never met. Good work by me.

Now, time to ask at the hair salon if I could do my work experience there. If anyone asks, I'll just say the restaurant was only able to take on one of us so I took the short straw and went to work at the hair salon next door. Genius. Deep breath, in I go.

The hair salon looks like an Irish attempt of a New York fashion salon. Small, warm shop, maybe the size of quarter of a tennis court. Everything looks brand new. Steady hum of hairdressers. Mirrors everywhere to give the illusion it's bigger.

Black and white tiled floor. Flattering lighting, spotlights popping up from all angles. Local radio station blaring out Top 40 pop and dance music.

No sign of Princess Jasmine but there's a woman dressed the exact same as her at the reception, just a shorter, plumper and paler skinned version. How dare she copy Jasmine's style! Nametag says Mary. Seems this lady is one of the owners along with Sheila, who's also dressed like Jasmine but looks more like Mary (as in Irish) just that Sheila's tall, skinny as a bony twig, has blond hair and a crooked nose. At least their hair looks stylish-ish, although for some reason they both remind me of characters from Roald Dahl's *The Witches*.

Convince them both with ease that I am genuinely interested in becoming a hairdresser when I grow up. Let them touch my fabulous woman-like hair. I compliment theirs. Seals the deal. Even though they've only ever taken on girls before they'll make an exception for me. Sorted. I'm in. It's on. Hairdresser Hayes all the way!

Week later Marcus arrives. Kind of excited to see him purely as I can now start work at the hair salon. Not just hang around outside kicking empty coke cans against the wall as I had been doing all week. Saw Jasmine a few times and she gave me a few polite smiles. Never really replied when I asked her what the best part of being a hairdresser was, but I put that down to her being shy. Nothing to do with that the fact it was raining and she didn't want to get wet or anything. I was the only wet one. Dummy just standing in the rain.

The minute Marcus arrived I knew it was going be a tough two weeks. He was perfectly fine and polite. I was the awkward one. Yay, great, so happy you're here. I tried. The drive home from the airport confirmed my wish that he didn't come. Nice, friendly guy but I can see he's going to be clingy. Listing out his passive-aggressive demands of tourist places he wanted me to bring him. Kept asking if he could watch TV with me, if I wanted to show him around to my friends, could he listen to music in my room with me? Come on Marcus buddy, give me some space man, you've just arrived. I think the fact I had to go solo in Germany and fend for myself without a host made me expect him to go do the same. I was now the Dirk to his Mirkus.

Not sure if he was best pleased when I told him he'd be working in an Indian restaurant for two weeks. Thought it was a joke but come Monday morning I made sure he was wearing his worst clothes as I guessed they'd be putting him in the kitchen to work. I myself wore my best black turtleneck and white jean combo along with my New Rocks Goth heels. Perfect hairdresser outfit, if I say so myself. The stylish Frankenstein of the hairdressing world.

Arrive at the salon around nine. Introduced to all the other employees in the small break room kitchen area out the back. Jacintha. Sharon. Noreen. Helen. Mary. Sheila. Some small, others tall, all bubbly and all dressed in black. All also potential witches. Made sure I left Jasmine until last when I was being introduced. Sweating with delight when I went to shake her hand, waiting to her what exotic accent she had,

"Are youse hawth? Why are youse swetting?"

That doesn't sound too exotic? Is she from Northern Ireland?

"Are you from Belfast?"

"Aye, I'm from up north. Were ye not expecting that, were ye not?"

"Ehm, no. Nice to meet you though."

"I'm a bit hungover so I am but very nice to meet you too."

"Yes. So it is."

Not what I was expecting but at least it was still technically foreign. Ish. Plus, everything Jasmine said sounded like she was on a hotline or something. Sounded older, as if she was naughty. I liked it. Didn't appreciate her telling me I reminded her of her younger brother though.

"Well you remind me of my mother," I blurted back.

"Cheeky one, so you are? Must keep my eye on youse."

"Oh I'll be keeping my eye on youse too, don't youse worry."

Wink. Start sweating a bit more. Is it hot in here? Am I flirting? Or is this being creeping? One and the same?

After Sheila gave me a rundown of what it takes to be a hairdresser, she soon realised I had no interest in being a one. Study the hair. Study the styles. Hours of practice (spoof). Yawned and nodded along as she listed out what it would take for me to really make a career for myself. The heat in the salon was ridiculous, almost had me nodding off standing up. In the end Sheila told me my duties would be to sweep the floors and read the magazines to see which ones were good. Maybe make coffee too.

"Can you handle that?"

"I can try."

As it happens, Jasmine was the soundest girl in there. Whenever she wasn't cutting someone's hair she would come out to the back office and hang out with me. Tell me about her night out in town the night before. Recall the drinks she had. Show me the new diet supplements she bought. Big bag of brown pills with the word PLACEBO printed on them. I don't think she knew what a placebo was so I said nothing. Told her she didn't need to diet, she looked good to me. This went down well.

Jasmine asked if I had a girlfriend. Well, I had become friendly with two American girls who lived up the road from me, Jenny and Jill. Their Mum was friends with my friend Daire's Mum so I met them through him, you see. Even though Jenny and Jill were born in Ireland they lived most of their life in America so had the accent and the healthy glow about them. Both blond, tanned and good looking. Hadn't actually hooked up with either of them or anything though. Kind of friendlier with Jenny because she was my age, sixteen too, but more pent up sexual chemistry with Jill who was a year younger. Alas, they had just moved back to America so I missed the boat there.

Obviously I didn't say any of this to Jasmine, all these thoughts were in my head. I just told Jasmine no, I didn't have a girlfriend. Might have also told her I was eighteen instead of sixteen when she asked me my age. Should have gone higher though, apparently that was still very young. She was almost twenty-five. Told her age was just a number. She laughed and went back to cut more hair. Did mention that she could set me up with her sister who was twenty.

"Does she look like you?"

"Even better."

Oh Jesus. She must be ridiculously good looking.

Once I heard this I was able to relax around Jasmine for some reason. Not sweat so much. Not as many awkward high-pitched voice moments. Her sister was now the target. Ended up having a good laugh with Jasmine over the next few days. Towards the end of my stint she even asked me if I wanted to help cut someone's hair. Seeing how badly hairdressers had messed my head up before I told her I wasn't qualified.

"Nah, if I can do it you can do it so you can."

"Better not. Maybe something easier."

"Fine. Mrs. Harris out there has got rollers in, go take them out for me while I have a cigarette."

Mrs. Harris was a small, old, frail granny about eighty-years-old. She came in to get her thin, scraggy, gossamer strands rolled every two weeks, I was told. Popped my head out of the break room and saw her tiny little body in one of the chairs with a big hair dryer over her head. Looked like a baby with a motorbike helmet on. Time for me to be a hairdresser. Never even spoken to a client before but I had heard the rest of them do it. Bluff on.

"Mrs. Harris, how are you today? Looking wonderful I see! OK, I'm just going to remove the hairdryer and take out the rolls before Jasmine comes back and cuts your lovely hair. Would you like some tea, coffee, a magazine?"

"Who are you? Do you work here?"

"I do Mrs. Harris, I do."

Spotted Sheila and Mary in the mirror looking over at me concerned. Don't let the witches get angry. Keep them happy. Gave them two thumbs up. Mouthed over,

"It's OK, I got this."

Shrugged their shoulders, went back to cutting hair. I went back to carefully removing the hairdryer helmet. While Mrs. Harris flicked through a magazine, half reading, half dozing, I sized up the rollers in her hair. She kind of looked bald with them in, lots of freckled scalp showing. Looked so delicate, just like most grannies really. Half afraid to touch her in case her head fell off. Never actually took out a roller before but how hard could it be? Just pull and it should come out, right?

Tried to pull one roll out but it kind of got stuck straightaway. Panicked and yanked at it, jerking Mrs. Harris' head backwards. She didn't really notice. Roll of thin hair got all tangled so I left it flop and dangle down from her head, looking like a sticky fly catcher. I'll come back to it.

Moved on to another roll, trying to more careful this time. Somehow made it worse. Even more tangled than the first. Tried to rip it out in a quick clean motion, like a plaster, that's how to do it, isn't it? Oh Jesus. No. Almost pulled a turf of Mrs. Harris' hair right out of her head. Did I leave a bald patch? No, but I did make her bleed. Start looking around panicked, thinking, *Blood coming out of the scalp, there is blood coming out of the scalp.*

Tried to hide this by rolling the roll back in, make it look like I did nothing. Didn't help. Kept flopping down. Is her hair going to just fall to the floor? Oh God. Tried to rip it out again. More blood. Sweet Jesus. Abort. Get out. Dodge. Patted Mrs. Harris' head,

"I'll be right back."

Scuttled off to the back room.

"Jasmine, quick, come, I did something."

"What?"

"You never told me there would be blood."

"Oh my God."

Almost choked on her coffee and cigarette. Calmly followed me back to Mrs. Harris. Looked at where I was pointing, blood trails down Mrs. Harris' head. While Jasmine delicately unrolled the roll, I shielded Sheila and Mary's view through the mirror. Mrs. Harris just kept on reading her magazine. Took five minutes of delicate prodding for Jasmine to undo my tremendous work but eventually we got the rolls out. The minute the last one was out Jasmine tells Mrs. Harris she'll be back in a minute. Drags me off to the back room where she breaks into laughter.

"That was so funny so it was. Are youse mad in the head? Hahaha."

I'm nervous and sweating thinking I'm in trouble so I break out laughing along too,

"Ha ha, heh, yeah, I know. Will she be OK?"

By now Jasmine is almost hugging me to keep herself from falling over. I'm hugging and pretend-laughing back.

"Never laughed so much, mental Mark, youse are hi-larious."

At this point I feel my ponder pipe is alive and alert in my pants. Oh Jesus. These random pop-ups had been happening a lot lately. The night before I had to go to a funeral for a relation of my grandparents. For some reason I kept feeling my ponder come alive then too. Not sure if it was the tight suit pants I had to wear or the fact being in a church was the worst place ever to get turned on. Maybe my mind was drifting to Jasmine being naked in my head. Couldn't tell. All I know is that I had an awkward mourning wood, as I called it. Now it's back again. Jasmine's touch triggered it off.

"Oh my God, we should go for drinks soon, I need to laugh like this some more."

My ponder is full on piping now. Do a twirl on the spot, subtly tucking it up and hiding the bulge in my pants. Don't want to look like a creep.

"Drinks? Sounds like a plan!"

For a split moment we touch and I thought we were going to kiss. I think Jasmine had the same idea, or at least saw what I was thinking. Abruptly stops laughing. Goes back out to finish Mrs. Harris' hair. I stay in the kitchen and fix my pants. Down boy, tame the beast.

For the rest of the week I daydreamed about us going for drinks, laughing and all that other stuff. Who cares if I was only sixteen, I could make this work somehow. I wonder if we would go for drinks this weekend? When would I go to Belfast too, I wonder? Too much, too soon? Let's just start with drinks. Her sister wouldn't be an issue between us so that was OK. She had wanted to know how much money I made a year before she would go out with me, so that was dead in the water. This Mrs. Harris incident had rekindled the fire with Jasmine.

Of course, these drinks never materialised. Always something else on when I asked Jasmine what the plan was going to be. I wouldn't have been able to get into the pubs anyway. I held no grudges against Jasmine or anything like that though, unlike say, the grudge Marcus held towards me. At the end of his two-week stay he told me he did not enjoy himself. He also no longer liked me. And, he was disgraced I made him work in an Indian restaurant's kitchen. In summary, he would never forgive me. So that was a shame.

On the upside, I did get a free haircut as my payment for working in the hair salon. Ended up getting highlights, as suggested by everyone in there. Now I was kind of blond and dark brown. I thought it looked good, my Mum didn't. I kept up this look for a good few months, mostly as it gave me a chance to go hang out with Jasmine.

Things were going well until just after Christmas. Went down in my new Christmas clothes to try and impress her - New blue jeans and classy looking cream turtleneck I had just bought in Next, the new, mod English clothing store that had opened up in Douglas Court. Great spot for turtlenecks. Time to sweep Jasmine off her feet.

Started well. Told me she had a new boyfriend. Well, that's nice. Nodded along and smiled as I sat down in the chair, my thoughts now racing. *What am I doing? Why am I here? WHO IS THIS OTHER MAN?!*

As Jasmine went to apply the bleach to my hair I noticed she was also busy texting on her phone. Probably her new guy. Bleach missed my head. Poured down my back. Burnt my neck. Turned my cream turtleneck orange. Apologies ensued but I never forgave her after that incident. No more hair bleaching either. Learnt my lesson the hard way. How could she? How dare she? I hate her! I joke.

Few years later I bumped into Jasmine out in a nightclub one night. As it happens, it would be her turn to try me at the bar that night. However, by then I was no longer blinded by the lights. Now I could see she was kind of just a bleary eyed, sloppy drunk who slurred her words. Those placebo diet pills had failed her too. And so, it was my turn to now turn her down.

Still though, we'll always have Mrs. Harris.

Chapter 20
Fisher Farmer Man

Sixth year of school. Last and biggest school year of my life. I'm seventeen-years-old. Becoming a man. Still a boy. Prancing like a fairy. Preparing for my Leaving Cert exams. Different kettle of fish than all the other exams I've done so far in my life. Pressure is on. Time to shine.

The Leaving Cert was the final exam you did in school, similar to the SATs in America. How it worked was you did seven exams and then added up your best six results giving you your overall score out of six hundred points. Three-four hundred was average, in the four hundreds was good enough but really you wanted to be getting over five hundred points to be a cut above the rest.

Each option in university had different points attached, the more prestigious the higher the points so these results determined what you could apply for. Basically laid out the rough work road map for the rest of your life. Doctor? Engineer? Fish farmer? It was all on the line, especially lifetime bragging rights with my brother Darren.

Since as far back as I can remember Darren and I have always been in competition. One area of constant rivalry was with our exam grades. Despite not doing the exact same subject choices, overall we could compare and compete. Who got more As, Bs and no Cs (come on now, please). We were both good at school and having parents who were teachers helped. Fair competition really. Bragging rights were split when it came to the Junior Cert results. I think we almost had the exact same results. Only a warm-up event, though. The Leaving Cert was the big one.

Darren had already done his the year before. He had wanted to do Electrical Engineering in university, not sure exactly why, liked mechanical drawing and architecture I think? Zoned out when he was telling me the reason. Forever lost. Points were about the four hundred and eighty-five yard mark, easily attainable number. I knew he'd be aiming for the high five hundreds. Down the well he went. Studied. Hibernated. Examined. Aims. Shoots. He scores! Results are in and Darren will definitely be doing Electrical Engineering next year.

While my parents and sister congratulated him around the kitchen table, I made sure to take a look at his exam results slip, just to make sure he's not lying. Scan down. As and Bs. Tut. He's not. Tot up. Well over the five hundred mark. Maybe not *fully* to the potential he might've wanted but he did well. Scrunch up the paper in disgust, then snap out of it and go give a congratulatory slap on the back.

"Well done, Darren, so happy for you. You're probably off to get drunk now, are you? Don't get too drunk."

"I can do whatever I want really. Finished school so the real fun starts now. Pity you've another year left slogging away."

Bastard. Eighteen and free while I was only stupid seventeen and still in prison-school. At least the gauntlet had been thrown down. Now knew what I had to beat. Time to wipe that smug smile off his face. Time to dominate these exams!

I started sixth year on fire. Study timetable laid out from the word go. Everything planned meticulously. Couple of hours of study every day after school ends and by the time summer comes around I'll be an absolute machine! Halloween exams are our first round of pre-testing, a taster of things to come. Ace every single one of them.

"Oh yeah! Who's your Daddy? Who's your Mammy? Who's the better brother now?!"

Back to school and I'm still in the zone. Nailing every maths question thrown at me. Dominating all the biology pop exams we're given. Debating German theology with Ms. O'Golden. This is on. I'm going to get full marks come summer. I AM SIX HUNDRED!

Christmas exams arrive. Do them with my eyes close.

"Outstanding results, simply outstanding! Outstanding, do you hear that," I say, reading my results report card out to my family over Christmas dinner. My Dad is busy carving the turkey while my Mum is making sure we all have enough gravy. Sarah is looking at me sucking her thumb (still at the age of nine?) as Darren pretends to ignore me. I repeat the word in his direction,

"Outstanding."

"If you don't stop shouting you'll be out standing in the garden eating dinner there."

"Now now, Darren, don't get jealous. Just simply *outstanding* results, is all."

Darren winces an annoyed smile at my direction, then swoops the biggest leg of turkey on me. Now his smile is big and happy. Some snake. I think my Dad had his eye on that leg too. We'll have to wrestle over who gets the other one. I'll have the last laugh, my friend.

What happened next was hard to explain. Unless I just take the easy route and use the explanation of me being an idiot. For whatever reason, when I went back to school after the Christmas break I kind of stopped trying. Had this whole thing wrapped up so I can take my foot off the pedal if I want. I was so confident, in fact, that I went ahead and took my foot fully off the pedal, got out of the car, climbed up onto the roof and then jumped off. Something to that effect.

Study plan, out the bedroom window. Cockiness, sky high. I'll just use my naturally acquired knowledge of biological processes, math theorems and scientific equations from here on in. I've peaked so there's no point in really studying anymore. Why bother pay attention in class? I'm golden.

Instead of working I'm actually just going to spend the next three months convincing myself I'm going bald.

Why did I think such a think? Because I saw the reflection of my wet hair one day in biology class when I was sitting next to a window and the sun was shining in on me. I saw my scalp in the reflection, you see, so that means I'm losing my hair and will soon be bald. Even though I have a thick head of lion mane hair flowing in full force, I'm now researching baldness cures instead of studying. Who cares if my Pre-Leaving Cert exams are coming up, you know the trial run that give a good indication of what you might get in the real ones. I saw my scalp. I'm going bald. This is the key factor in my life right now. And I bet it's because of all the hair bleach Jasmine poured on me. HOW COULD SHE?!

Did the pre-exams. Barely got in the mid-three hundreds. Failed three exams. Maths (I blanked), Biology (I mixed up ferns and mosses big time) and Irish. Bloody Irish. School system beating it into us to make sure the language doesn't die out. It's weird, if only they taught it better we'd probably enjoy it. Instead the teachers are all always angry and yelling. Appears a lot of heavy drinkers teach Irish. Red whiskey noses up on them. Deep-rooted misery and hardship put in to each lesson, which is always fun. Each class feels like the worst chore ever, up there with folding socks fresh out of the dryer and putting clean sheets on your bed.

Only thing that mattered was I failed. Not good. Got a low B in Irish at Christmas but Maths and Biology were my two best results, both high As. They were my bankers. Now I was actually going bald, ripping my hair out in despair. What had I done? How did I become so stupid? Did I give myself enough time to fix it? Maybe I should've ditched school earlier and pursued my dream of becoming a rock star instead. Who needs these academic notions of grandeur? Should just sail off to America and make it big there. Way easier than learning bloody Irish.

Spent the next month in the darkness of my bedroom, mulling over where it all went wrong and what this now meant. Looked over my options that I put down on my university course wish list. You could apply for up to twenty and were offered the first one you got enough points for.

My first choice was a new course called B.I.S, Business Information Systems. Only the third year on offer so the points were high, about five hundred and twenty the year before. Expected to go up this year too. Not sure exactly what it involved, computers and business or something. It was seen as one of the best courses to do though, unless you wanted to be a doctor or a dentist. No interest in either of them. Plus, if you did B.I.S you got to go to Boston for six months in third year on work experience and you were meant to be guaranteed a high paying job once you finished. Get paid savage money to go work in America, the land of blond beach beauties? Maybe I could be a rock star on the side too somehow? Sound good? Chalk me down! Except now I had ruined that dream by wasting my time on my bald theory.

Second choice was Actuary even though this had higher points, five hundred and sixty. Never really knew what an actuary was until I read *The Big Book of Careers* in the career guidance office one day. Big, emerald green, hardcover book as thick as three encyclopedias, kind of like *The Book Of Kells*, just for careers. Actuary was one of the ones near the front. Risk assessor. Assess risk. Suss out risk. Something to do with risk. Sounded risky. Not sure really what it was all about. I just knew that actuaries made at least £100,000 a year within three years of starting. So that was appealing. Although I don't think you could travel from country to country being an actuary. Each qualification was purely for the country you were in. Hampered my hopes of being a global actuary superstar. Either way, that option was gone now too. Maths was key to that. That'd never happen now. Funked it all up.

Worst of all, I put my third choice as joke. That's how stupidly cocky I had been. Last place on the points charts went to Fish Farming. Ongoing joke throughout the year in school was that some people were definitely off to become fish farmers. Let's call them the people who still struggled with doing the alphabet in one go. Now, in a bitter twist of stupidity, I was going to be left with that option. Only needed one hundred and eighty points, which you more or less got when you signed your name to the exam papers. Too late to change my choices as well. What a great joke I didn't even tell anyone about, had some laugh with that one.

At least I wasn't freaked on my own. Misery does love company. My best buddy at this time was the man, the myth, the legend: Derek Peyton. He too had failed some exams and was not a happy camper. I had known Derek for years before becoming really good friends with him. Derek was a strapping, fully-grown man by the age of ten. Developed physically way before anyone else. Taller, faster, stronger. Hairier.

In primary school we used to have a sports day where we all competed at various sports, like a mini-Olympics. The big one was always sprinting, where the top three would go on to represent our school at the City Sports. Like a young Carl Lewis, Derek would win with ridiculous ease. I, on the other hand, would always come fourth, narrowly missing out. That stung.

Derek would go on to do a clean sweep of every race he was able to enter in the City Sports, beating everyone and anyone before returning to school like a Greek hero dripping in gold plated medals. On the surface I clapped along whenever Derek went on his victory parade of the classrooms but underneath I promised myself, *Someday that'll be me, some day, I swear.*

When we moved on to secondary school I got to know Derek better from swimming competitions. Here, again, Derek excelled. However, I was a good swimmer as well. Used to run him close on occasion. Never actually beat him, *ever*, but at least I was second best.

We did question Derek's legitimate age at the time. There was no way he was only thirteen. Whereas the rest of us looked like scrawny or flabby, pube-less little boys, Derek strutted around like a young Burt Reynolds. Thick hairy chest, built like a little ox and the confidence of someone who knew they were the best.

In fairness though, Derek was never overly cocky. Just ridiculously better than the rest at us when it came to sports. As a result, everybody liked him and always had a good word. Even teachers stopped him in the corridors for a friendly chat and some adult-like banter. Derek was the man of the school. We were all just little boys in awe.

Soccer was where Derek really shined. An absolute beast, like a minotaur creature from Greek mythology. Our coaches on the school soccer teams used to give us one tactic: Give the ball to Derek. He'll take care of the rest. Again, Derek always did, even when he was singled out for special treatment by the other team.

We played an All-Ireland final one year in Belfast where hundreds of people started making monkey noises every time Derek touched the ball. Shut them all up when he scored a hat-trick. After the match, like always, the other team's coach came in to our dressing room to congratulate us on winning and then asked to shake Derek's hand,

"Where's number seven? Jesus, fair play to you today, you're something else. You're going to go all the way."

We'd all nod and clap along, knowing he was right. Derek was going to go on to play for one of the top teams in England. Professional soccer player. Live the high life. Derek was on his way to the top, no stopping him now!

And then fifth year came along. Over the summer something happened that no one could do anything about it: Derek stopped growing. The warnings signs had been there in fourth year but we all chose to ignore it. Closed our eyes. Looked the other way. Tut. Some friends.

Whereas Derek had always been about strength and pace, now we were all kind of taller, stronger and quicker. Growing into young men, something Derek had been since the age of nine. For some reason (God?) Derek plateaued in height at about 5'7 while the rest of us got taller, more skillful or faster. Sports wise, Derek peaked in fourth year, an All-Ireland champion now on a fast and steady decline.

By the end of fifth year he had almost lost his place on all our soccer teams, forever living on former glories. We all tried our best to coach his confidence back, willing him to regain the swagger he once had on the pitch. Just made things worse. Shots were no longer nestling in the top corner of the goal. Now they were hitting the corner flags. Passes no longer pinged around the pitch with grace but instead shanked and sprayed out of play.

This affected Derek off the pitch too. Started berating girls for wearing heels and accusing them of looking down on him. Mentally and physically, Derek was a broken man-boy minotaur. This once great hero was now down and out, reeling on the rocks.

As it so happened, Derek's decline coincided with us becoming really *great* friends. Playing on the same soccer teams for a couple of years laid the seeds while both of us being good at taking the piss really cemented the bond. While Derek was on the down I was on the up, physically at least, growing over the six-foot mark and beyond. This had Derek coming to me for tips on how I shot up out of nowhere, asking for inside knowledge on how to grow,

"Not sure really, I eat a lot of cereal. Oh yeah, I eat slices of white bread all the time too, you should try that maybe."

Little did we know my clueless theory on how I managed to keep growing led Derek to piling on the extra pounds. Started wolfing down loaves and loaves of white bread (this being a time before the healthy whole grain wheat option was ever really around). This extra weight might have contributed to Derek no longer getting every girl he wanted, which gave him more free time to hang out with me. At least now in sixth year we both had each other to fall back on, two chumps freaked about their futures.

When I wasn't up at Derek's I was busy sitting in my room mentally preparing myself for a life at sea touching fish eggs and wondering how long it would take before I stopped realising how bad I smelt. This was now my future. Living on some small island off the coast of Ireland, forever wearing wellies while twiddling my thumbs and wishing on a mermaid, big bald head up on me itchy to be a star.

Thankfully a teacher in school told me to cop myself on when he heard I was moping around. My buddy Vinnie's Dad was a teacher in the school, Mr. Motherway (looked a lot like Vinnie, a square Lego Man with a shaved head). Clipped me around the ear and told me to start studying. He'd tutor me if needed. Might have let it slip to Vinnie about the fish-farming joke. Handy he told his Dad.

Within two weeks I was back on track. Irish lessons were going well. Maths was beginning to make sense again. Even my biology teacher Mr. Huggard dispelled my fears of going bald by pointing out all the biological facts of why I wouldn't. "Is your Dad bald?" No. "Is your Mum bald?" No. "Granddads?" No. "Is your hair falling out?" No. "Is your hair thinning?" No. "Are you wearing a wig?" No. "Then you will be fine. Stop wasting my time."

Once June came around I was no longer massaging my scalp with aloe vera and sudacreme in a homemade bald cure remedy I had concocted afterhours in the chemistry lab. Worked well as a gel at least, gave my spikes a natural bouncy feel to them. Should've patented that paste. Or maybe I was just a babbling, rambling, Irish version of Doc Brown from *Back to the Future*. No more hair distractions. Too busy down the well, studying again. Back on track for my Leaving Cert exams. I think. I thought. No clue.

The two-week exam period was a blur of sleepless nights, Red Bull laden days and a steady, superstitious diet of pistachio nuts. I'd start off with a five-pound bag of salty pistachios. Count out fifteen nuts. Take one. Suck the shell. Crack it open. Eat the nut. Place the shell on the table. Repeat for the next fourteen. Take a slug of Red Bull. Sip of water. Line the nutshells up in a straight line next to my essay pad. Five across, three down, shells about a centimeter apart. Make sure they were all in line. Study for fifteen minutes. Go back for more nuts. Repeat over and over. Wired and nutty. Sleep for a few hours every night. And so on until all my exams were done. Nailed that routine to a tee.

Seeing as I had thought my pre-exams went well, I'd no real clue how these final ones actually went when I did them. I had gotten stuff to add up and balance out but had I used the right equation? My experiments and samples used in biology seemed right but what if I got the genealogy wrong? And the essays I learnt for Irish, did I use the right one or did I black out and misread the question? Why did I spend so long perfecting my nut routine? It was all a blur. One big, caffeine induced daydream, a horrible, anxiety-ridden, Red Bull, pistachio nightmare.

By the time August came around and the results were about to come out, every possible scenario had been played out in my head. Fish farming mightn't be so bad after all. People liked fishermen, didn't they? Although I would be more a farmer of fish but still, people liked farmers too, even if they did stink of fish. Maybe I could combine the fish with my new love of pistachios and create a new wonder product. Fish-flavoured nuts? I'd be a millionaire. People like fish-flavoured stuff, don't they? Oh Jesus.

My stomach really dropped to my bowels when Darren started being nice to me the night before the results, telling me not to worry about the twenty-pound wager we had on the results. Not only was he being condescending but now he's also giving me *pity*? Had I really sunk this low? Kill me now.

Next morning I made my own way to school to collect my results. Took the long route. Drizzling with raindrops dripping off my nose but I didn't care. Let it ruin my hair, I'll be bald soon anyway knowing my luck. Who needs hair? My life is done. Just going to be a bald, nut obsessed fisherman from now on.

Slowly strolled to my demise. Didn't eat all morning in order to offset any puking/diarrhea that might occur from disappointing results. Led to me being pretty woozy and light headed as I walked in the school gates on that cold, wet September morn. Steeled myself to be strong.

Strode up the footpath toward the main doors. Inside at the main office a little brown envelope with my results waited for me. Counting the steps as I walked along, I tried to make the numbers in my head somehow increase my confidence "One-and-two-and-three-and-four, let's be confident as I walk in the door".

Instead they started reversing in my head going down from ten. Just made me weaker, as if I was counting down to my own doom

"Ten-nine-eight-sevenyouregoosedandyouwontevengetintoheaven."

"Hayes!"

"Vinnie. Jesus, you scared me."

"You don't look good."

"Yeah, it's just fish farming and stuff. Where would I even live?"

"Huh? What are you on about, boy? Have you seen your results?"

"No, getting them now."

"How did you get so high?"

"Pardon?"

"I've seen them."

"How?"

"My Dad showed me."

"He *what*?"

That's an invasion of my privacy, how dare they!

"Yeah, how did you get so high? You're not smarter than me."

Who cares about my privacy? Felt a surge of confidence and energy flow back throughout my veins.

"Oh yeah? Apparently I am!"

"Prick. Go get them, I'll meet you here."

"Are you serious? WhatdidIgetwhatdidIget WHAT-DID-I-GET?"

"Can't remember exactly, five hundred and something."

No way. Race inside the main doors. Stop for a second - Is he lying? No. Wouldn't do that. Would he? He would, the funker. Give the secretary my name. Hands me back an envelope. Wait for a split second. Should I have some sort of ceremony for such an occasion? No. Rip the envelope in half, ripping my results slip into pieces by mistake. Put the pieces back together. Scan it quick: A – A – B – A – A – OH. YES. WAHEY! Vinnie wasn't lying, that big-headed delight! I did it. I got what I wanted. Dancing!

Phoned my parents, they were pumped. High fives from teachers. Everyone was happy. And that was that. End of story. Giddy up. Well, I suppose you're wondering about that brotherly bet. Look, at the end of the day it doesn't really matter who won between Darrem and I, now does it? Who cares if I did? Or he did. Just the difference of five points, but still. There was a difference.

Although, in my defence, there was a report out that year that the Irish exams had been marked unfairly and people were docked extra points when they shouldn't have been. We could even get them re-checked if we wanted to, see if we got extra points. I would've jumped at the chance to get mine rechecked but the letter sent out to me informing me of this option seemed to got lost in the post somehow. Dose. Not sure how such a thing might've occurred.

Rumour has it (according to my sister Sarah who I had to pay for such information) Darren was spotted opening said letter and throwing it into the fire before I even knew it existed. Sarah retracted her statement when I confronted Darren about it though, so my case was dismissed by my parents.

After assessing my risk of making it an even bigger deal than it already was, I decided to let it go. Let Darren have his day. I had bigger fish to fry. And thankfully, they weren't going to be pistachio flavoured ones. Farewell, fish farmer man Hayes!

CHAPTER 21
SUMMER LOVIN'

I lie in bed contemplating me navel. Finished school. Leaving Cert over. Eighteen-years-old. Now ready to take over the world! Well. Actually. Not sure what to do with all this freedom. Daunting. White abyss of endless possibilities. Not starting college until the end of September. Extra-long summer holidays. Four months to go do something amazing. But, emm, what should I do? No clue.

See, when you grow up in Ireland summer never really has anything to do with the sun coming out. More the time between final exams ending and the next year of school beginning. Those were your summer holidays come rain, sleet or shine, so go out with your friends and enjoy them.

In primary school this was a doddle. Just play sports all summer long, two weeks of summer camp in the middle, more sports to cap the summer off. Great hoot. This feeling of summertime elation continued into secondary school as well. Pass away the months getting into some sort of adventure. Unreal. Felt like it would never end.

And then the last week of August came along. Dread of returning to school appeared out of nowhere. Looming. Ominous.

Foreboding. Felt it inside your gut. Days started to feel like a panic attack. Shorter. Faster. Spiraling. Gasping for air. Where has the summer gone?!

Pretty sure that last week of August feeling is where the now infamous Sunday Night Fear comes from as you grew older and started dealing with hangovers. Your weekend is like a summer holiday from the dreary workweek. So much mirth and merriment, buckets of rejoicing and romping, spades of frolicking and festivities! Then you realise it's over already. Flew too close to the fun. Back to the real world again with an existential 'What am I doing with my life?' bang. What's the point of going on? Why did I spend all that money? Surely there's a better way to live?!

That fear would all be in front of me though. Right now I'm all about the freedom and not knowing what to do with it. At least I wasn't alone. My best buddy would be along for the summer ride with me as well, the man, the myth, the legend - Derek Peyton, the young Burt Reynolds lookalike. Just the two of us, a pair of chumps aimlessly making our way through this new stage of life.

My Mum and Dad had always been a huge fan of Derek, initially due to his ability on the soccer pitch,

"Pleasure to watch him play!"

But then also because Derek was quite possibly the world's greatest small talker when it came to chats with parents.

"Mr. and Mrs. Hayes, may I say ye both are looking fantastic this eve, I won't interrupt you, I can see you're eating, just wanted to say hi and goodbye."

"Goodbye Derek! What a great chap." my parents would reply in unison.

At times they did find it weird that I would go to Derek's house all the time. What they didn't seem to realise was how good it was up there. He lived in a place called Grange, about a twenty-minute cycle from my house, including a slow steady incline of a hill. Worth the slog though.

Even though Rochestown was viewed as a nicer place overall, Derek's park was the fanciest estate in Grange. His house was like a mini version of Will Smith's mansion in *The Fresh Prince of Bel Air*. Decked out. Similar looking to my house in a way but his was wider and bigger than mine, meaning Derek more or less had his own computer room/sitting room downstairs. Big screen TV, two couches, Nintendo 64 and a Playstation along with the fact no one would come in and try to watch the news or a soap opera while we played soccer competitions on the computer. Well, except for his gran every now and again but she usually fell asleep on the couch midway through what she was saying.

Although come to think of it, I also had a second living room where I could play computer if I so wished. Maybe it was more the fact that Derek's parents were more lenient about him drinking before he was eighteen (the legal age in Ireland) than mine were so we ended up hanging out there more during our last year of school. Can't beat drinking cans of stale Dutch Gold beer indoors to make you feel like an adult. It was cool, comfortable and cheap for us but by the time summer came around Derek and I both realised we needed to get some beautiful, luscious women in our lives who could take care of our raring needs. Now that our exams were over we had no more excuses. Hibernate off. Summer of lovin' on!

Well, that was the plan. Turned out to be one of the wettest summers ever recorded in Ireland. This meant for the first month of the summer of freedom, myself and Derek spent an awful lot of time indoors watching the sports news channel, Sky Sports News, repeat the same soccer transfer gossip over and over throughout the day until we could finally take no more and started playing soccer computer competitions of *International Superstar Soccer* instead.

Fill up that free time. Two chumps consumed by soccer and surreptitious booze.

After four weeks of this daily routine we decided we needed more out of life. Maybe we should get a job of some sort. Derek's Dad, Frankie P., a local legend, offered us a gig delivering betting slips to various bookies (gambling shops) in different towns around Munster. Frankie P. looked like a slightly taller version of Danny DeVito. Sound guy. Always shaving corners when he could. Hooked us up with a cushy number. Just drive around and drop off boxes of paper. Sixty-euro each. Sounds good. Should be easy. Probably boring. Legal? Think so.

Plan was I'd drive and Derek would run into the shops with each box. Shift started at five in the morning. Job involved us driving to all these little postcard like village towns that looked the same as they did three hundred years ago, spread out all over Tipperary, Wexford, Waterford, Kilkenny, Limerick, West Cork and back to Cork again. At least I could just wear my pyjamas. Driving along, looking at green fields, wet sheep and majestic mountains covered in thick forests. Nice views, if we weren't so used to them. Wouldn't have minded seeing some Malibu beaches or New York skyscrapers for a change. Grass is always greener, over there in the concrete jungles and sandy shorelines, I do suppose.

The main roads were grand to drive on but some of the little country lanes were about the width of a single bed. Not sure how my car fit down some of them. Got stuck behind a good few tractors every now and again, moving at three miles an hour.

At one point we got stuck behind a flock of sheep blocking the road in both directions. Funny if it was a scene from the TV show Mr. Bean or the likes, not so much when you're stuck in the midst of it. Not sure how we got ambushed by all those sheep but I've never seen Derek curse so much. Those poor, dopey balls of wool.

No time to lose I suppose, we were on a four-hour round drive time schedule. Might have to bend the speed rules of the road slightly to make that happen, technically it was a five-hour drive. Tearing it along in my old, white Mitsubishi Colt. Not the prettiest fish in the sea but she did the job. Wind rattling the windows. Window wipers on full blast. Hot air pumping out to keep us warm. Foot down. Drive on!

After the first two shifts the sheen of the job wore off. Too early. Too dull a drive. Radio stations are crap. Why is it always raining? Where is our sunny summer? Why don't we make some good tapes to listen to? Frankie P. had seen us coming.

Derek and I started baying for each other's jobs. I was annoyed he could have a sneaky sleep between the drop off points. He was annoyed I didn't have to leave the car and go run around little villages carrying heavy boxes as he got wet from the rain. Tit for tat.

The driving and the hot air pumping used to almost make me fall asleep so at least that meant Derek had to stay awake to make sure I stayed awake. Sneaky move out of me. We did come up with a great idea of sticking our heads out the car window as we belted along the motorway, like two dogs with our tongues out, letting the rain and the wind smack us in the face as we made "WUU" noises at the top of our lungs. Great wake up technique, if you're ever looking for one.

At least the job gave us some spare cash to spend. Not just stuck on pocket money. Enabled us to go out gallivanting in town at night. Cork City, the big smoke! Well, the biggish smoke. Both of us had just turned eighteen. Legally allowed go to pubs. We just didn't really know what to do or how to act with all this new legal freedom. We had been in pubs before but the fact we were using fake IDs kept us on edge. Can't get too drunk. Needed to get the last bus home at eleven. Might get caught. Arrested. Jailed. Locked up for life. Even worse – What if my parents found out.

At least the drink helped to ease us into this new legal pub life. Presume everyone was in the same boat. Nodding hellos to people while trying to look cool as we stroll into Doyle's, the most popular pub for eighteen-years-olds at the time. Doyle's was right in the middle of the city. Dark. Stonewalls. Black trimmings. Two floors. Kind of trying to look modern despite being old. Cheap drink. Student specials. Crowd was young, borderline pikey-ish at times. Lots of mutton girls dressed as lamb too. Some genuinely good-looking girls as well though so you took the risk. Lamb dressed as lamb. Feed me those succulent chops!

All awkward and nervous in my best, freshly ironed white shirt and blue jeans, spiky fringe and black leprechaun shoes. (Apparently tap dancing shoes with shiny buckles were now in fashion, I was just a few years ahead of the curve, as always.) Good buzz being in the dim, dank pub with people smoking all around me. I'm a real boy now. Cobbled grey walls wailing out for all the hopes and dreams lost in there. Bleached blond haired girls caked in make-up, most of them too big for their tiny clothes. Boob tubes and miniskirts seem to be the name of the game, fashion wise. Ordering pints. "Cheapest you have please, barman!" Meeting buddies. Wait until a few drinks kick in. Warming up. Fuzzy feeling. Fun begins.

Leave the dark, smoky pub behind. Head to a club called One, a new, modern looking nightclub located in an old building down the street from Doyle's. New on the inside, eighteenth century on the outside. Queue up. Check out all the bleached blondes. Outside light highlighting their true looks. Harsh. Pay the door cover. Skip through the mirrored hallway. Straight to the bar. Have a few shots. Courage kicks in. Music pumping. Two rooms. Hip-hop. Electro. Dance. Pop. Weird mix. Who cares. Time to go dance. Try and pull a few girls.

Start dancing one on one with this good-looking girl. Little brunette, hair in a ponytail. White jeans. Black top. Both skin tight. Slightly sweating from all her dancing, in a good way, (not panting like a paedophile way). Stomach showing. Tight body. Big voluptuous boobs. Hot girl. Never seen her before. She can dance too. Turning me on. Getting me going. Better tuck my ponder pipe up. Almost poking straight out of my zipper. Do a swivel. Tuck it up. Between my waist and my belt. Safer there. Girl moves in. Says something to me. Her name? Sara? No clue. I nod and laugh back,

"Ha ha ha."

She smiles. Closes her eyes. Hips come closer. Now we're lip locking. Dancing the tongues off each other, going for broke, entwined. Coming together as one on the disco ball lit dance floor. Purples, pinks, silvers and blues swirling around and meshing in my head with all the cheap beer and sugary shots.

Girl pulls back. Puts her hands around my body. Seems she likes what she feels. Backs away and lifts up my shirt a bit. Looks at me quizzically. Stops dancing. Lifts up my top some more. Exposes my fully dancing, tucked up ponder pipe to anyone who might be looking. Slipped up over my belt barrier. Popped his head out to say "Hello!" People around me look at me like I'm a weirdo. The girl gives me an awkward/disgusted look like somehow I'm a pervert. Checks to see if her friends saw. They did. Lets go of my top, turns and disappears into the crowd, never to be seen again. Huh? Am I not supposed to be turned on with you dancing like that? Come back!

Alas, she didn't. Foiled. Kind of liked her too, looks and dance wise at least. In fact, that would be the way of the summer. The months came and bundled away and while Derek and I got some girls, we never really got our first choices. Always either taken or else looking for older guys with more money/frightened by my ponder pipe poking out of the top of my jeans due to it being tucked up.

Derek had some joy with a beautiful blonde named Abbey who looked like a young Pamela Anderson. Unfortunately the drink didn't always agree with Derek. There was always that one shot too many that caused him to take off his top and run around like a wide-eyed crazy cave man. Some laugh. Just not for getting women. Scared her away.

This kind of thing was also had I ended up giving Derek the nickname 'Dino Patsy'. At first I used to tell girls his parents wanted to name him Patsy if he was born a girl and preferably Dino if a boy but Derek changed his name when he was ten. Derek was not a fan of this tale but at least it gave us an icebreaker chatting up girls. When drunk Derek reared his head I let people know by saying he turned into Dino Patsy, an Irish Jekyll and Hyde. Derek by day, Dino Patsy by night. Still sticks to this day actually. I was always good at nicknames.

Back to the women. I had a few tasty girls in spurts too myself. There was one beautiful beauty who reminded me of Farah Fawcett a bit. Tall, blond, slim, heavy eye make-up, push-up bra giving her an extra bounce, all an oasis but who cares. Well dressed, hot hair that you wanted to grab, cherry like bum behind. She had a classy yet also a dirty look. A classy, dirty look. Dirty hot. Beautiful. Think she went on to win the Ms. Cork beauty competition in the years to come, maybe Ms. Ireland too.

Hooked up one night in a nightclub. Dance floor. Getting it on. Retired to get a drink. She was sitting on my lap at one point. I remember thinking she must be very happy to be sitting there, kept gyrating up and down my knee and thigh. Don't think she was wearing any underwear. Felt her happiness on my leg, if you know what I mean. Her hen house was on fire. My lap was wet with delight. Then she just got up and left all of a sudden, while we were kissing. Not a word, just a weird look and she was gone. Didn't think much of it. Had a few more shots with Derek then laughed as he strutted around topless like Burt Reynolds once more.

Next day my Mum came into my room to wake me up. She was about to do a wash and wanted to know,

"Any idea what this weird red stain on your jeans is, Mark?"

"The ones I wore last night? No clue."

Took a look. Strange stain all right, right on the lap section. Looks a kind of red- no, crimson colour. Oh Jesus. I know what that is. That girl. Farah Fawcett. Did she really? Time of the month. Sweet funk. She bled on me. No way. Mank. And there's me thinking I was turning her on.

"Eh, I think I spilt some ketchup on my pants when I went to the chipper after the pub, Mum. Just ketchup, that's all."

Farah avoided me for years after that. Somehow made it out like it was my fault. Maybe that's what embarrassment does, makes the other person the bad guy for witnessing it. Anyway, things dipped after that incident. The well dried up, so to speak. Some summer of freedom for Derek and I, we really took over the world.

After we first blamed girls in general for our lack of steady giddy upping, Derek and I then started to see the light and turned on ourselves. Derek blamed his height and fluctuating bread weight (he still had a thing for eating full loaves in one go thanks to me) while I blamed my inability to talk to women.

It wasn't that I was bad, it was just it took so much effort to put on a front of what I thought girls wanted me to say all the time. All an act to appear cool. Very tiring. When I did happen to let my guard down and act myself, the difference would be so dramatic I'd come across like a schizophrenic and scare them off. At least that's what I told myself. Delusional. Dopey. Doomed.

That is, until the very end of summer, an evening late in August. On my drive home from Derek's I stopped off to get petrol in Douglas. The Colt needed a top up. While I was fiddling with the gas knob I happened to get a text from my cousin Gillian. Beep beep!

"Did you just drive past us in a white car?"

"I did."

"Any chance of a lift home? It'd be good to catch up!"

Seeing as Gillian lived close to me, I said no problem. Nice cousin that I am and all. I knew she was spoofing about catching up too, just didn't want to take the bus home. Lift on.

Picked Gillian up down the road. Not alone, she was with her hot friend, Aisling. Light brown, almost blond hair, flowing just past her shoulders. Smaller than me, but not too small. Good fit if we were to stand next to each other. Pretty saucer eyes and big wide pretty smile. Perfect white teeth. Smooth tanned skin. Nineteen, I think, a year older than me. Sound as a pound too.

Met Aisling once before years ago. Foreign object. Made her hotter. Irish but she lived in Saudi Arabia for years so never around, not your typical Irish girl. Added to her mystique and allure. Local legend. Also gave her that healthy tanned glow not found on many Irish people. Was she fully Irish? Hadn't a clue. Most of us are kind of an unhealthy, blotchy, pinky-porky pig colour.

Anyway, while living in Saudi Arabia Aisling stayed best friends with my cousin Gillian. Turns out Aisling's Mum, Ger, was best friends with my aunt Marie and her Dad, Bert, was best friends with my uncle Harling. Plenty for us to talk about. As we drove along and chatted on, I realised I was at ease talking away. Not putting on any act. Gillian was my cousin so that was grand but Aisling was a girl I found hot. How could this be? And, she seems interested in me. Keeps laughing at my witty (horrendous) jokes.

"What's orange and sounds like a parrot? A carrot! Good, huh?"

In fact she's invited me down to her house with them. We're actually driving past my house, past Gillian's and all the way down to Aisling's abode - Wait until I tell Derek!

Aisling lived in a place called Monkstown, which is about ten minutes past Passage West where my grandparents live. Turns out that Aisling's house is unreal, even nicer than Derek's. It looks exactly like the Fresh Prince of Bel Air's abode. White pillars. Three levels. Sports cars outside. Built next to a castle. Golf course running alongside it. And, best of all, it even has a better living room with a bigger TV and an even more comfortable couch than Derek's house. If only I could get him down here, it'd be the perfect spot!

As things do, one thing leads to another, then some drink is involved and before I know it Aisling and I are kind of together. The Irish way of things like that working out. Now, instead of going to Derek's all the time I'm going down to Aisling's house. Start seeing each other every day. Hanging out all the time. Feels good. Having a laugh. Seeing this new way of life. So this is what 'being friends with a girl and liking a girl and her liking you back and she's cool and hot and how weird is this' feels like.

At the time I still had a bit of a curfew from my parents, had to be home by two o'clock-ish. Slowly but surely I was coming home later and later though, sometimes almost spending the night at Aisling's house. Whenever my Mum asked where I'd been, I'd always say Derek's house. Easier on me, less questions, less probing. My poor Mum, cutting her out of my loop.

When September time came around Aisling had to go to Dublin to start university at Art College. This led to us talking on the phone a lot. Every day and night, hour-long conversations, rambling on about everything and nothing at all. All grand until the phone bill came for the month. My Dad calls me into the kitchen,

"Could you close the door as well, please?"

Oh no - The dreaded phrase. Close the door means trouble. In I go. Draft blows the door shut. Ominous. My Dad is sitting at the kitchen table. Stern face. Says nothing. Silence. Just the smell of cabbage and peas we had for dinner the night before and the tick tock of the grandfather clock, intensifying whatever I did wrong this time.

"Any idea why the phone bill is two hundred euro dearer than usual?"

"Eh, no clue Dad. Maybe ask Darren."

"He said it might be you. There's one number in particular appearing a lot, do you know it?"

Take a look at the number - Aisling's mobile phone.

"Don't think so."

"Well I'll call Darren in and see if he does. Are you sure?"

"Just let me check my phone, looks familiar now you mention it."

Pretend to check the phonebook on my mobile phone. The reason you didn't phone someone from your mobile was that it cost so much phoning mobile to mobile in Ireland. So, whoever was at home would take the hit and phone the other person's mobile to help them save money. Unwritten rules which I was now getting stung for.

"I'm waiting Mark. Do you know the number or did they bill us extra by mistake for a number we don't know. I'll phone it and find out."

Oh God. That's the worst thing ever. Don't want to get Aisling in trouble. Panic time.

"No, I know who owns that number actually."

"Who?"

"Eh, Derek."

"Derek Peyton?"

""Yeah, Derek. I must've been phoning it by mistake."

"You phoned Derek for three hours last Monday at two in the morning?"

"Yeaaah… Just having a chat about stuff."

The Derek angle threw my Dad off.

"I thought it might be a girl's number?"

"No. It's Derek's. I better be off actually, told him I'd call up to his house right now. His Mum is making us a quiche for dinner. Can't let Mary P. down, you know how nice she is. Sorry about the bill Dad, I'll keep the calls to a minimum from now on."

Left my Dad in a confused haze. Skedaddled out the door. Hopped in the Colt. Drove up to Derek's house. Munched down Mary P.'s mighty quiche. Hid out there for a while. Distance myself from the phone bill.

When I arrived home later that night both of my parents were still up. That's strange. Thought the matter was dealt with. Hmm. Dodge on. Creaked open the front door as slow as I could, trying not to make a murmur. Crept inside then tried to tiptoe up the stairs to bed without them hearing me. First step of the stairs creaked. Balls. Caught.

"Mark? Could you come into the kitchen for a minute."

Here we go again.

"Close the door please."

Dose.

"Mark."

"Yes Mum?"

"Are you in a relationship with Derek?"

"Ha, what? No."

"You can tell us if you are Mark, just don't lie."

"I'm not Dad, I swear. I don't even know what you - I'm not gay if that's what you think?"

"Well why else are you always up in his house and now you're phoning him so late at night staying on the phone for hours to each other? I heard you whispering you missed him one night. I'm sorry, Mark, it just doesn't make sense. Are you two plotting to run off somewhere together? You can tell us, just be honest, *please*."

"No, Mum, it's not that! It's-It's-It's a girl."

With that, the whole room breathed a confused sigh of something. I told my parents all about Aisling. The clock struck midnight. And summer was officially over.

Chapter 22
Toaster Head

Seeing as I was not going to fish-college to learn how to be a fish-farmer, I instead went off to University College Cork (U.C.C) to do Business Information Systems (B.I.S), my lifelong dream (L.L.D). Yay.

To be honest, I had no real clue what B.I.S was all about, business and computers of some sort. However, I did know that the U.C.C campus was pretty slick. Darren had filled me in from going there for a year doing his course but I also had an orientation day to see it for myself in the last week of September, a week before class was due to begin. Apparently it had been named *Irish University of the Year* numerous times and was ranked in the top two per cent in the world. Glamorous.

The main section was called the Quad, a rectangular green area of manicured grass trimmed with red roses, white daisies and yellow tulips, all living free together as one, sweet smelling and not a sign of flower racism in sight. Two long, grey, gothic Tudor halls and a commanding clock tower, all covered in lush green ivy, ran along the width and length of the Quad, facing it. I think the building is called The Long Hall which was lined inside with Ogham Stones, these old stones that recorded the earliest forms of writing in Ireland, going back to about 4th century A.D. Whole place looked like something out of Harry Potter, almost made up. Postcard scenery. Pretty sure the clock was broken though, never heard it chime. Typical.

Spread out in all directions on the opposite side of the Quad there was a huge, speckled white pebble, five-story library; a sprawling, modern, exciting looking four-story glass building filled with computer labs; an odd oval shaped art gallery that looked like a wooden bowl turned upside down; a small historic Roman-Catholic chapel called the Honan Chapel, which dated back to 1894, that was situated just next to a modern, expansive, glass, three-story student centre that had a bar (called the New Bar), dining hall, shops, book store, café and hall space.

Over a bit to the right of the Quad there were all the older buildings, the more rundown but also more lively pub called the Old Bar, a ragged looking theatre building, a rundown looking, grey, dining hall that actually wasn't too bad inside, almost inviting you might say, along with an ominous, horrible looking, 1960s East Germany with a splash of communist Russia , food science building that made you feel violated and hopeless when you stepped inside.

Further down along by the banks of the River Lee (where the Vikings once sailed in back in 795 A.D. and started raiding the whole place), just past the fancy Juries Inn Hotel (where Michael Jackson once stayed), there was a state of the art gym, running track, soccer pitches, football pitches, tennis courts, hockey pitch and a swimming pool, along with lots of other university buildings scattered here and there. Even had part of an old prison wall in one section, I think. Some of these buildings were going back thousands of years. Pretty cool, all mixed in with all the modern looking ones. Old blended with the new. U.C.C had it all. Most importantly, it had two pubs. Right there on campus. Boooze on! This was going to be a great laugh. Right?

Well. Actually. Nay. My first attempt at university did not go too well. First day set the tone. Now I was out of school and considered kind of a man (despite still looking like a fresh faced eighteen-year-old boy, a blend of Zach Morris, AC Slater and Screech), it was down to me to make my own way to class.

Back in my school days I'd either get a lift with my Dad who dropped me off on his way to work or else a lift from one of my friends who had their own car when we got into sixth year. Not sure if owning a car was somehow related but none of those friends made it in to U.C.C. Dose. My Dad could only bring me part of the way there as well seeing as it wasn't really on his route to work, so I'd have to walk for thirty minutes or else get a bus. Double dose. Only other option was get to take two buses and leave my house at half seven in the morning to make sure to get be on time for nine. Messy affair. Plan D on.

My buddy Ronnie (*Hey Arnold*) was really the only friend from school who had made it into U.C.C as well, doing B.I.S like me. Everyone else either went to Dublin for university or else didn't really get what they wanted and ended up in C.I.T (considered the second rate technical college in Cork). A few others decided to repeat the whole year to try and get better results. Derek Peyton was included in this repeating crowd. Dose. Our paths would have to diverge. See you on the other side, boss. I knew other people from my school who were going to U.C.C to do other courses but no one really whom I was too friendly with. Just Ronnie and I. It'll be grand, I told myself, I'll make more friends soon enough.

Just before university started Ronnie bought himself a new motorbike. His Dad was a big bike head. Trickled down into Rob's blood. Not really a fan myself, always seemed a bit dodge. Comfort of cars was far more appealing. When Ronnie was sixteen he got a scooter and gave me a go. Managed to crash it into a curb and almost kill a few people on a path. Turned me off bikes for good after that. Clearly they were the dangerous factor, not I.

Anyway, now Ronnie was eighteen he upgraded to a proper bike. Not sure what kind exactly, some kind of sports bike. Big. Shiny black. Complete beast. Powerful machine with a victorious sheen. Looked like a weapon. A canon meets a panther on wheels. Dangerous bastard.

Due to my 'how to get to class?' conundrum, Ronnie offered me a spin in on our first day. Said yes. Dubious call. Never actually been on the black beast before. Whereas the scooter had the power of a lawnmower, this beast clearly had some oomph.

Ronnie showed up at my house at half eight in the morning. Class was at nine. With no traffic it might take twenty minutes to get from my house to U.C.C. Ronnie assured me that being on a bike was like there was no traffic. Could just zigzag between all the cars. Sounds mighty, and *very* safe. Even better, it was pouring rain outside. Bucketing. Horrible, grey, slippery wet. Typical October morn in Ireland. Charming.

Heard Ronnie honk his horn outside. Whipped on my wet pants and big, blue, bulky bomber jacket. Said goodbye to my Mum. Waved me off to my first day of university with a tear (probably a fly) in her eye. Scuttled out the door. Soaked the minute I took a step outside. Funk - The rain, my hair! Then I remembered - Balls, the motorbike helmet, my hair! This was another reason I wasn't the greatest fan of bikes, the helmet hair issue. My level of vanity was ridiculous, I know.

Ronnie nods hello at me and says something through his helmet that I don't quite get. Nod hello and thumbs up back.

Bucketing down, I can barely see. Rain is pelting off my face like little tiny snipers taking shots. Stinging. Weather's dodge, isn't it? Hands me a helmet. Ah for funk sake – It's his old crappy back up one. How am I meant to look cool in this?

At first glance it looks like a weary old turtle shell mixed with a faded piece of Lego. It's even worse than a bicycle helmet and they're quite possibly the worst looking things in the world when worn. At least his helmet is cool, sleek and black. Looks like I'm wearing a toaster on my head. Toaster Head, as my buddy Vinnie used to call me. (Claimed my head looked like a toaster, long and narrow. Great insult, best I've ever had. In return I called him Lego Head due to his head being the same shape as a Lego man. Poor comeback.)

Sign language an offer to Ronnie to swap helmets with me. Declines. Tut. Toaster on. Back of the bike is one long, wet, slippery slope of leather covered in water. This is where I'm to sit. Jump on. Realise this is dodge for balance. Two options to steady myself: Hold onto the small, tiny little rail on the back of the seat behind me. Or. Hold onto Ronnie. That's a bit feminine. Only ever seen women hold onto men like that. Never guy on guy. What if I slide forward? Bump parts? Junk to trunk? Seems like awkwardness waiting to happen. Only one option really. Attempt to hold the slippery rail. Just grip my knees tight against the sides of the bike. Hold on for dear life. I'll be *graaand*.

Ronnie shouts something at me again. Muffled words. Rain pelting down. Can't understand a word. Still, I tap his helmet twice to indicate a yes, I do understand. Whatever you said, yes. Looks at me oddly. Starts the engine. Vroom vroom. Monstrosity takes off. Away we go. Head first into a gale force wind that's now pelting down hailstones. This is fun. This is what university's all about. My Mum was right - I'm going to love it!

Ronnie skips past traffic in Rochestown like it - and I - aren't even there. Swaying back and forth, rubbing cars with my elbows, clipping wing mirrors. Get as far as Douglas village before we're held up by a traffic light. By now I can't even see out of the helmet visor. Delightful combination of condensation from the heat wafting through my head from my big wet jacket mixed with the thunder humidity on the outside. Can't feel my hands from the hailstones battering down. This is very pleasant. Like all the comforts of riding in a car, just without any of the actual comforts of riding in a car. Bikes are great.

Ronnie turns his head and lifts his visor. Says something to me again. Wipe my visor with both hands and lift it up. Let the cool, wet air hit me in the face. As the lights go green, Ronnie slams down his visor, yelling at me. Before I can mull over what "Hole gone?" might mean, Ronnie does a wheelie. Bike rears up like Black Beauty on its back wheels. Ronnie revs the motor. The horse lets out a ferocious "NEEEIIIGGGHHH!" as I let out a dismayed "NAAAYYY!" Both of my hands are still on my visor. Bike takes off mid wheelie as I take off the back of the bike, barely missing the back wheel. Splash! Land with a heavy thud on my back into a puddle filled pothole. Yes! Soaking wet clothes. Happy days. My school bag and toaster head helmet break most of my fall, bar the sweet spot on my tailbone.

Lie there for a second before the thought pops in my head that the car behind me might not see what happened. What if they just drive over me by mistake? Roll with all my might to the right, struggling in my big wet jacket. Roll over five times, like an overweight James Bond trying to dodge some very slow bullets. Right into a gutter filled with flowing water. Lovely. I had no need to worry though, everyone saw what happened. They all saw. Rush hour traffic and I took quite a dopey fall. Few people got out of their cars but the rain didn't make they come over or anything. Once they saw I was OK, they all laughed. Raise my head up to see Ronnie has pulled in up the road. Waves at me: Run! Hurry up. No apology. Just,

"I've been telling you to hold on since we left your house! Come on, we're going to be late."

And we were late to our first class, statistics. This was on in the Boole Basement, an underground, labyrinth like, Bat Cave section in the campus below the old dining hall. The largest lecture halls were here. Seeing as it was the first class of the year the whole place was packed, about a thousand students all crammed into a roasting hot, stuffy auditorium. Old heating system cranking out a thick blanket of muggy warm air. Wet from the rain. Sweat from the heat. Walking into class late trying to find a seat. Flustered. Uncomfortable. Out of place. Lovely.

Even worse, while standing at the top of the hall scanning the room for any open seat, my toaster helmet slipped out of my wet hand. The lecture hall sloped downward so the helmet just banged and clanged as loud as it could down the aisle, similar to a metal toaster smashing its way down a ladder. Didn't stop until it hit the podium that the lecturer was standing on. BOOM! Made a huge clatter as it landed by his feet. Stern faced lecturer who looked a bit like a milder version of Hannibal Lecter. Older, balding man with a grey wispy comb over. Glasses perched on the edge of his nose, wearing a tattered grey cardigan with brown elbow patches and black slacks. Fiddled with a pen slowly as he took his time, let out a slow sigh, then looked up at the crowd with disgust and asked,

"Who owns this toaster helmet?"

"Emm, I do. Sorry."

Made my way down to the front of the room to pick it up. Cumbersome jacket. Sore tailbone. Wet pants. Sweaty, flushed red face. Tried to apologise to the lecturer for interrupting class but as I did I broke into a fit of nervous laughter.

"HA HA HA." Couldn't stop. "HAHAHAHA."

Lecter the Lecturer waited for me to take in air, then politely kicked me out of class.

"HAHAHAIMSORRYICANTSTOPITWHENISTARTHAHA."

Told the entire room he wouldn't start again until I had left. So that was fun. Ahem.

Exited the roasting hot lecture hall and basked in the cold air drafting in from an open exit door nearby. Closed my eyes and took a deep breath. As I did Clash's song *Should I Stay Or Should I Go* started humming inside my head. Must've heard it on the radio having breakfast earlier. Stood outside the door, scratching my toaster head hair and singing softly to myself, trying to figure out what just happened. No clue.

I do know that I more or less decided there and then: Funk this. Funk that. I'm not ready for college. Or else college isn't ready for me. I'm going somewhere fun. See you later, Lecter. College off. Adventure on!

CHAPTER 23
FIRST-CLASS. ISH.

Adventure on. Indeed. That was the plan at least. Easier said than done when you're eighteen, not sure what to do with your life and have no money. I did give college a go for a few more weeks after the toaster head incident but between the lack of enthusiasm for the course I chose, the lack of friends that made it to college from school, along with a dash of getting my head turned by Aisling (technically my first proper girlfriend), I dropped out and went to work in an apple factory instead. Great move.

Apple computers' European headquarters are based in a rough, pikey filled area of Cork, way up the north side of the city. Tax breaks and all that. Derek Peyton and a few other buddies started working there part-time so I got a mind-numbing job in the factory warehouse as well. Loading up orders and offloading stock. Riveting, stimulating, top level stuff. My plan wasn't to stay working here for life or anything. Promised my parents I would return to college the following year so that gave me some breathing room. Helped ease them in when I told them of my newfound career as a factory boy. After all my hard work to get such high points as well. Tut. I still wanted to go see the world and adventure on. Just needed to make some money first.

The main Apple building looked like a Mac computer. Shiny, elegant, sleek. This was the business/call centre side. The other half hidden in the back was the warehouse, definitely the more common section. Just looked like a well maintained but typical factory floor. Sparse, harsh lighting, rows and rows of shelves filled with brown boxes all with the partially eaten apple on each and every one, along with a dark hole shoot to dump rubbish.

The whole building was located right next to a hauling site where pikeys lived. Every lunchtime we would watch them from the safety of the cafeteria as they raced their horses around the car park, fight each other to a bloody pulp, and, in one case, burn a caravan down to the ground over a dispute between two brothers about where their mother should live. Typical pikey stuff.

On the call centre/business side there were loads of good looking women, all nationalities, all dressed in sleek business outfits, looking all hot with their foreign flair. Brunettes, blondes, red heads, the lot. We used to see them at times in the cafeteria that everyone shared but us factory folk never really had a chance with them. We were all either eighteen-year-old boys or foul-mouthed, overweight men (the guys in charge) who looked like toads and moles in our itchy, grey wooly jumpers and black tracksuit pants. Comfort and warmth needed in the cold warehouse, obviously.

Not sure if I was really the next Steve Jobs, don't think I was ever up for employee of the month. All I seemed to do was cause some sort of accident. Crashed a few too many forklifts, surprisingly easy to topple. Overloading was my fault, too many brand new computers stacked up on empty boxes. At least I only ended up in the hospital once for stitches. Nowadays when girls see the scar on my back where I cut myself, I tell them I was knifed one time in Greece "you should see the other guy". At least give them a tale. They seem to respond to it better than me saying,

"I sliced a mole on my lower back off a sharp metal shelve in a warehouse when I was wrestling my buddy Kevin Madden and I needed stitches to stop the bleeding, you see."

Quite a hoot.

Not so much of a hoot was my relationship with Aisling at this time. While it started in a whirlwind of heat, emotion and bliss, it quickly descended into a murky land of unknown feelings and other people. It had been this way for a few months. Things started great. We got on unbelievably well. Her family loved me. I thought they were all sound as a pound. Brother, sisters, the lot.

Then, things slowly soured. Exes appeared out of everywhere. Odd outbursts. On the scene, off the scene. Good. Bad. Ups. Downs. Young. Dumb. Impetuous. Always on, always off. Eighteen. No clue how to control my emotions. Wildfires, running away from me with blissful glee.

What I didn't realise when I first met Aisling was that she was kind of seeing another guy, Trevor. Tall, skinny, skateboarder dude. Just like an American only with an Irish accent. Kind of looked like Ernie from Sesame Street. Fuzzy head, dopey looking, always wearing a stripy jumper and forever carrying a yellow duck around with him. Despite myself and Aisling becoming a couple, Trevor was always an issue. We did not see eye to eye.

There was another ex of hers still on the scene too, Ronan (a slightly chubbier, smaller version of Trevor, more of a Bert lookalike, cocky as could be, skateboarder dude as well). He was also still professing his undying love for her at every opportunity he could get.

On top of Bert and Ernie, it appeared a lot of other skateboarder guys seemed to be quite smitten with Aisling as well. I was surrounded by muppets, all of them dressed like skateboarders with baggy pants and loose fitting hoodies, just not sure if any of them ever skated, none of whom were too happy that I had suddenly appeared on the scene.

Best of all, all these guys were actually in Aisling's group of friends along with a good lot of girls who mostly didn't like me because that meant Aisling wasn't going out with one of the guys in their friends group and that was just the worst thing ever. Poor Tom, Dick, Bert and Ernie. How could I have done that to them?

So that was great fun, hanging around with all these fine folk all the time when I was with Aisling. To make matters worse, the majority of them were two-faced and back stabbers to their own friends in the group. You had Count Van Count, pronounced without the 'o', hooking up with his best friend Biff's girlfriend behind Biff's back. Then you had another girl, Ms. Piggy, who seemed to love to get drunk and say horrible things about her so called best friends, Granny Bird and Gladys the Cow. No clue how they were all friends. Fake as Chinese rubber plants, a relentless pool of muppets unwittingly out-snaking each other on a daily basis.

Few of the friends were sound though, like Fred the Wonder Horse (guy with big teeth and a hearty, snorting smile) and Hoots the Owl (guy who hooted every time he spoke, although maybe he had Tourettes, not sure) so I just chatted with them whenever they all came to Aisling's to play basketball in her court and booze on in the kitchen. Still, I was always a complete outsider. Kind of felt like that English girl in *Friends* who Ross marries (apparently she said none of the cast made her feel welcome, you see, in real life that is, off set).

Anyway, for about three months things were always on then always off between Aisling and I. It all stemmed from one night in particular. Ernie (Trevor) had asked Aisling to his Grads dinner, which is like the Prom at the end of high school in America. Promises me she's going as friends.

"OK, sure thing, I trust you!"

Next day I go down to Aisling's house before a big event her family were having that night, the opening of their new brewery in a town in County Cork called Kinsale. Aisling's family were minted, particularly for Cork standards. Never been to the opening of a brewery before, so I had been looking forward to this night for weeks.

Anyway, as I'm down waiting for Aisling to get ready for the opening party, I notice she's being weird with me. Ask her what's wrong. She informs me that she kissed Ernie the night before. Oh. Right. Mighty. Stunned. Although I had a feeling it would happen. Still, good old gullible me giving the benefit of the doubt.

First reaction was to call her a plonker, which is a nicer way of calling someone a dope, an idiot or a wally. Maybe I should've been harsher but my manners were still intact despite what she had done. Then my emotions kicked in and I asked to know every detail. Not sure why, but I felt a need to know everything. Already felt like a fool. While Aisling is sobbing and saying sorry, her Mum calls out for us downstairs.

"Hurry up you two, we'll be late!"

Oh yeah. The party. How am I meant to go now? Although how do I pull out at this late hour without causing a scene? Don't want her family knowing. Making me more embarrassed. Funk. What to do? I don't know. Shut down. Go through the motions. Ride the night out. Tell Aisling to stay away from me for the night. Then we both go downstairs and get into the back seat of their brand new, black 7-series BMW. Look at Aisling and grimace a smile. *Let's just enjoy these lovely heated leather seats and pretend like nothing's happened in front of your parents, OK?*

In one last attempt at getting away from the whole event, I pretend to Aisling's parents that I need to go home and get something. I forgot it. Never actually said what 'it' was but I needed to figure out what to do. The brewery was a forty-minute drive away, did I really want to be here? BMW pulls up outside my house. I run in. Greet my Mum. Asks me why I'm home. Tell her I forgot something. Run upstairs to my room. Darren and his buddy from college, Shane 'Wanchope' Hennessy, are playing computer in my bedroom. Before they can ask me why I'm back, I fill them in and ask for their advice: Should I stay or should I go? Darren's not sure. Wanchope shrugs his shoulders,

"Put it this way: How often do you get to go to the opening of a brewery? Go for it, kid."

Good point. Cheers Wanchope. Brewery on. Go back outside to the waiting car, rattling a box of Tic-Tacs I took from my room.

"Got it, thanks."

Strange looks seeing as I went back home to get some mints but fair enough. To the brewery we go. Cool set-up. Place looks slick, a two-story, vintage style brewing house with big, brass vats and shiny silver machines that somehow make booze, along with a bar and patio area upstairs, kind of like a mini version of the Guinness brewery in Dublin.

I'm not really in the mood for it all but the booze helps. Don't talk to Aisling for most of the night but later on she apologises again to me. I have some booze, then some more. Mixes in with my complete lack of awareness and first strong feelings for a girl. The doe-eyed, sad manipulation gets to me. My Dad always told me on of my best traits is that I never hold a grudge too long. I held out as long as I could. Plus, the weird manipulative, heartstring, narcissistic mind games work on me. So. I forgive. Back on. Weak man I am.

A few days later it was my own Grads. Final big party now that school was over. Rented a tux. Combed my hair. Posed for photos in front of my family. Aisling came up to my house in her full-length pink gown dress. All our families delighted to see us going out. Noticed that Aisling was a bit quiet at my house though. Turns out that she went out the night before with all her friends. Boozed on. Heavy session. Now dying with a hangover. Too goosed for my Grads. Delightful.

Go to the hotel up the road for the event. Aisling spends most of the night sitting at our table nursing water and trying to make sure she didn't get sick. I drank on and danced around like a clown with my buddies but having to look after her for most of the night put a dampener on things big time. At least I won the award for *Best Hair In School* though.

Few days later I broke it off with Aisling, seeing as I found out she had been texting Ernie the whole night of my Grads. And so the next few months would be like this. On. Off. On. On. Off. On. Boozing together usually led to it being back on. Dangerous liquid.

During one of the on-periods flights were booked for an indefinite trip to Hong Kong. Her Dad was the CFO of a big financial company (I think that's what they did anyway) and was currently based in Hong Kong where they had a nice apartment. Might as well see some of the world now I was taking a year off college. Aisling's art college course finished in January so we decided to go then. After a few months of dull, repetitive factory work I had enough saved for a flight and spending money.

Adventure time. No clue what we were going to do there but giddy up!

January came. Time to depart. First, one last night out with my friends before I go. Aisling goes out with hers. Separate pubs. Arrange to meet in a local nightclub Redz at the end of the night. Arrive in with Derek and a few more buddies, Kevin Madden, Robert Heffernan, my brother Darren and the likes, all drunk and merry. See my cousin Gillian, ask her where's Aisling? Points to a table. Aisling is huddled over a drink talking to Ernie. Oh right. Spends most of her night talking to Ernie. I booze some more. Derek asks me why she's spending so long talking with him. I say I don't know. I go talk to Aisling outside the club afterwards. Cold night. Foggy air. Blurry feelings pour out of my mouth.

"I've had enough. I'm drunk. I'm done. We're over!"

So we break up. Go home to our separate abodes. Sleep for three hours. Wake up at five in the morn. Pack my bags. And my Mum and sister Sarah drive me to the airport. They don't know what's happened. Aisling is at the airport with Gillian. All very awkward as everyone pretends like everything is mighty. This is wonderful: I'm going to Hong Kong with my ex.

We say our goodbyes and then go through airport security. The minute we're out of sight the waves and smiles are dropped. Stroll in to duty free. Get in an argument over the night before. Both exclaim,

"I don't want to talk to you."

"Well I don't want to talk to you!"

So neither of us say a word to each other on the flight to London. Fall asleep. Land. Alight. Heathrow. Arrange to meet at the gate for our next flight in three hours. Go our separate ways. I get breakfast. Check out the magazines and books. Find a seat where I can chill out and do some people watching. Sit on my own, listening to music on my minidisc player, watching people scurry by.

After listening to about ten songs on a minidisc Aisling made for me, I spot her running around looking frantic. Chuckle to myself. She must realise what an idiot she's been and now desperately wants to apologise to me. I'll let her stew a while and run around. Slide down in my seat like a snake. Pull the collar of my jacket up around my ears to hide myself some more. Does the opposite of what I intended. Aisling catches my eye line. Runs over. Time for her apology,

"WHAT HAVE YOU BEEN DOING YOU IDIOT?!"

"Huh? This is how you apolo-"

"DO YOU NOT HEAR THEM CALLING OUR NAMES ON THE INTERCOM OVER AND OVER? WE'RE GOING TO MISS OUR FLIGHT!"

"Oh. Right. Funk. Balls. RUN!"

Peg it to our gate. Thank God our bags were on board. Angry looking flight attendants scowl and take our tickets, then usher us through the gates. We made it. We're on. And I'm getting abuse. Why did I hide? It's *my* fault we almost missed the flight? So *I'm* in the wrong? No. Well. Yes. But she's the one in the wrong too, right? Don't know. Too much abuse. And now we're meant to sit next to each other, for - how long's this flight - fourteen hours? Jesus. We're going to kill each other. Maybe we should've just canceled the trip, lost the money we paid for flights and called it quits. Funk that actually, although this is brutal.

Hmmm. Notice lots of free seats as we walk through first-class. Follow Aisling down to our seats way back in the cattle ranch section. Settle in. Eat some mints. Get ready for takeoff. Devise my plan to sneak into first-class. All the usual pre-flight stuff. Once we're in the air, I excuse myself to the bathroom. Add on in a hushed whisper,

"I'm going up to first-class, see you in fourteen hours."

Aisling just glares back at me, obviously not hearing what I said over the hum of the engines. I did tell her at least. With that, I made my way through cattle ranch, past business class and back to first-class. Slide into one of the open seats. Grab a blanket and a sleeping mask. Recline the seat. Lie there pretending to be asleep, waiting to be kicked out. After half an hour, I think I'm safe. Just bumped myself up to first class for a long haul flight - Success!

Slightly dodge when the stewardess came over to me but it was only to ask,

"Would you like champagne or orange juice, sir?"

"Could I try both?"

"Certainly, sir."

So that was nice.

Never really flew long haul before. This was a fourteen-hour flight. That's over half a day, if I do the sums correctly. Kind of forgot it was that long too as we were mid-flight. For some reason I had the figure ten in my head. Might explain why I started panicking after eight hours. By that point I slept for a chunk, watched two movies and six episodes of *Friends*, all the ones with Emily the English girl, my new favourite hero (not really, to be honest I didn't like her much myself either). Felt like we had been flying for days. Surely almost there by now. Asked a different stewardess how long was left,

"Only six more hours."

"*Six*? Six more? Can't be that long? I JUST SLEPT FOR AGES!"

Think I caused suspicion when I jumped out of my seat. Must've looked delirious. Stewardess then asked,

"Is this your seat?"
"Yes."
She then asked,
"What's your name?"
So I said,
"Hubulla."
She asked for my ticket. I said,
"I'm not too sure."
She told me,
"This is not your seat."
I said,
"Isn't it?"
She asked me to leave.
I asked her to,
"Ah come on, it'll be just our secret?"

And then she kicked me out of first-class. Banished. Culled. Returned. Shuffled back down to my original seat to a confused Aisling,

"Where have you been? Did something happen?"

"Huh, me? Just at the bathroom."

Realised this was a poor answer. Abuse starts again. Can't hack more abuse in this mental state. How do we still have six hours left? Also can't hack being back here in the cattle ranch after swimming in the ocean of first-class legroom. I need to be in business class at the very least. So. Excused myself once again. Walk down the aisle towards the back of the plane. Back up the aisle on the far side. Ignore a fuming Aisling hissing at me. Pop my head through the curtain: Business class has lots of room. Mighty. Grab two blankets. Hide in what I think is the most inconspicuous option. Wake up five and a half hours later. Rudely being shaken by Aisling as she's leaving the plane.

"This is where you've been hiding?"

"Are we here? Jeez, that flight actually wasn't too bad at all, huh?"

Good way to travel halfway across the world. First-class. Ish. Rocky start, but, I made it. Now, time to have some fun!

Well, first I have to wait for Aisling. She must make a quick call to Ireland. Already? We just got off the flight! Do that later. We haven't even got our luggage yet. I thought we left Bert and Ernie behind? Gives me a dirty look. She's making this call.

And then it hit me: Maybe I'm Kermirk, the biggest muppet of the lot. Mighty. Well, at least I'm a muppet in Hong Kong. Adventure on!

Chapter 24
I Am Batman

Muggy. Sticky. Heavy. Oh Jesus. This weather. Just stepped outside the airport exit into the warm midnight air. Heat hit me like a hammer to the face. Stinging my eyes. Losing my bearings. Seven hours ahead. It's midnight. I think that's about dinnertime back home in Cork. Not sure. My body clock's all over the shop. Feels like we've been traveling for days. Goosed. Wired. Pumped. Spaced. Aware.

See a small, refined, older looking Chinese driver with grey hair dressed all in black and a driver's hat holding up a sign with Aisling's name on it. Kind of looks like a Chinese Alfred out of Batman. Chauffeur on. Barely have to walk twenty feet to the black town car. It was enough though. Leave the cool A/C and the sleek modern airport behind. Straightaway I'm clammy. Moist. Sweating. Clothes sticking. Wet body. Sweet Lord. Some heat. Feels like I was drenched with a bucket of warm seawater. Felt woozy.

Nod a hello as Alfred takes my luggage. Climb inside the back seat of the air-conditioned car. Inhale back on the complimentary bottles of water like a calf sucking on a nipple. Leather seats didn't help the sweating situation but after the twenty minutes or so it took us to leave the busy airport, I acclimatised. Aisling wasn't as bad as me but still struggling a bit nonetheless. We bonded over our discomfort. So that was nice. Managed to enjoy the car ride to her apartment.

Drove along the coast on the freeway. On our left in the night sky were miles and miles of magnificently lit up skyscrapers stretching way up into the clouds and beyond. Never seen so many. Not just one or two either, they were all over the place. Massive, vibrant, neon pillars of steel and glass. City of Lights. Huge glowing metropolis, all red, purple and blue, lighting up the dark night sky of a futuristic looking world. Seems we traveled forward in time, into the future like *Blade Runner* or *Total Recall*. Where are all the three-boobed women?!

On our right was water. Sea. Ocean? Not sure. Calm. Few waves. Lots of boats. Old, wooden, red Chinese style rowboats with dragon heads on the front that looked like pirate ships. Big, white, expensive yachts that looked alien like as they just glided over the smooth water. Small, black speedboats that you might see in a James Bond movie. Also a few slow moving, weary looking ferries that we have in Cork. Cool mix. Almost like a fishing village on one side, Gotham City on the other.

Look up into the sky to see if there are any Chinese symbol Batman signs (or Kermit the Frog ones) being lit up. Not yet. At one point we drove through this slick underground tunnel with purple, blue and yellow lights that made me double check in the rearview mirror whether or not I was Batman. Stuck out my chin, gritted my teeth and sucked in my cheeks as I peered mysteriously in the rearview mirror. Alfred our Chinese driver caught me looking so I gave him an awkward, double eyed wink for some reason. Pretended to fall asleep for the rest of the drive.

Arrive at Aisling's abode. Doorman who looks like Alfred's twin greets us as the car pulls up outside the foyer and lobby area of the apartment complex. Hop out. Suck in the warm night air. Take a look around. Reminds me of The Ritz hotel I remember seeing in the first Batman movie. White marble floors with lavish black marble walls. Spot lights and drop lights lighting up the empty foyer. A/C pumping. Elevator music tooting. Small waterfall art piece in the lobby peacefully bubbling over. Mighty spot.

The complex is made up of four skyscrapers facing each other, three huge ones stretching high into the sky plus a smaller one with a leisure centre, restaurant and swimming pools. Hop in the elevator. Shoots us up all the way up to the fiftieth floor of Building A. Takes about ten seconds, zip! Doesn't feel like we even moved. Step out. Oh yeah. Top floor. Penthouse on.

Two apartments per floor. Must be big. Rich mahogany door to my left, dark oak door to my right. We go right. Quietly open the heavy oak door. Aisling takes an immediate left to use the bathroom. I shuffle inside and inspect my new headquarters. Oh Betsy. Now this is an apartment. Looks like something out of American Psycho, in a good way of course. Dance around as I give myself a tour.

Wooden floors and wide-open plan as you walk in to a tennis court sized apartment. Huge kitchen. Massive living room. Modern. Sleek. Slick. Everything looks new and expensive. Shiny sterling silver kitchen appliances, thick black leather couches, plush white rugs, polished bleach dining room wooden floors, enormous widescreen TV on the living room wall, I'm guessing seventy inches, and floor to high ceiling windows, giving me almost a 180-degree view. Mountains to my left, the City of Lights over to my right and I presume there's a view of the ocean out straight ahead.

Dark outside so can't see too much, just my smiling reflection beaming back at my goofy head. Lap of luxury on!

Aisling's parents are in bed. Two in the morn and they just got back from a trip to Australia. Aisling is fairly goosed too, wants to go to sleep as well. We're in different rooms. Family abode and all that. Shows me where I'll be staying. Nice sized guest room, about the size of my bedroom back home. It's one of five bedrooms. Everything neat, tidy, modern and minimal. Chilled from the A/C. Queen size bed with a white duvet and a ramp of plump white pillows. Light blue walls make me feel nice and serene. This will do me nicely, already feel at home. My new Batcave for the foreseeable future. Wish Aisling a good night. Not sure if we should hug or kiss or what? She gives me a weary grimace of a smile back. Says it all. Night so.

Wait until I hear her door close then go back out onto the balcony by the living room for a look. Ridiculously high up. Gusts of warm winds hitting my face. Balcony isn't the safest place to be, seems like I could be whisked off at any minute. Railing is up to about my chest but still feels dodge being so high up. Get an odd urge to throw something off. What would happen if I jumped? Feet and palms get sweaty at the thought of it so I settle with seeing how far I can throw a Tic-Tac. Wonder if I'll hear it when it hits the ground. Throw it out with all my might. Wind takes it and lashes it – crack! – back against the window next to me. Thought it almost broke the pane, which would've been a wonderful start to my stay.

Make out a few boats in the harbour. Looks like an island or two as well dotted around the place. Everything looks so tiny all the way down there. Pretty sure the tallest building I've been in in Cork is five stories. Spot the roof top pool on the smaller skyscraper. Open twenty-four hours? Late night dip? Quickly change into my white soccer shorts. Down I go in my flip-flops. No top, I am on holiday after all. Pale white body needs a tan though. Spikey hair still up despite the ridiculously long flight at least.

Nod polite hellos at all the doormen like I've known them for years. Explain who I am. They've been expecting me. Wave me in with a big smile. Scamper up. Now this is a pool with a view. Harbour. Boats. Village. Mountains. Lights. Oh Betsy. Jump in. Water feels unreal. Luke warm. Cools me down. Do a few laps underwater. Start saying the mantra "King Kong, Hing of Hong" over and over again to myself for some reason. I'm a fan of here already.

Float around on my back for a while. Stare up at the sky. Can't see any stars. Just a glazey-haze from all the lights. Cork skies are far clearer. That's where I was yesterday, looking up at that sky. How the funk did I end up here? Living the high life. Feels right but also like I stumbled here by accident. Not sure. Say nothing. Mighty dancing.

Head back upstairs for a shower. It's as if I'm in a rain forest with the water pouring over me, a shower with power. Dry off. Notice I'm still dripping wet. Doused in sweat. Not good. I might have made a grave mistake coming to this foreign land. Didn't realise I'd be sweating this much. Never really had a problem with hot weather. It's the humidity I can't hack. Always been an issue, Ireland is brutal for it. Murky. Grimy. Mank. Sweating like a paedophile in a Barney suit. Red head. Clammy body. Puffy hair. Some catch. Some pity.

Oddly my face and head rarely perspire. I'd sweat more trying to talk to a girl I liked than after playing a soccer match. My sweat glands basically dominate my body and mind. Weak boy. At least I never get B.O. Just an abundance of uncontrollable wet patches. Way better, right?

Wrap a towel around my waist and go sit on my bed trying to think of ways I can combat this sweating problem. Unpack all my stuff as quietly as I can. I like to unpack as soon as possible when I get somewhere new. Settle in. Make sure they can't get rid of me too easily. Almost four in the morn by now. Not really tired. Too excited to sleep. I want to see all of Hong Kong straightaway. Take everything in just in case I wake up and it was all a dream.

Still feeling fairly fresh after the nice kip (nap) on the flight. Maybe I'll just test out the pillows on the bed for a second. Head barely grazes the silk case. Pass out. Bruce Wayne has retired for the night and then some. Wake up about sixteen hours later. Dry, cotton mouth. Confused. Goosed. Was I boozing? Am I Batman? Whose room is this? Oh yeah - Hing Hong on!

Chapter 25
Love, Death & Monkey Balls

Plan on our first night is dinner with Aisling's Mum and Dad, Ger and Bert, followed by meeting up with Aisling's friends somewhere in downtown Hong Kong. Ger and Bert are sound. Both in their fifties, fit looking, always with a smile on their faces, funny, generous and laid back.

Aisling's Mum Ger and I get on unreal well. She kind of looks like the actress Helen Mirren. Spends most of her time in Cork and only just got out to Hong Kong herself. Whenever Aisling and I ever got in an argument she would always take my side. Dead right too, as they say.

Bert was a great laugh as well, he looked a bit like Sean Connery. We always had some good chats about soccer and the likes when he was back in Cork for a week or two. Good old sports, the great male bonder. Dinner should be a good hoot.

Plan is to go to their favourite restaurant down the road, Bombay House. Casual affair I'm told. Throw on a t-shirt and jeans. My pants are sticking to me from the get go. Feels like my t-shirt has shrunk as well. Clung to my body. Humidity seems to be getting worse. Attempt to put gel in my hair. Pointless. Big, frizzy, ball of cotton wool. Knock on the bathroom door. Nothing I can do now. Time to go. First night out on the town!

Restaurant is close enough to the apartment. Instead of waiting for the car service to swoop us up, Ger suggests that we just walk.

"Only a five to ten minute stroll, it'll be nice."

"Sure thing. Sounds great," I smile back.

Worst call ever. Exercise builds up a thick layer of sweat. Humidity feels like I'm wrapped in heavy blanket. Every step I take encourages more beads of sweat and gel to drip from my brow into my eyes and mouth as if I'm trying to water-board myself. T-shirt glued to my back. Boxers clinging like clams to my legs. Socks squelching. Foot sweat. Lovely.

By the time we reach Bombay House my stomach's warbling like a drunk bird staggering home from the pub. Losing a lot of fluid. Severely dehydrated. Everyone else seems a tad hot but nowhere near the pain I'm in. Restaurant is small, tight and busy. Reminds me of the Indian place back home in Douglas where Marcus did his work experience (you remember him, the German student exchange replacement for Dirk who came to stay with, and hate, me). Same music. Feel the wafts of smoke and heat pumping out from the kitchen as we sit down. Lively waiters bellowing orders at one another in frantic Chinese. All their bustling gets me more flustered. This is not going well.

Can't focus on the menu with all the heat so I just nod along when asked if I want to share plates with everyone. Starters are ordered along with beers all round. So far I've managed to hide the impending doom I can feel bubbling up in my stomach. Did well with the small talk on the stroll down with the parents. I think Aisling noticed something's up though, especially when I started panting like a pregnant woman trying to get air into my body as the waiter was taking orders from everyone,

"Are you OK?"

"It's hot, is it hot, anyone else hot? Some heat. Jesus. Is it me? Or is it hot? It's hot."

Ashley hands me a Tiger beer.

"Calm down, drink this."

Oh no. Panicked gibbers. Smile at Ger and Bert. Nod a friendly chuckle at the people sitting at the table next to us. Americans? Europeans? Not sure. No one in here is Indian or Chinese. They don't say anything back to me anyway. Maybe they're German. So I nod again. Cheers them with my bottle. Oh ja. Play it cool, Marky boy, keep yourself together. You can beat these hot flushes. Make a speech or something. Distract yourself. Turn back to our table,

"Well I'd just like to say this is lovely, isn't it? I love Hong Kong already. Bit hot but it's unreal. Thanks for heating me- I mean having me. Thanks. How hot is it in here, ha ha, funny. Can anyone open a window or something?!"

Cheers to the bewildered table. Take a slug of the bottle. Warm beer rushes through me. Attacks my bowels and stomach. Diarrhea really is the terrorist of the body. Evil forces hit you hard. Shakes you to the core. Leaves you frightened in the aftermath. I knew it was coming being so dehydrated from the heat but that mouthful of beer triggered an immediate onslaught against my weak digestive system. Grab a glass of water and chug for dear life. Refill, refill, refill. Drink two pitchers of water in two minutes. Feels like I've steadied the ship. Taking a stand against the body terrorism. I *refuse* to let diarrhea ruin my night.

While Ger and Bert ask Aisling how the flight was, I sip on my warm beer once more, slowly testing the brown waters. OK, I can do this. Calm down. Just smile and try not to let the sweat rolling off your face drip onto anyone's plate. Mind, body: Are we in this together? Come on, we can do it!

Starters arrive. Plates and bowls of filled with sauces of all kinds - Brown, yellow and green looking dishes. Chicken in the yellow stuff, beef in the brown bowl and no clue what's in the green dish, fish? Everything looks like how my stomach feels.

"What kind of food is this? Hong Kong is amazing."

"Indian, have you had it before?"

"Oh yeah, *love* Indian food. Eat it all the time back in Cork."

"Great! We weren't sure if you liked hot spicy foods."

Christ Almighty. Never had Indian food before in my life. I'm doomed. This is going to be dodge. My stomach can't hack spicy stuff at the best of times. Ger shows me what to do. Just grab some naan bread that looks like a pizza crust. Dip it in one of the bowls. Scoop it up. Eat it down. OK, looks easy. Grab, rip, dip, scoop, eat it down. Oh God, I dipped too much. Huge scoop. Why did I eat it all in one go?! Feels like an atomic bomb has been dropped into my stomach.

Brief pause as my body readjusts to the horrendous mistake I just invited in with open arms and big dumb mouth. Mustn't let the terrorists win. Feels like they're opening bottles of champagne in my stomach. Sweet Lord. Save me. Grimace. Concentrate. Battle. Pregnant pants. Calm. Sweating stops. Everything goes quiet. I think. I beat it. Maybe I just needed food? Cured myself. Good work Marky b- Oh no. Oh Jesus. Here it comes.

Tidal wave of doom sweeps through my body, crashing against my stomach and rushes downward from my bowels. In one of the quickest moves I've ever made, I leap up from the table, excuse myself feverishly, smile like a mad man, look around with my crazy eyes for the appropriate sign, run, skip and hop, burst into the bathroom, karate kick open a stall door, rip open my belt, whip down my pants and manage to get my cheeks on the toilet seat just as my stomach unleashes a feast of fury the kind I've never seen or felt before. Unable to move as my insides pour and splatter themselves out into the toilet. About to pass out. Maybe I'm having a stroke. Feels like my body is weeping. I'm crying at this point. Tears of fear. Joy. Relief. Terror. Some sort of dam has opened. Keeps gushing and flowing, an endless, relentless, ongoing assault. There are moments when the waves subside and I think I'm done but the minute I go to stand up the bouts returned. This is not going to be a quick knock out fight. We're going twelve rounds. All I can do is take off all my clothes, including my socks, and try to cool down. Let nature do its worst.

After half an hour there's simply no more to give. Every bit of sweat, shame, blood, tears and mud has been released from my body. Exhausted. Naked. Beaten. But. Not defeated. Drag myself to my feet. Dry myself off with flimsy toilet paper that must be the cheapest stuff ever made, disintegrating the minute it touches my wet body. Take a deep breath. Put back on my drenched clothes. Pat down my messy, cotton candy, wig like hat of hair in the mirror. Looks like I have a scarecrow style going on.

Return to the table like nothing has happened. My stomach and I have a newfound confidence in ourselves after what we've just been through. Been to the battlefield and made it back again. Nod a friendly hello to everyone at the table. Start picking at the food in front of me, trying to act like I haven't been missing for the entire meal. Aisling looks at me like I must look like death,

"Are you OK?"

"Yeah. Just a really long queue in the bathroom. Ahem. Which one's the chicken again?"

Despite everyone at the table telling me I look pale and asking if I wanted to go home to lie down, I insist I'm fine. Minor blip.

Stronger for it. Manage to eat the least spiciest dish going. Move from beer to vodka-coke. Small talk starts flowing once more. Start to gain back a bit of energy. First night in Hong Kong after all, can't ruin it with some stomach trouble. Finish dinner. Made it through. I survived. Ger and Bert stroll home and wish us well as Aisling and I head off into the night.

Plan is to meet her friends in an area called Kowloon, somewhere in central Hong Kong that's filled with lots of bars and clubs. We're in Stanley, which is out a bit. Need to get a subway. Nine o'clock now. There's a subway leaving in ten minutes. Aisling thinks if we run we can make it. Hurry. Scurry. Run. Go!

Follow Aisling as we scuttle through the streets. Stanley looks cool. Cobbled streets. Tourist looking town with restaurants, stalls and pubs. Beach and ocean to my left, mountains and forests to my right and the big bright city lights in front of my way in the distance. Hong Kong is slick. Big fan. By now we're sprinting towards an underground sign in the distance, ducking and weaving around people. Run inside. Follow Aisling's lead by jumping the barrier. Renegades. We run this city.

"Quick quick," Aisling keeps calling back at me.

"I am, I am!"

Skipping down stairs. Pelting it along. Don't stop me now! And then we reach the platform just as the doors of the subway shut close. Dose. Missed it. Hopes dashed. Out of breath. Out of time. Out of - Oh God. Here it comes again. Underground. Heat. Running. All kicks in. All too much. Vodka, coke, nan, chicken. All come flooding back.

Like a burst balloon my sweat glands erupt. Freak out. Entire body instantly wet. Arms. Pits. Hands. Back. Bum. Cheeks. Gushing geysers. Slippery slopes. Moist marshes. Funk me pink. Can't hack this. Feel like I'm going to die. Feel a rumble in my stomach. Bomb about to explode. Need to find a bathroom. Right away. This is going to get messy. Fast. Out of my way please, Hong Kong folk, this is life or death.

Spin around in circles. No bathroom here. Oh Jesus. I need to stop sweating. Too many people. Surrounded by Asian folk. Young, old, unknown age thanks to unreal genes. Schoolgirls, grandparents, hipsters. All so small. All staring at me. Freaking me out. Feels like I'm on another planet. Where's Aisling? Over there checking the time of the next train. I need to cool down. Fast. Right now. I'm spiraling. Sweating. Profusely. Freaking. So I start stripping clothes off in the subway station. Pants down. T-shirt gone. Cool on.

Nothing's working. Slump down on a bench. Naked. Mostly. Just in boxers and runners. T-shirt on the floor next to me, pants around my ankles, close to giving up and letting it all go. Who cares if I die (arrhea) here? I had a good eighteen-year run. We had a laugh, right, life? Time to let go. People are taking photos of me now as I sit here in my boxers. Smile a delirious smile and thumbs up. Give them a good photo at least before the explosion about to erupt out of me. Calm before the s**t storm.

Just as I'm about to pass out, onlookers and photographers come over to me. Bottles of water are thrust in my direction by a little old Asian couple. Young Hong Kong skateboarder teenagers start rifling through their backpacks, pulling out Pepto Bismol, Tylenol and Imodium. Huh? How the funk did they know? Do I have to pay for all this? Who cares. Slurp. Chug. Swallow. Repeat. Slurp. Chug. Swallow. Repeat. Slurp. Chug. Swallow. Repeat. Thank you, I cry with my eyes, thank you, Good Samaritans, my saviours, helping me through this desert. Thank you, I croak again, water spilling out of my mouth, ruining an old man's shoes.

By the time the next train arrives I feel way better. Sweats are back to a normal level. Stomach feels strong once more. Mind still feels weak but nothing some booze won't fix. Even the fact I can have this thought makes me feel OK. Must be able to go on with life (and my night)!

Aisling offers that we go home and cancel the plans she has made with her buddies, not sure if she's concerned or embarrassed. Mix of both perhaps. No, no, I insist. We must go on. Mop up the last bit of body sweat with my t-shirt then put it back on. Lovely. Don't want to ruin her night any more. Plus, I'm not sure how to get back to the abode, not by foot anyway. Nay nay, on with the night! She immediately agrees, ha.

Bid goodbye to all my new doctor and nurse friends and offer them all some money. They laugh and wave me away. Jump on the subway. I'm over the hump. Fun on!

Well. That was the plan anyway.

Kowloon is slick. Never been in a place like this before, whole new world. Looks like Times Square in New York, except full of Asian folk. Skyscrapers lit up yellow, white, purple and blue under the black night sky. Computer screens the size of houses everywhere. Karaoke jingles. Ads and billboards for all sorts of futuristic gadgets. In some parts you can barely see the sky because of all the crowded signs overhead.

Streets are packed full of people, throngs and throngs and throngs, as if they were all coming out of a stadium after a big game. But nay, just the normal foot traffic. Closest experience to this commotion back home was taking a packed bus ride to school on a stuffy day. This amount of people is another level. Mental how many people there are around me. I'm barely a drop in the human ocean. Way taller than almost all of them though, some sort of distinction at least. I feel like Bill Murray in *Lost in*

Translation. Every white person I see passing me by looks like a model. None of them look back at me. Might be my scarecrow head perhaps.

Head to an area filled with classy bars and outdoor restaurants lining the cobbled streets. Met Aisling's friends at a fancy social club that reminded me of a golf club with its wooden décor and diamond design carpets and wallpaper. Had to put on a Hawaiian shirt and a blazer provided by the club to even get in. Apparently my attire was too casual. Mighty.

Given a group introduction to Aisling's friends who were sound if not a little prudish. Mostly English and Australian. All well to do and well lived. Private school heads. All the guys had stiff upper lips, fat wallets and a probable coke problem. Group of girls all looked like Daddy Girls, very waspy and proper. Very different from Aisling's friends back home but in a way, very similar. I think they got a nice thrill conversing with a common scarecrow like myself.

"No no, my parents aren't royalty or hedge fund bankers. And, guess what – I didn't go to a private boarding school. I know! Never played polo either. Amazing, right? Yeah, you can touch me, I'm real."

After a few Sherries we left there and went to a more relaxed, underground bar nearby. Looked like the bar in Cheers. People here started buying me lots of drinks and shots because I was Irish. Ergo, I was drinking lots of shots and boozes. Stomach felt strong at least. I'm back, Marky Boy has arrived!

Playing pool against two of the guy friends, Hugo and Clancy. Both English and their dads were heads of banks over there. Looked like Prince William and dressed like cricket players, cream jumpers thrown over their shoulders. Not sure if those were their names or nicknames either. Beat them easily at pool, which they seemed to enjoy (probably fuming on the inside). More shots. More pool. Repeating these activities. Clock strikes twelve. Night starts getting darker. Let the fun begin!

Around one in the morn Aisling tells me she's going to get a cab home with her friend Tonsy, a blond English girl. Asks if I want to stay or go. Only one o'clock. Early doors. In the middle of a pool competition as well with Hugo and Clancy. Aisling says stay. So I stayed. Got the address of the abode written on my hand. Everyone celebrates me staying with a round of tequila, "TO MAAAARRRK!" Drank it even though I knew it was my arch-nemesis. Things are going to get dodge.

Blurry. Tequila. Pool. Dancing. Amazement that I'm actually here in Hong Kong, half way across the world from Ireland playing pool with two guys named Hancy and Clugo. Hear a bar man scream out "LAST CALL!" One of Aisling's friends buys me another round. Beatrice I think her name is, a small, curvy brunette who looks like trouble despite not being great looking. Think she's cracking on to me. Looks like she wanted a roll in the hay with the stable boy. Simmer, roaming hands of yours. Down the shot. Smile her off. Time to dodge.

Flag down a red taxi. Ride home solo. Back seat. Show the local Chinese driver my hand with the address on it. Older guy, millions of wrinkles on his face. Keeps smiling and nodding at me. Drive on boss! Look out the window with delight at all the sights and buildings we passed on the way home. Start singing a song to myself. Gibberish.

Realise I'm getting the spins. Close my eyes. Feel carsick. Ask the driver to pull over. Doesn't hear me. Or understand. Says something to me. Shut my eyes. Gulp hard. Open my mouth. Puke out the window as we sped along the highway. Hear the cabman say stuff in Chinese to me that doesn't sound nice. I thought we were friends! Wonder to myself if it was Chinese or Cantonese. Pull into a garage. Cabman drags me out of the back seat. Fall asleep for a bit until he starts hosing me down with water. Rip off my t-shirt as I feel a need to be naked if I'm this drunk. Use my t-shirt to clean the backseat of the cab while the cabman hoses it down with water. Throw my t-shirt away. Get back in the cab. Drive home.

Fall out the door at Aisling's apartment. Crawl into the elevator. Push all the buttons. Lie face down on the floor as I'm swooshed up. Wonder if this is my bedroom floor. Cursing tequila. Feel sick thinking of drink. Doors open on Aisling's floor. Take off my shoes, pants and socks. Leave them in the elevator. Crawl into the apartment. Make my way to the bathroom door. Take off my boxers. Drag myself to the toilet. Hug the bottom of the bowl. Fall asleep.

Wake up some time the next morning. Aisling standing over me. Lying there. Naked. Fully. Clueless. Wondering. Again. Where the funk am I? Who is this girl? And where are all my clothes?

Fun first night in Hong Kong.

After that rocky start the next few months in Hong Kong were amazing. Fell in love with the place. Old world meets new. Used to love the bus ride from Stanley into the heart of Hong Kong. Driving up mountains, passing huge old graveyards running down the side of mountains while seeing skyscrapers and a skyline that looked like something from the future, all with chaotic alleyways squeezing out every available drop of space possible. Never thought I'd see anything like it.

Aisling and I got on well for most of the trip. In the future we would split up for good but at the time Hong Kong was a fun experience. Great laugh together. Ups and downs, but all good. Friends. Maters. Boyfriend. Girlfriend. Friends again. Waves and spurts. Made me realise that love is kind of like diarrhea really. Comes and goes. Stronger for going through it and better when you come out the other side. Something like that.

Hong Kong was surprisingly safe for such a big city. You could amble down what looks like a dark, dangerous alley and all you'd bump into was a kind stranger asking if you were lost. Hong Kong folk were the friendliest people I've ever met actually, even though we didn't even speak the same language.

Locals would give me directions to places by walking with me in silence to wherever I needed to go. Sometimes this was a ten-minute walk. There were some signs in English which was handy but usually it was just a cluster of cluttered Chinese symbols on countless signs that were all battling for space and eye lines. When we reached my destination, which was usually just a corner shop where I could buy more Tic-Tacs, my impromptu tour guides would just smile, wave me goodbye and then disappear down a different alley. Vanish. Gone. Good luck!

Some days I'd go explore the local markets for cheap clothes. Hoodies were popular at the time so I bought a few bags of them. T-shirts, I bought about ten bags. Jeans, four bags more. Within a month my money was running low so I tried to find some work to tie me over. Lack of a working visa was a big problem. Working in a pub was a non-runner. Nor was being an English teacher for Kindergarten folk. Traipsed all over Hong Kong going to pointless interviews.

Good few people suggested I should try modeling. Laughed them off. I've never been able to pose or smile for photos. My face twists and torts in a weird cheek sucking, pout face. Same one I use when I look in the mirror. It's not good. Ruined many a family photo. Gave in to giving modeling a go though when I heard it was mostly down to me being tall and white, two rarities in Hong Kong.

Put on my best new clothes and made my way to the main modeling agency in Hong Kong, Elite Models. Unfortunately this involved a bus ride, a subway, and a twenty-minute walk in severe humidity. By the time I arrived I was sweating, panting, pink and puffy. Took one look at myself in the mirror in the waiting room. Decided to cut the gibber. Left before they could say no. Trust me, I looked like I had just emerged from living in a hole underground for a month. No one in their right mind would've hired me as a model, not even a foot one.

At least on my way home that day I found a cool outdoor market area full of stalls. Clothes, jewellery, food. All sorts. It was here where I bought a nice silver chain for myself. Sterling silver, I was told, with a nice cross at the end. Memento for my mighty trip to this foreign land. Didn't realise that this was the money I needed for the bus ride home. Stranded in downtown Hong Kong. Stupid call really by me.

As was eating monkey balls for the first time. Free sample. Street vendor. What was I thinking? Another evening spent on the bowl. Still though, live and learn. Better to have love and lost and all that, right?

That trip opened my eyes in lots of ways really. Expanded my little mind. More to life than just Cork and Ireland. Big world out there, plenty to see, plenty to duu. Maybe I'll go west next. Californication time. All about taking a chance, going on an adventure. Or, as a wise Chinese woman once said to me: Monkey. Balls. On!

Chapter 26
This Isn't The End

So it's the first of May, I'm twenty-four-years-old and it's six years to the day that I arrived back to Cork from my trip to Hong Kong. I'm in my car, half naked, driving out of the Navy base in Cork and there's a guy in my backseat. He's about fifty, lying face down on the seat with his legs on the floor, trying to hide underneath my jumper and t-shirt with a plastic bag that has a sandwich in it covering his head. I'm smuggling him out of the base. Smuggler Hayes. How did I end up here?

At this point of the book, dear reader, I was going to go through all my college tales. However, I realized I have a lot of good college stories. As in a *huge* bucket. So I might just write another book about them. Would that be all right with you? We've come this far I'd hate to cull them short and not do them justice. Plus I don't want this book to be extra-long. This way you'll get more stories out of it and another book to read, think of it that way? I'm too nice.

For the time being I'll just summarise what has gone on so far up this point. I wrote this book mainly out of narcissism. It's the reason I wrote my other two books as well, *RanDumb* and

PREDUMB

RanDumber. I have a story. Listen to me cry! Hear my words! Middle child syndrome!

Not all narcissistic reasons though. Maybe a lot of it was the fact I'm not a huge fan of repeating stories over and over so having them all in one place where I can direct people to helps me out a lot.

Which leads me to another reason why I wrote this book: To show people why I am like I am. Why do I make certain decisions? How do I end up in certain situations with recurring themes? What is going on with my hair? These were three of the most popular questions I got from readers after my first two books. Some critics claimed that stories could not possibly have happened. "All made up! No one is like that! Nobody could be so stupid!"

Well. I'm afraid. I am. But I wouldn't call it stupid. I'd call it open. Naïve. Clued in. Willing to go with the flow. Down for an adventure. Up for a laugh. Easy going. Let's see where this takes us. Maybe it's because I'm Irish and we're like that? I'm not sure but I think that helps. Which is why I wanted to show where I'm from. And how also, I do like to gibber on. Little spurts of poetry, a verbal jig, a tip of the wig, a dash of phonetic joy amongst the everyday normal mundane, or normane as I like to call it.

That's not all critics say either, in case you're wondering. There are the anonymous folk who like to send you hate mail. Always tremendous. People leaving lovely messages for me on my blog, or else emailing me directly, which is handy. I've noticed their spelling is always a bit off. One girl informed me I was a 'cumt'. Also misspelt a few other words in her message so I don't think it was intentional. Another guy signed his name as Johm. These people seem to not like the letter N for some reason. Also did not like *RanDumb* or *RanDumber* at all. Seem to have offended them somehow, even though they managed to read both books start to finish. And yet they *hated* them.

Hated me too. I was a prick. A cumt. And a prick. Did I say that already? Their vocabulary was limited enough when it came to insults. Or else they were just very specific and knew exactly what it is that I am.

Thing is, when you first read these kinds of messages your initial thought is: Oh no. They know. How did they find out I'm a cumt?! Stomach drops. Heart sinks. Mouth goes dry. They know the truth!

Once the disgust settles you calm down. Have a glass of water. Gather your thoughts. Realise they had to leave an email address on my blog in order to leave a comment. Or else they emailed me straight from their real email address. So I can just plug their email into Facebook and see who they are.

Oh, looks like this guy has a lot of friends in Cork that I have too. This girl is a complete stranger. As is this guy in Boston. One thing they share in common though is that they all look like complete winners who are fully happy with their lives. They also have this deep, bitter, angry look in their eyes, like a guy who once found out his online girlfriend of two years was actually an obese gay man named Roger.

I can imagine them now. Rage bubbling over as they read *RanDumb* or *RanDumber*. Keep reading the book all the way through, even though they hate it beyond belief. Keep reading. Finally finish. Scream. Curse. Shake their fists. "I must tell that prick Mark Hayes that he is a PRICK! AND A CUMT!!!"

Open up their laptops. Turn it on. Wait for it to load up. Anger. Rage. Hatred. Coursing through their bitter bodies. Must. Release. Somehow. So they have a hate-filled Tommy Tank while waiting for their computers to load up. *RanDumb* in one hand, self-gratifying with the other. Screaming at the cover: YOU F**KING PRICK!!!

Computer is ready. Time for them to type. Hands shaking in anger as they type: *"Just read your stupid book in a day. You. ARE. A. P.R.I.C.K!"* Body shaking and convulsing, still tugging away at themselves like they're trying to pull a stubborn carrot out of the ground. Beating off. Beating keys. *"And I kept the receipt and tried to return the book but they wouldn't let me because you are such a CUMT!!!!"* Looking at the screen, then staring in the mirror. Grunting. Snorting. Wheezing. Climaxing as they press 'Send'. Ughhhhhhh. Screen takes the brunt of their anger. Toss the book to the floor. Their job here is done. "I showed that cumt. Never again will he write another word."

At least that's how I imagine these folk go about their hate mail sending activities. Similar, in fact, to that travel guide guy in one of the Sunday papers in Ireland who was another victim of *RanDumb* rage. Not happy as he wrote *"It is surely some sort of crime against humanity that I had to read this. The fact that a tree was felled so paper could be made to print this is also shocking."* Happy enough he had to read it all. Thanks for giving me your time, buddy.

Special thank you as well to that guy on Amazon who left me a one-star review saying: *"ALL LIES. THIS BOOK IS NOT REAL. NOT TRUE. RACIST. INSULTING. HE IS NOT IRISH-AMERICAN."* At least he got the last part right.

Oddly enough, the same guy's only other review was a five-star one that he wrote for a can of corn. As in the yellow vegetable, sold in a can. He really loved that stuff too. *"I couldn't be happier with this can of corn. It was everything I hoped for AND MORE. I will never buy a different brand and quite frankly, why would I? Even though I usually prefer white corn, this really hit the spot. My corn casseroles have never tasted so good!"* Special man.

Although saying that, we all have our problems so I can relate to all these folk in a way. And it's not like lots of people didn't say lots of things and my books haven't done me proud and helped me out and opened doors, hearts and legs for me. It's just you always really notice the bad things people say, don't you, which is weird. Maybe that's just me.

I remember when I was young and felt sick my parents would try to make me feel better by being nice to me but it never worked. Only when they had enough of me crying and told me to cop on in a sterner voice did I stop crying and copped on. Wonder if I'm the same now. Perhaps that's just the way I am with that sort of thing. Or perhaps those two things aren't even related. Good analysis.

Looking back at it now though I do see that there have definitely been issues and events that have followed me around for life. Let's have a mini quiz. Clearly I have had a reoccurring history with:

1. Shoes
2. Hair
3. Girls
4. Bowels
5. Sweating
6. German grannies?

If you guessed all six, congrats! You have won the prize of smugness and good memory. If you guessed only one, you need to go back and read this book along with my other two. No no, I insist. Go back and read them all. What else would you be doing with your life?

From the burst open shoes to the leprechaun shoes to the Goth heel shoes to almost having a meltdown in San Francisco (*RanDumber*) mostly triggered by shoe shopping, shoes have caused me an odd amount of strife in life. *Shoes?* Not sure why I have so many problems with them, or them with me. Troubled soles, as they say.

I remember the first time I went shoe shopping with my Mum, I think I was six. We went to a place in Cork called Clarks, an old shoe shop institution in the middle of the city. The elderly, grandfather like salesman in a burgundy cardigan brought me an array of shoes to try on. I remember thinking they all looked the same. Whenever I would pick a pair I liked and wanted to get, he would ask "Are you sure? Are you sure now?" Over and over, for every pair. In the end I wasn't sure of what I was sure about and couldn't decide. I think I asked my Mum to choose in the end. So maybe that's where my shoe syndrome stems from, not sure.

Hair is always an issue, a daily one even to this day. Long, short, puffy, spikey, tall, flat, combed, messy, wet, dry, frizzy, straightened, I actually have very little idea what I'm going to get when I look in the mirror every day. It has been like a temperamental wife who dictates and dominates my life. Some days she's happy and looking wonderful. Other days she looks like a wet dog and has an angry, raspy bark to match. If my wife is having a bad hair day I will invariably be in a bad mood for the day, whereas if she's dancing and looking well (even if only to my own demented eyes) I too will be dancing and brimming with confidence. Thin hair line which one it might be. Every morning there is a new hairstyle to discover, which wife will roll out of bed with me. Exciting times.

Girls have always been a bit of a tough nut for me, in a way at least. From the social awkwardness from not mingling with them when growing up, mostly due to not going to school together, to then having feelings and wants, needs and desires, followed swiftly by realizing booze helps break the ice, followed by realizing you don't really know how to make a move without booze, which can lead to making wrong moves with too much booze (passing out prior/mid-deed) it has always been a confused spectrum of not ever really knowing what's going on.

Then again, as Oscar Wilde once said "Women are made to be loved, not understood." Go on the Oscar, a wiser man than I. Although he was gay so it's easy for him to say, not in the thick of things, so to speak.

My bowels have given me trouble at various points throughout my life. Stomach issues. Dehydration issues. New climate issues. New culture issues. Trips to prison, none of which I can recall of right now, well maybe that collection box affair and that close call with the two police helicopters and six police cars and having guns pulled on me in L.A. Both events weighed heavily on my poor bowels. As did the trip to Hong Kong. Women. Angry men. Booze. Shots. God knows what else. All culminating in a very sensitive and fragile stomach that I still batter with all sorts to this day. At least my new motto of "Eat what I have to so I can drink what I want" has served me well. Healthy food. Offsets the booze.

Sweating is in a similar vein. Nerves. Exams. Girls. Realisations. Heat. Humidity. Awkwardness. Thoughts. Premonitions. Projections. Memories. Bungee jumps. Leaps of faith. Dire situations. High living. My sweat glands have been put through a lot. On the upside they are still working well, which is good apparently for ensuring you don't go bald. People who only sweat out through their head go bald easier, the sweat pushes the hair out of the head if my biology memories serve me correctly.

And, of course, then we come to German grannies. I'm including not only Dirk's granny but also Dirk himself in that category as well. Marcus can be put into this one as well. He really did have a grandmother like haircut, big fluffy blond perm, kind of looked like Napoleon Dynamite now I think of it. Those two German lovers who both looked like Gary Glitter in their red thongs and muumuus who I met at spring break in Mexico that time in *RanDumb*, they're in the German granny category as well seeing as almost everyone in our resort was a gran or granddad. Fun times at the old folks home during spring break. Although that might make me a German granny too. Probably. I am Angela Merkel. Something for you now to mull over and decide.

Back to my Smuggler Hayes story from above. It's my first official day as a German gun translator for the Irish Navy (odd story how I ended up here). I've just gone down to the naval base in Cork to pick up the gun manuals. They were left in a bag for me outside an office door. The woman I was meant to meet left a note on the door saying she was out for lunch. As I'm driving back up the docks wondering who goes to lunch at eleven, I spot an older guy with grey hair in uniform waving me down. Stop. Roll down the window. Wonder if I'm in trouble.

"Do us a favour?"

"Pardon?"

"Will you give me a lift out the gate?"

"OK?"

"Good lad."

Open the locks on the car. Expect to see the guy get in the front. Hops in the back instead.

"I'll just sit back here. Must keep a low profile."

"Are you sure?"

"Yeah. Any jumpers or anything?"

"For what?"

"Must hide."

"Why's that?"

"Meant to be at work."

"Where are you going?"

"The pub. Security won't let me leave if they see me though. Say nothing, all right."

"Fair enough."

Hand him my jumper on the passenger seat so he can hide underneath it. Looks dumb as funk. Tell him I can clearly see him still.

"Give me your shirt so as well."

"Ha, no."

"Come on, give it to me. Turn up the heater. It's sunny out too, just say you were hot if anyone asks."

"Sorry man, I can't."

"I'll give you a tenner."

I'm a cheap man. Whip off my shirt. Feel exposed with the sun shining in on me. Navy guy slides down on the seat. T-shirt and jumper over him. I grab an umbrella and throw that on him too. Still see his head. Grab the plastic bag from the passenger seat. Throw it at him. "Put that on your head and you'll be hidden." He does. "Don't eat my sandwich." He promises he won't.

Drive on. Reach the main exit gate. Have to go through security to get out. Guard stops me. Walks to the car. Looks in. Gives me an odd look over my topless attire.

"Are you all right?"

"Yeah, just a bit hot. Need a tan."

"Did you get what you needed?"

"Yeah," I say as I pat the folders on the seat next to me, "Sorted."

Guard looks in again. Nods his head. Waves at the other guard in the hut to raise the barrier. Away we go. Drive on for about twenty minutes. Nothing but road. Guy in the back finally pops up.

"Good work lad. You can drop me off up here by O'Shea's Pub and I'll be on my way. Say nothing if anyone asks."

"Loose lips sink loose ships, as they say. Your secret's safe. Just don't forget that tenner."

"Oh yeah, don't worry, you did me well."

Pull up by O'Shea's. Leave the bluffer out. Takes out his wallet and looks through it. Pops his head down by the passenger window.

"Sorry, I've no change. I'll get you next time."

Before I can say a word he's gone. Off into the pub. Boozing the day away. Some sneak. At least I got a feel for how tight a ship they ran down there in the shipyard. Not the covert smuggling mission spy novel I half hoped for when the guy asked me to sneak him out of the base. Nay. Just a RanDumb chancer being an Irish RanDumber, as we like to do.

On that note, I too must depart. I have six more years to write about. Plenty to look forward to. Wuu huu for you. Guinness for me. Until then, go forth and adventure on. Follow your dreams. Chase the highs! Suffer the lows. First, I must go eat. Which reminds me of an article I read the other day, where an author's big wish was that one day he would be able to finish a book with the word mayonnaise.

ACKNOWLEDGEMENTS

Thanks to my delightful Mum and Dad, you are mighty as always. Getting mightier it seems. Good work. I must've brought ye both up well.

Big thanks to Charles, my editor. You pushed, preened and plucked. Churned out the good stuff from my drivel. Cheers for your patience.

To the Kaw bird, mucho gracias for your fine fecking ways. Especially those times you pretended to read the drafts I sent you and told me they were great, even if you couldn't recall what the chapters were about.

Thanks to everyone who pretended to proofread the book, couldn't have done it without your pretend help. Cheers to Jimmy B for actually reading it all and thanks to Darren for reading those few chapters.

Special thanks to you, the reader, and all the other fine readers. Particularly the RanDummies on Twitter and Facebook who write such wonderful reviews on Amazon and keep me entertained. Mighty dancing!

BOOKS BY MARK HAYES

RanDumb: The Adventures of an Irish Guy in LA

RanDumber: The Continued Adventures of an Irish Guy in LA

www.ingramcontent.com/pod-product-compliance
Lightning Source LLC
Chambersburg PA
CBHW031948070426
42453CB00006BA/136